Wills *and* Administration
of
Isle *of* Wight County
Virginia

- 1719-1760 -

By:
Blanche Adams Chapman

Southern Historical Press, Inc.
Greenville, South Carolina

Please direct all correspondence and orders to:

www.southernhistoricalpress.com
or
SOUTHERN HISTORICAL PRESS, Inc.
PO BOX 1267
375 West Broad Street
Greenville, SC 29601
southernhistoricalpress@gmail.com

ISBN #0-89308-467-0

Printed in the United States of America

TO

MARTHA WOODROOF HIDEN
(MRS. PHILIP W.)

To whom all persons of Virginia
ancestry owe a debt of gratitude,
for her untiring and successful
efforts in behalf of the preser-
vation and restoration of the
court records of the State.

BOOK II

THE GREAT BOOK

Pierce, Ann: Of the Lower Parish. Leg.- John Keighly, the plantation on which I live for seven years, at expiration of time, I give it to John Teasley's son John; to Patience Carver; my movable estate to John Keighly.
D. March 14, 1718/19   R. June 22, 1719
Wit. John Teasley, Thomas Altman, Peter Davis.
Page 1

West, Francis. Inventory, signed by John Gilliam.
D. January 10, 1718   Page 1

Ridley, Nathaniel: Leg.- beloved wife Elizabeth; son Nathaniel; daughter Mary; son Thomas land adjoining Anthony Quant; daughter Elizabeth; daughter Lydia; Godson, Robert Hodges. Wife Extx.
D. March 10, 1718/19   R. July 27, 1719
Wit. James Day, Julia Day, Roger Hodges.   Page 2

West, William: Leg.- son Thomas; daughter Sarah, if she marries Samuel Williams; my son-in-law John Williams; daughter Elizabeth; daughter Mary; daughter Ann.
D. May 4, 1719   R. July 28, 1719
Wit. Richard Price, Joseph Goden (Godwin)   Page 3

Howell, Thomas: Leg.- son Thomas the tract of land lying upon Blunt's Creek, which I bought of Samuel Godwin, Jr.; son William; daughter Sarah; wife Rebecak.
Wife, Extx.
D. March 16, 1718/19   R. August 24, 1719
Wit. John Dawson, Joseph Bradshaw, John Lucas.
Page 4

Bevan, Mary: Of Newport Parish. Leg.- son Thomas; son Peter; daughter Mary; daughter Elizabeth. Ex., son Thomas.
D. March 2, 1718/19   R. August 24, 1719
Wit. William Taylor, Jeremiah Proctor.   Page 4

Darden, Jacob. Inventory, signed by Ann Darden and Jacob Darden. 28th of 7ber 1719   Page 5

Holladay, Anthony: Appraisal by Henry Pitt, George

House, Thomas Copeland.　　　　R.　September 28, 1719
　　　　　　　　　　　　　　　　　　　　　　Page 6

Johnson, William:　Leg.- wife Sarah; son John; son
William; son Thomas; son Benjamin; friend Hardy Council.
Ex., son John Johnson
D.　April 10, ----　　　　　R.　September 28, 1719
Wit.　Hardy Council, Robert Council, James Council.
　　　　　　　　　　　　　　　　　　　　　　Page 9

Rayner, Francis:　Of the Upper Parish.　Leg.- wife
Joanna; my two daughters, Joanna, the wife of Thomas
Ward and Frances, the wife of William Little; grandson
Samuel Rayner, the son of my deceased son John Rayner;
to Joseph the son of Thomas Ward until Samuel Rayner is
seventeen; reversion of bequests to the said Joseph Ward.
Aforesaid sons-in-law my Exs.
D.　September 29, 1716　　　R.　September 28, 1719
Wit.　Charles Goodrich, Sr., Charles Goodrich, Jr.,
　　　　Lawrence Baker　　　　　　　　　　　Page 9

Pitt, Henry:　Leg.- my children, John, Joseph and Mary;
to son John the gold seal ring, which my father gave me.
Wife Extx.　　D.　February 6, 1718　　R.　October 28, 1719
Wit.　Arthur Smith, John Turner, Mary Smith
　　　　　　　　　　　　　　　　　　　　　　Page 10

Wrenn, Francis:　Of the Upper Parish.　Leg.- wife Eliza-
beth; to my children.　Friends, George Goodrich and Thomas
Wrenn to see my will performed.
D.　January 29, 1718　　　　R.　September 28, 1719
Wit.　William Gainor, Richard Jordan, William Allen.
　　　　　　　　　　　　　　　　　　　　　　Page 10

Williams, John.　Appraised by Philip Rayford, John
Mackmial, Jacob Darden.　Signed Mary Williams
　　October 26, 1719　　　　　　　　　　　　Page 11

Johnson, William, Sr.　Inventory presented by John
Johnston.　　October 26, 1719　　　　　　　Page

Ridley, Nathaniel.　Appraised by (pages transposed)
September 24, 1719　　　　　　　　　　　　　Page

Pitt, Henry.　Appraised by John Chapman, Richard Wil-

kinson, Thomas Moscrop. Signed Mary Pitt. Ordered
October 26, 1719.   R. 28 of Xber 1719
                                                    Page 17

Sikes, John. Of the Lower Parish. Leg.- son Joshua;
wife Sarah. Exs., wife and son Joshua
   D. August 5, 1719   R. February 22, 1719/20
   Wit. Thomas Moore, Rebecak Howell, John Davis.
                                                    Page 18

Murphery, William. Account estate, to the widow's
third, to be paid the four orphans. Signed by Barnabie
and Mary Mackinnie.   February 22, 1719/20   Page 19

Monro, Mr. Andrew. Appraised by Thomas Moscrop,
William Wilkinson, William Price. Ordered January 25,
1719. Signed, Sarah Monro.   R. February 22, 1719
                                                    Page 20

Exum, Jeremiah: Leg.- daughter Elizabeth; daughter
Mourning; daughter Christian, the land I bought of James
Collins; granddaughter Catherine Scott; my cousin Jane
Exum; daughter Sarah; daughter Mary; daughter Jane; wife.
   D. September 3, 1712   R. March 28, 1720
   Wit. John Gibbs, Thomas Godwin, Jr., Mary Godwin
                                                    Page 21

Webb, James: Leg.- William Wilkinson and his wife, 250
acres, at their decease to be equally divided between
Giles and Richard Webb. Exs., William Wilkinson and his
wife.
   D. January 19, 1719   R. March 28, 1720
   Wit. John Watts, James Snowden, William Leune (?)
                                                    Page 22

Wade, Edward. Appraised by William Spivey, John
Teasley, John Powell. (No dates)   Page 22

Evans, William. Appraised by John Chapman, Robert
Richards, Thomas Bevan. Ordered, January 25, 1719
   R. March 28, 1720   Page 23

Joyner, Bridgman. Appraised by Thomas Mandew, Giles
Driver, Andrew Griffin. Ordered in October last past.
   R. December 4, 1719. Signed, Ann Joyner   Page 23

Bevan, Mary. Appraised by John Wright, Daniel Riggins, Charles Fulgham.   R. December 21, 1719

Page 24

Hunt, Lawrence. Appraised by Edward Simmons, Edward Brantley, Richard Smith, John Person, Jr.
D. November 7, 1719   R. April 20, 1720

Page 25

Watkins, George: Leg.- friend Joseph Bracher (?)
D. August 15, 1719   R. April 25, 1720
Wit. Elizabeth Luter, John Bowen   Page 25

Stricklin, Samuel: Leg.- son Stephen; son Samuel; son Joseph; daughter Rachell. Ex., wife Abigail
D. May 27, 1718   R. April 25, 1720
Wit. Mathew Stricklin, Joseph Stricklin   Page 26

Howell, Mathew: Leg.- son Thomas; son Joseph, unborn child; to wife due me from John Gant, also money due me from Richard Braswell, John Edwards and Henry Flowers. Exs., my father Joseph Lane, Sr., Joseph Lane, Jr. and my wife Mary.
D. January 11, 1719   R. April 25, 1720
Wit. Thomas Jarrett, Arnale Pew   Page 26

Boddie, John. Leg.- son William; son John, wife Elizabeth. Wife, Extx.
D. March 10, 1719/20   R. April 25, 1720
Wit. Mary Applewhite, Robert Hadley, Richard Gent

Page 27

Rodwell, John: Leg.- sister Elizabeth Atkins, wife of Christopher Atkins; to Lucy Atkins, daughter of aforesaid; to their third child, Christopher Atkins.
D. January 20, 1719   R. April 25, 1720
Wit. John Simpson, Frances Cocke

Lanquishear, Robert: Of the Upper Parish. Leg.- wife; granddaughter Unity Lanquisher; grandson Samuel Lanquisher; grandson William Lanquisher my plantation on the Blackwater at the death of my wife; granddaughter Lettis Pitman; granddaughter Ann Pitman; grandson Samuel Pitman; son Samuel Lanquishear; son-in-law Thomas Pitman; daughter Elizabeth Pitman; son Robert Lanquishear; to son Robert's eldest daughter. Exs., wife and son Robert Lanquishear.

D. April 28, 1720   R. May 23, 1720
Wit. James Piland, Benjamin Hoddg (Hodges), Roger
        Ingram   Page 28

Tiller, John. Appraised by Edward Symonds, Edward
Brantley, Richard Smith   R. May 23, 1720
                                                  Page 29

Larner, Bartholomew: Leg.- kinswoman Mary Laughle;
Thomas Copeland and his heirs; Joseph Weston.
D. March 8, 1719/20   R. May 23, 1720
Wit. Thomas Applewhaite, John Gray   Page 30

Lancaster, Robert. Appraised by John Brantley,
Richard Gray, Benjamin Hodges. Ordered May 23, 1719
R. June 27, 1720. Signed Robert Lancaster   Page 30

Caroll, Jone: Leg.- son Thomas Cooke; Elizabeth
Weaver, Joannah Burah (?); son William Cooke; John
Carroll; son Reuben Cooke.
D. March 31, 1720   R. June 27, 1720
 Wit. Edward Chitty, Abraham Baggett   Page 32

Wilson, John. Appraised by George Goodrich, Thomas
Wrenn, Joshua Copeland. Ordered June 21, 1719
R. June 27, 1720   Signed by Frances Wilson
                                                  Page 33

Legg, Ann: Inventory, signed by William Warr (?)
D. May 19, 1720   R. June 27, 1720 Page 34

Shelly, John: Of the Upper Parish. Leg.- to brother
Thomas Shelly; to Elizabeth Ogburne, the dishes at John
Harris'; to my son John Phillips Shelly. Ex., brother
Thomas Shelly.
D. June 23, 1718   R. June 27, 1720
Wit. George Riddick, John Brantley   Page 35

Matthews, Alexander: Of ye Lower Parish. Leg.-
daughter Sarah ffulgham; to my three grandchildren,
Thomas, A------ and Catherine Joyner; son Alexander
Matthews; wife Catherine. Exs., wife and son Alexander.
D. May 23, 1713   R. June 27, 1720
Wit. John Jones, Joshua Turner, Joseph Chapman
                                                  Page 36

Hunter, William: Leg.- wife Elizabeth; daughter Mary;
daughter Ann; daughter Martha. My brother James Hunter,
Thomas Moscrop and William Green to divide my estate.
Wife Extx.
   D. April 29, 1720   R. July 25, 1720
   Wit. William Green, Robert Smith   Page 36

Smith, Mary: Leg.- daughter Mary Kelly; grandson
Nicholas Ogburne; daughter Martha Smith; daughter Mary
Smith; my grandchildren, Simon, Elizabeth and Mary Og-
burne. Joseph Smith, William Weston and Joseph Weston
to divide my estate. Exs., daughter Martha Smith and
Joseph Weston.
   D. August 12, 1719   R. July 25, 1720
   Wit. Joseph Smith, John Daniel   Page 37

Shelly, John. Appraised by Lawrence Baker, James
Briggs, James Sampson.   R. Jly 25, 1720' Page 38

Harrison, William. Appraised by ----- Miller, -----
White, ------ Lee.   R. July 25, 1720 Page 39

Hill, Thomas: Leg.- wife Mary; son Thomas; son Joseph;
daughter Mary, the land bought of Mr. Alexander Forbes,
which formerly belonged to Mrs. Silvestra Hill; daughter
Ann. Exs., wife and son Thomas Hill
   D. May 3, 1719   R. July 25, 1720
   Wit. (torn)   Page 39

Watkins, James. Appraised by Thomas English, Philip
Pierce, Nicholas Tynes.   R. July 25, 1720
Signed, Martha Watkins   Page 40

Bennett, Richard: Of ye Upper Parish. Leg.- son
Richard; son ------ land to be taken out of Mr. John
Coffer's patent of 1450 acres; to Jane Coffer and her
sons, Robert and John Coffer, the land where I now live
which I bought of Mr. William Miller; to Richard Coffer;
to Magdalen Coffer; to my granddaughter, Frances Manggum;
daughter Silvestra. Exs., Jane Coffer and William Allen.
Friends, John Carter and James Carter to see that my will
is performed.
   D. March 30, 1720   R. May 23, 1720
   Wit. John Carter, James Carter, William Allen, Sr.
                                      Page 41

Woodley, Andrew: Leg.- son Thomas; ----- ye two
brothers, Thomas and John Woodley; grandson John Copeland; granddaughter Elizabeth Copeland; to my daughter
Copeland. Ex., son John Woodley
    D. September 25, 1718   ·R. August 22, 1720
    Wit. A. Forbes, George Bell, Thomas Wilson
Page 42

Hodges, Roger. Appraised by George Goodrich, Thomas
Wrenn, Edward Miller.   R. May 8, 1720   Page 43

Branch, Francis: Leg.- son Francis; my wife; son
George; son Benjamin; daughter Elizabeth; daughter Mary;
daughter Sarah; daughter Liddia; daughter Jane; daughter
Hannah; daughter Martha; daughter Ann; to my cousin Catherine Branch. Exs., son Francis, wife and daughter Mary
    D. April 22, 1717   R. August 22, 1720
    Wit. John Joyner, Elizabeth Doiel,
            Elizabeth Benson   Page 44

Bennett, Richard. Appraised by Arthur Jones, Thomas
Ward, William Bell. Signed, Jane Coffer
    R. August 22, 1720   Page 45

Harris, George: Leg.- son George; son Robert; daugh-
ter Elizabeth; daughter Sarah; son Joseph; son William
Wife Martha Harris, Extx.
    D. December 15, 1719   R. August 22, 1720
    Wit. Martin Harris, Daniel Doyle, John Bowen
Page 47

Larner, Bartholomew. Appraised by Charles Norsworthy,
William Best, Humphry Marshall. R. Aug. 22, 1720
Page 47

Smith, Martha. Appraised by Tristram Norsworthy,
Robert Richards, Henry Pitt. Ordered July 26, 1720
R. August 15, 1720. Recorded as the estate of Mary
Smith. Ralph Frissell an Appraiser
Signed by Joseph Weston   Page 49

Watts, John. Appraised by William Wilkinson, Thomas
Uzzell, William Price. Ordered May 24, 1720
    R. August 22, 1720   Page 49

Exum, William: Leg.- son John; son William; son Joseph;

son Robert; daughter Anne; daughter Sarah; wife Susan.
   D. April 25, 1720   R. August 25, 1720
   Wit. Thomas Atkinson, Francis Exum, William Crocker
                                             Page 51

   Godwin, William: Leg.- son William; son John; son
Joseph; daughter Sarah G-----; daughter ----- Bridger;
daughter Mary Whitehead; daughter Martha Cotton; daugh-
ter Jane. Wife Elizabeth, Extx.
   D. November 21, 1710   R. September 26, 1720
   Wit. William Pope, John Whitley, James Edwards
                                             Page 52

   Dukes, John: Of the Lower Parish. Leg.- son -----;
son John; son James; son Robert; estate between my wife
and children, sons to be of age at 21 and daughters at
marriage
   D. March 16, ----   R. August 3, 1720
   Wit. (torn)   Page 53

   Hill, Thomas. Appraised by ------ Wrenn, John Goodrich.   R. September 26, 1720   Page 54

   Barnes, James: Leg.- son Thomas; son Edward, ye gun I
bought of Philip Thomas; wife Sarah
   D. March 2, 1719/20   R. October --, 1720
   Wit. William Thomas, Susannah Gregory, John Dunkley
                                             Page 55

   Doyle, Samuel: Leg.- son Daniel; son Edward; daugh-
ter Elizabeth; daughter Mary. Wife Jane, Extx.
   D. March 1, 1719/20   R. October 24, 1720
   Wit. Richard Batman (?), Joseph Bradshaw
                                             Page 55

   Matthews, Richard: Leg.- daughter Mary Howell; grand-
daughter Mary Howell; granddaughter Mary Matthews; son
Richard ------
   D. (torn)   R. November --, 1720
   Wit. Jacob Darden, Thomas E------, Edward ------
                                             Page 56

   Bodie, John. Appraised by Arthur Pursell, Thomas
Woodley, James Bragg   R. November 28, 1720
                                             Page 57

   Kirle, William: Leg.- eldest son William Kirle, the

son of Margaret Cobb, daughter of Robert and Elizabeth·
Cobb; to my son Robert Kirle, the son of Margaret Cobb,
daughter of Robert and Elizabeth Cobb; wife Ellinor; --
my ------ to wit., George, William and Joseph the sons of
-----, when their mother Elianor marries again; my son
William Kirle, the son of Elionor Kirle. Wife, Extx.
    D. December 24, 1719   R. November 28, 1720
    Wit. Michael M-----, John Murphrey, Sarah -----
                                            Page 58

Colwell, John: Of ye Lower Parish. Leg.- Elizabeth
Harris; Edward Green; to Benjamin Crocker, the son of
Robert Crocker; to Arthur Crocker, land adjoining John
Rochell; to William Crocker; Joseph Crocker; Elizabeth
Crocker; Mary Crocker; Sarah Crocker, all the children
of Robert Crocker. Ex., Robert Crocker
    D. August 10, 1720   R. January 23, 1720
    Wit. Needham Bryan, Nathaniel Powell   Page 59

Lawrence, Robert: Leg.- to my ----- during her natural
life; to my ----- to him and his heirs forever; son
Robert; after decease of my wife, certain bequests to my
son-in-law Henry Gay. Ex., son-in-law John Gay
    D. April 20, 1720   R. January 23, 1720
    Wit. Ambrose Sanders, Jane Gay   Page 59

Page, Thomas: Leg.- wife Alice; son Thomas; daughter
Rebecka; daughter M-----; daughter Alice; granddaughter
----- Gay. Ex., son John Page
    D. February 20, 1719   R. ----------, 1720
    Wit. Mary Ricks, Abraham Ricks, William ------
                                            Page 60

Green, John: Leg.- daughter Mary, the wife of Peter
Williams; son Peter; daughter Sarah, the wife of Robert
Coggens; son Edward; son Thomas; wife Ann. Wife, Extx.
    D. March 21, 1719   R. January 23, 1720
    Wit. Arthur Smith, Patrick Sweeney, Mary Bryan
                                            Page 61

Davis, Mary: Leg.- daughter Prudence; grandson
William Da---; son Samuel and all my children. Daughter
Prudence Davis, Extx. I request Captain James Day and
my brother William Green to assist her
    D. September 20, 1720   R. January 23, 1720
                                            Page 61

Terrell, Joane. Appraised by Reuben Cooke; Thomas

Holliman; John Stevenson, Christopher Holliman
   R. January 23, 1720   Page 62

Hayes, Peter: Of ye Upper Parish. Leg.- son Robert;
to my ------ John and Peter Stevens; to ----ther Hayes.
Wife Elizabeth, Extx.
   D. November 10, 1720   R. February 27, 1720
   Wit. Arthur Jones, William Crocker, Robert Hayes
                                        Page 63

Wilson, James: Leg.- son William; son George; son
John; son James; son Gutridge; son Joseph; son Samuel;
son Benjamin. Extx., loving wife
   D. March 28, 1720   R. February 27, 1720
   Wit. George Goodrich, John Goodrich   Page 64

Frissell, John: Leg.- sister Mary Frissell; to the
widow of my brother George Frissell; Cousin Ann Frissell;
cousin, Violet Frissell; cousin, Mary Frissell; cousin
John Driver; to Thomas Smith. Sister Mary Extx.
   D. August 24, 1720   R. February 27, 1720
   Wit. Arthur Smith, Bridgett Ducke   Page 64

Lawrence, Robert. Appraised by Thomas Gale, Jacob
Darden, Thomas Sikes, John Pope.   R. February 27, 1720
                                        Page 65

Meecum, John. Appraised by John Crews, John Brantley,
Richard Gray. Signed by Susanna Meecum
   February 8, 1720/1   Page 67

Duckes (Dukes), John. Appraised by Ambrose Adley (Had-
ley), Timothy Tynes, Jeremiah Fly. Signed by Bridgett
Duckes. Ordered, November 8, 1720
   R. February 27, 1720   Page 67

Davis, John. Appraised by John Screws, Jr., Richard
Blunt, Edward Crocker, Arthur Davis. Signed Susanna
Davis. Ordered January 23, 1720/21
   R. February 27, 1720   Page 68

Murre, John. Appraised by Philip Wheadon, John Miller, Ellis (Elias) Hodges   R. February 27, 1720/21
                                        Page 69

Lawrence, Robert. Additional Appraisal. Signed by
John Gay   Page 70

Pardue, Phillip. Appraised by John Brantley, John
Fiveash, Richard Gray. Ordered March 11, 1720/21
R. March 27, 1721   Page 71

Bulger, Sarah: Leg.- brother William Smith; sister
Parker; brother Nicholas Smith; to Mary Loathlin; sister
Martha Smith; brother Joseph Smith; to Anna Barnes; cou-
sin William Smith; sister Weston, at her decease to Jo-
seph Weston; remainder of my estate to be divided be-
tween Nicholas, Joseph, Annar and Martha Smith
Ex., brother Joseph Smith
  D. January 4, 1720/21   R. March 27, 1721
  Wit. James Benn, William Hawkins   Page 71

Barnes, Jacob. Appraised by Thomas Copeland, Henry
Pitt, Humphry Marshall. Ordered October 22, 1720
R. March 27, 1721   Page 72

Logan, Elizabeth. Appraised by Edward Driver, Giles
Driver. Ordered February 27, 1720/21
  R. March 27, 1721   Page 74

Wood, Elizabeth: Of ye Upper Parish. Leg.- James
Pyland, my whole estate. Ex., James Pyland
  D. November 22, 1720   R. March 27, 1721
                                                 Page 75

House, George: Leg.- brother James House; my wife
Elizabeth. Wife. Extx.
  D. Anthony Holliday, Brian Dogan, Ann Cuningam (?)
     Robert Lawrence   Page 76

Williams, Thomas. Appraised at the plantation of
Mary Williams, by Nathaniel Parker, William Hawkins,
Thomas Parker, William Weston. Ordered March 27, 1720
  R. April 24, 1721   Page 77

Driver, Mary: Leg.- son Giles; son Charles; daughter
Hardy Goodson; daughter Mary House; daughter Susanna

Bulls (?); granddaughter Sarah Driver; son Thomas. Exs., sons Thomas and William Driver

    D. August 24, 1719   R. April 24, 1721

    Wit. Christopher Reynolds, John Butler   Page 79

Benbrigg, George: Leg.- whole estate to John Butler, Sr. D. December 28, 1720   R. April 24, 1721

    Wit. Edward Driver, Thomas Driver, John Driver

                        Page 80

Denson, James: Leg.- son James; daughter Frances; daughter Sarah; son Joseph my plantation in Nansemond County, also my land in Charles City County, in Parish of Weyanoke; wife Sarah; cousin James Denson, the son of John Denson; to unborn child. Wife Extx.

    D.   July 15, 1720   R. April 24, 1721

    Wit. Richard Hutchins   Page 80

Luck, John. Appraised by Philip Wheadon, William Baker, John Miller, Thomas Renn. Ordered March 16, 1720/21   R. May 22, 1721   Page 82

Mathews, Richard. Inventory, signed by Richard Mathews.   May 22, 1721   Page 83

Driver, Charles. Appraised by Richard Casey, John Butler, Christopher Reynolds. Ordered May 12, 1721

    R. May 22, 1721   Signed, Giles Driver

                        Page 84

Jones, Richard: Of ye Upper Parish. Leg.- daughter Ann Bell, the land on which she and her husband William Bell live; son Samuel; son Richard; daughter Elizabeth; daughter Christian; daughter Sarah; daughter Mary; daughter Martha Davis; wife Elizabeth; son Joseph; son Benjamin. Wife Extx. Friends William Bell and Thomas Harris to see my will performed.

    D.   R. May 22, 1721

    Wit. William Gainor, Arthur Davis, William Allen

                        Page 84

Amos, William: Of the Lower Parish. Leg.- my friend Elizabeth Whitaker, the daughter of Elizabeth Whitaker of Denby (Denbeigh), Warwick County; friend, Col. John Allen; friend James Pyland all my books on Physick, Surgery and all my instruments. Elizabeth Whitaker, Extx.

D. May 10, 1720   R. June 26, 1721
Wit. William Drew, Mathew Jones, Lawrence Baker
Page 86

Ingrum, John: Of the Upper Parish. Leg.- son Roger;
son John; daughter Elizabeth; son William. Ex., son
John Ingrum
D. December 21, 1720   R. June 26, 1721
Wit. James Pyland
Page 87

Murphry, William: Leg.- son Micaell the land I purchased of Robert Hooks and of Jacob Darden; son John;
wife Sarah; son William; daughter Catherine; daughter
Margaret Lawrence; daughter Elizabeth Farrow (?); daughter Elinor Kirle; daughter Sarah; daughter Ann. Exs.,
sons Michael and John Murphry
D. November 14, 1717   R. June 26, 1721
Wit. Roger Tarleton, Jr., Joseph Tarleton, William
     Tarleton
Page 88

Seward, William: Leg.- son Benjamin; daughter Sarah;
daughter Elizabeth; daughter Mary; son Samuel; wife
Elizabeth
D.   R. July 24, 1721
Wit. Joseph Holt, John Dortch
Page 90

Brantley, Edward. Aged 72 years. Leg.- son Edward;
grandson John Balmer. Exs., wife Ann and Dave Evans
D.   1720   R. July 24, 1721
Wit. John Brantley, James Madree (?)
Page 90

Browne, John: Leg.- son James, my land on Timothy
Walker's road in Surry County; son Thomas land on the
same road; daughter Elizabeth; daughter Mary; daughter
Ann Camerine; daughter Bridgett Wresbury.
Exs., sons James and Thomas Browne
D. January --, 1720/21   R. July 24, 1721
Wit. Thomas Nickson, George Goodson, Peter Green
Page 90

Murphry, William. Appraised by Jacob Darden, John
Pope, Richard Pope, Thomas Gale. Signed by Michael and
John Murphry.   R. July 24, 1721 Page 91

Hall, Pool: Leg.- my second son Joseph; if he pays my

debt to Capt. William Wilkinson; third son John Hall;
first son, Thomas Poole Hall; between my wife and all my
children
D. November 20, 1720   R. August 28, 1721
                                                    Page 95

Amos, William. Appraised by James Wilson, George
Riddick, John Brantley, Richard Gray. Signed, Elizabeth
Whitaker   R. August 28, 1721   Page 96

Wormington, Jeremiah. Estate sold by order of
Court. Signed, Joseph Godwin, Sheriff
R. August 28, 1721   Page 98

Martin, George. Estate sold by order of Court.
Signed, Joseph Godwin, Sheriff. R. August 28, 1721
                                             Page 98

Ridley, Nathaniel. Account of the stock, returned
by Joseph Copeland and Ellis (Elias) Hodges
R. August 28, 1721   Page 100

Gibbins, John: Leg.- Mr. William Kinchen; Henry
Harris; Mathew Harris; Mary Adkins, the daughter of James
Adkins; John Jackson; Thomas Harris, the son of Edward
Harris; Robert Harris. Ex., Mr. William Kinchen
D. August 20, 1721   R. September 25, 1721
Wit. Edward Chitty, Edward Harris   Page 101

Dowles, Thomas: Leg.- son Thomas; son Joseph; daughter
Ann; daughter Elizabeth; daughter Martha; daughter Chris-
tian; daughter Easter; daughter Rebecca; daughter Rachell
Wife, Catherine, Extx.
D. February 19, 1720/21   R. September 25, 1721
Wit. Edward Chitty, Thomas Stevenson   Page 102

Howell, Mathew. Appraised by Thomas Jarrell, John
Edwards, Robert Newsum. Ordered April 21, 1720
Signed by Joseph Lane   R. September 25, 1721
                                             Page 103

Hall, Pool. Appraised by John Long, John Wright,
William Price.   R. September 25, 1721
                                             Page 105

Goodrich, George: Leg.- daughter Elizabeth; at the death of my wife, I desire that William Seward to take care of her
 D. March 15, 1720/21   R. September 25, 1721
 Wit. Alexander Forbes, John Goodrich   Page 106

Coles, Sarah. Appraised by John Miller, Henry White,
George Bradshaw   R. October 23, 1721
                                                Page 107

Parmenter, Na. Estate sold by order of Court. Signed
by Joseph Godwin, Sheriff.   October 23, 1721   Page 107

Thropp, John: Leg.- sister Sarah Batt; sister Strat-field Pierce; after the decease of my mother-in-law Mary Bell, to my sister Sarah Batt's two sons, she had by William George, Elias and William George; to Mathew Jordan ten pounds with which to repair the Meeting House at "Levy Neck"; friend Susanna Jordan; my cousin Thomas Pearce Ex., friend William Batt.
 D. January 20, 1720/21   R. November 27, 1721
 Wit. John Miller, Abraham Cole, John Bradshaw
                                                Page 108

Bracey, Francis. Inventory. R. February 26, 1721
                                                Page 109

Goodrich, George. Appraised by Joseph Copeland,
Thomas Wrenn, Elias Hodges. Presented by Thomas Walton,
Sheriff.   R. February 27, 1721   Page 110

Rigins, Daniel. Appraised at the house of Ann Rigins
by Charles Fulgham, Robert Richards, Jr., Christopher
Dickinson.   R. March 26, 1721 Page 111

Bell, John: Leg.- son John; son George; son Benjamin;
son Edward; daughter Alice Miller; daughter Olive Bell;
wife Sarah and her three daughters and son. Exs., wife
and friend John Miller
 D. April 21, 1721   R. March 26, 1722
 Wit. William Dixson, Thomas Roberts, Thomas Goodson
                                                Page 113

Davis, Thomas: Of ye Upper Parish. Leg.- son Thomas
and William the tract of land, which I bought of the widow

Blake, on which my son John lived; daughter Frances
Williamson; son George Williamson; wife Elizabeth, the
plantation bought of William Exum; son Benjamin; grand-
son Thomas Davis; son Edward. Wife, Extx.
  D. March 4, 1721   R. April 23, 1722
  Wit. William Bridger, Thomas Ryall, William Story
Page 114

  Kea, Robert. Appraised by James Wilson, James Pyland, George Riddick   R. April 23, 1722
Page 116

  Driver, John. Appraised by Timothy Tynes, William
Brock, John Butler. Ordered March 26, 1722
Presented by Elizabeth Driver, his widow
  R. April 23, 1722   Page 117

  Williamson, George: Leg.- son George; son Robert;
grandson Jacob Darden; to son John and son Robert my
tract of land on the Blackwater; son Thomas; daughter
Hester, the plantation on which Mr. Rueben Proctor lives,
being land escheated by Col. Joseph Bridger and so made
over to my mother and my brother Robert Williamson by the
said Col. Bridger; daughter Mary; daughter Patience;
daughter Elizabeth; daughter Juliana. Son Robert, Ex.
  D. April 26, 1721   R. May 28, 1722
  Wit. Francis Williamson, William Vasser, Joseph Price
Page 118

  Williamson, George. Appraised by William Crocker,
William Vasser, William Moore, Edward Chitty
Signed by Robert Williamson   Page 120

  Bell, John. Appraised by John Woodley, Reuben Proctor, Thomas Goodson. Signed Sarah Bell
  R. June 25, 1722   Page 121

  Lowery, Arthur. Appraised by Joseph Parnell, John
Dowles. Signed by Jane Lowery   R. September 24, 1722
Page 123

  Morse, Richard. Appraised by William Arrington,
Owen Myrick, John Sorjiner (?)   Signed by Mary Chapman
  R. July 23, 1722
Page 122

Larner, Bartholomew. Additional Inventory. Signed
by Thomas Copeland. 24 of 7ber 1722   Page 123

Clarke, John: Leg.- loving wife; to Thomas Davison,
the son of William Davison; to William Phillips, the son
of John Phillips, the tract on which my son James Clarke
lived until he died; to Jane Hunnifort; son William; to
Mary Davison and Mary Phillips. Ex., William Davison
     D. March 17, 1721/22   R. November 26, 1722
     Wit. Edward Chitty, Joseph Parnell   Page 124

Lancaster, Sarah: Leg.- granddaughter Ann Craft;
granddaughter Sarah Meacor; granddaughter Ann Kea; to
Mary Mangum, the daughter of John Mangum; to Sarah Mangum
the daughter of John Mangum; to Bridgett Bennett, the
daughter of James Bennett; to Sarah Bennett, the daughter
of James Bennett; granddaughter Elizabeth Meacor; granddaughter Martha Meacor; granddaughter Susan Meacor; to
Mary Ussery; to my sister Elizabeth Hood; to Mary Sowdell;
daughter Susanna Meacor; grandson Lewis Meacor; to Mary
Jonas; to Benjamin Bell; to Samuel (?); remainder of my
estate to my daughter Mary Bell. Mary Bell, Extx
     D. October 31, 1722   R. January 29, 1722
     Wit. Thomas Roser, William Hood   Page 125

Gray, Richard: Of ye Upper Parish. Leg.- son John
daughter Elizabeth; daughter Mary; daughter Martha; grandson Benjamin Gray, if Mary, the wife of James Maddera will
allow my Executors to keep him; to my grandchildren, John,
Rodgers and Elizabeth Delk; daughter Patience. Estate to
be divided by Mathew Wills, Thomas Moreland and Lawrence
Baker. Exs., son John and daughter Mary Gray
     D. October 21, 1722   R. February 25, 1722
     Wit. Mathew Wills, Francis Wills, Lawrence Baker
                                                  Page 126

Goodson, Edward: Leg.- daughter Joan Floyd; daughter
Martha. Joan Floyd, Extx.
     D. December 3, 1722   R. February 25, 1722
     Wit. Nicholas Tines, Jr., William Couldson
                                                  Page 127

Watts, John. Appraised at the request of Joseph
Wright, by John Hurst, Thomas Uzzell, John Wright
     R. February 25, 1722   Page 128

Underwood, William. Appraised by Thomas Gale, Giles
Driver, John Sellaway. December 24, 1722   Page 129

Goodson, Edward. Appraised by Thomas Uzzell, John Dawson, Theophilus Joyner. Signed by Joane Floyd
  R. March 25, 1723   Page 129

Evans, William. Additional Inventory. Signed by
Charles Fulgham.   R. March 26, 1723   Page 131

Dees, Manll. Appraised by Benjamin Chapman Donaldson, James Turner, Edward Simmons. Ordered November last
  R. April 22, 1723   Page 132

                      Appraised by Henry Pitt, Thomas
Muscrop, Thomas Copeland   Page 133

Fuller, Ezekiell: Leg.- son Ezekiell; son Solomon;
daughter Ann; daughter Mary; son Benjamin; son John;
son Joseph; son Arthur; son Timothy; son Henry; daughter
Martha Whitley, daughter Onner Allen; wife Deborah
  D. November 19, 1722   R. June 24, 1723
  Wit. Arthur Smith, Mathew Lowry, William Ward

                                        Page 133

Clarke, John. Appraised by Thomas Williams, Thomas
Ward, George Carter, William Davison
  R. August 26, 1723   Page 134

Matthews, Alexander. Appraised by Arthur Smith, John
Dawson, Thomas Woodley, Ambrose Hadley
  R. July 22, 1723   Page 135

Price, Thomas. Appraised by Christopher Reynolds,
Thomas Pinner, Benjamin Beale. Signed by Abraham
Cornall (?)   R. September 23, 1723   Page 137

Amos, Dr. William. Estate settled by James Day and
Mathew Jones.   R. September 24, 1723   Page 140

West, William. Estate settled by Arthur Whitehead
  R. October 29, 1723   Page 140

Norsworthy, Thomas: Leg.- cousin Elizabeth, the daughter of my brother John Norsworthy; cousin Leah Norsworthy; cousin Julian, the daughter of my brother John Norsworthy, to John Marshall the son of Humphry Marshall; to Martha Baker, the daughter of my sister Martha Baker. Ex., brother Charles Norsworthy
D. July 31, 1723   R. October 29, 1723
Wit. James Benn, Thomas Goodman   Page 141

Giles, Thomas. Appraised by Robert Richards, Jr., Thomas Green. Ordered September 5, 1723
R. October 24, 1723
Arthur Benn also an appraiser   Page 141

Meacome, Thomas. Appraised by James Wilson, James Briggs, Thomas Skelton. Ordered September 20, 1723
R. October 28, 1723   Page 143

Atkinson, John: Of ye Upper Parish. Leg.- wife Ann; son Christopher; son John; daughter Ruth; daughter Hannah Cooke; daughter Ann Carrell; daughter Mary Richardson; daughter Olive Bruce; daughter Elizabeth White. Wife, Extx. D. April 18, 1717   R. October 28, 1723
Wit. William Atkinson, Joseph Chapman, Hugh Hunniford
Page 144

Atkinson, James: Leg.- daughter Mary; son James; wife Mary. Exs., wife and daughter Mary Atkinson
D. July 28, 1723   R. December 23, 1723
Wit. Thomas Atkinson, John Stevenson   Page 146

Moscrop, Thomas: Leg.- wife Susanna; daughter Mary; daughter Jean, reversion of bequests to brother Mathew's son Thomas, if living, if not to his son John and James Middleton the son of Jane Middleton. Exs., daughter Mary, Robert Murry and Christopher Dickinson
D.   1723   R. January 27, 1723
Wit. Elizabeth Shaw, Robert King, Robert Murry
Page 146

Everitt, Thomas: Leg.- son Thomas; son John; son Samuel; loving wife. Exs., brother Samuel Everitt and Thomas Dixson
D. October 9, 1723   R. January 27, 1723
Wit. Samuel Everitt, Thomas Dixon, Jennet Jenkins
Page 148

Moscrop, Thomas. Appraised by Robert Richards, John
Butler, John Hurst   R. February 24, 1723
Page 149

Day, Thomas: Of ye Upper Parish. Leg.- aunt Elizabeth Lear; cousin Thomas Day, all the land that I bought
of John Thomas, with reversion of the bequest to my cousin James Ridley; to sister Jones; brother James Day; to
brother-in-law Mathew Jones; to brother-in-law William
Bridger; to the three daughters of Nathaniel Ridley and
the daughter of Mathew Jones. Ex., Mathew Jones
    D. January 19, 1723   R. February 24, 1723
    Wit. Joseph Seward, William Bamer, Elizabeth Hodges
Page 151

Edwards, James, Sr.: Leg.- son Robert; son Joshua; son
James; daughter Sarah Poope (Pope). Wife Ann, Extx
    D. July 16, 1723   R. February 24, 1723
    Wit. John Whitley, John Williams, Joshua Turner
Page 151

English, William. Appraised by James Piland, James
Wilson, Benjamin Hodges. Signed Anne English
    Ordered, February 14, 1723/4   R. February 24, 1724
Page 152

Lundy, James, Sr.: Leg.- son James; daughter Burchel;
son Edward; son Robert; daughter Elizabeth; son Thomas a
tract of land after the decease of John Tiller and Susanna his wife; wife Elizabeth. Wife, Extx.
    D. February 20, 1717   R. March 23, 1723
    Wit. Thomas Harris, Thomas Addison, Catherine Harris
    Presented in Court by Elizabeth Perry, formerly Eliza-
beth Lundy   Page 153

Weston, Stephen: Of Newport Parish. Leg.- loving
mother; brother Joseph; sister Anne; sister Mary; brother William, brother Benjamin. Ex., brother Joseph
    D. February 20, 1723   R. March 23, 1723
    Wit. Peter Lugg, Nathaniel Parker   Page 154

Day, Thomas. Appraised by Joseph Copeland, James
Wilson, Thomas Wrenn. Signed Mathew Jones
    R. March 23, 1723   Page 155

Ricks, Isaac: Leg.- son Isaac; son Abraham; son
Robert, the plantation on which my son John formerly

lived; son James; daughter Jean; two grandchildren,
Isaac and Martha, the children of my deceased son Jacob.
Exs., son James and daughter Jean Ricks
   D. September 26, 1721   R. April 27, 1724
   Wit. John Sellaway, Thomas Sikes, John Page, William
        Denson, William Wilkinson   Page 157

Sellaway, John, Sr.: Leg.- wife Margaret; son Richard;
son John; daughter Margaret, now the wife of Henry Sanders;
grandson John Sanders; son-in-law John Allen and my daughter Elizabeth, his wife; grandson John Allen; daughter
Martha; daughter Mary; daughter Katherine. Wife Extx
   D. January 24, 1712   R. April 28, 1724
   Wit. William Havett (?), Robert Cogen, William Cogen
                                             Page 158

Vasser, William: Of ye Upper Parish. Leg.- daughter
Mary; son Joseph; son Benjamin; daughter Ann; son William;
daughter Olive; son Jacob; son Jonathan; daughter Rebecca;
son Peter. Wife Ann, Extx.
   D. June 25, 1723   R. May 25, 1724
   Wit. John Williams, Francis Williamson, George William-
        son, William Moore   Page 160

Kea, Robert. Account of estate returned by Ralph and
Alexandera Murry   R. June 22, 1724 Page 161

Jordan, Richard: Leg.- wife Rebecca; son Richard; son
Joseph; son Benjamin; son Mathew; daughter Elizabeth;
daughter Mary; daughter Patience. Exs., wife and bro-
ther James Jordan
   D. December 26, 1723   R. October 26, 1724
   Wit. John Howell, Edward Haile, Robert Tyler
                                             Page 161

Ennis, Walter. Appraised by Joseph Parker, Francis
Myrick, Joseph Turner. Signed by Winifred Ennis
Ordered October 30, 1724   R. November 23, 1724
                                             Page 163

Long, John: Leg.- son John; daughter Martha; reversion
of bequest to son John to Henry and Samson West. Wife,
Extx.
   D. March 16, 1720/21   R. December 28, 1724
   Wit. John Long, William West, John Wright
                                             Page 163

Rayford, Phillip: Leg.- son Robert; daughter Mary;
daughter Anne; daughter Patience; to son Robert all the
cattle at John Person's; daughter Sarah; son William; son
Mathew; son Phillip; wife. Son Robert, Ex. Brother-in-
law William Kinchen and brother-in-law William Crumpler,
trustees. D. July 23, 1724   R. December 28, 1724
  Wit. John Crumpler, William Crumpler, Jr.

                                              Page 164

  Driver, Joseph. Appraised by William Green, John
Wright, Richard Wilkinson, Epaproditus Williams
Ordered February 24, 1724   R. February 23, 1725
Signed by Edward Driver   Page 165

  Murry, John: Leg.- son George; son William; daughter
Elizabeth Woodson; grandson Thomas Murry, the son of my
deceased son John Murry; grandson William Murry, son of
my son William; grandson George Murry, the son of my son
George; son Thomas; grandson James Woodson
  D. October 1, 1724   R. March 22, 1724
  Wit. Richard Hurst, Edward Miller, John Miller
  Codicil changing bequests
  Wit. Thomas Wrenn, Elias Hodges   Page 166

  Norsworthy, Tristram: Of Newport Parish. Leg.- youngest son George, the plantation on which Mycell Rogers lived (not 18); second son John; Eldest son Tristram; wife
Sarah; daughter Sarah; daughter Elizabeth; daughter Frances; daughter Martha. Son Tristram, Ex. Friends, John
and George Norsworthy, overseers
  D. March 5, 1709/10   R.
  Wit. Joseph Bridger, Thomas Walton, William Williams,
       George Norsworthy   Page 167

  Note,-that the above and subsequent wills were left in
the office unrecorded by Mr. Henry Lightfoot, late Clerk,
my predecessor, wherefore, I have committed them to re-
cord, lest the County, sustain damage. Signed,
                                    James Ingles
                                              Page 167

  Arrington, William: Leg.- son Arthur; son William;
son John; grandson William Arrington; son Benjamin; daugh-
ter Mary Sykes; daughter Elizabeth Crumpler; daughter
Sarah Riggan; granddaughter Ann Riggan; wife Elizabeth
Exs., sons John and Benjamin Arrington and wife
  D. May 4, 1725   R.
  Wit. James Cooper, John Dunkley   Page 169

Fulgham, Nicholas: Leg.- son Nicholas; the land I purchased of my cousin John Fulgham to my son Charles; to
grandson John Lucks, land on the Blackwater; daughter
Martha, the wife Robert Richards; daughter Susannah, the
wife of Thomas Whitley; grandchildren, Susannah, Robert
and Mary Richards. Exs., Nicholas and Charles Fulgham
   D. January 6, 1719/20   R.
Wit. Mathew Lowrey, Arthur Smith, Arthur Smith, Jr.
Page 170

Best, Mary: Leg.- daughter Ann; son William; son
Thomas; grandson Daniel Batten; son John. Exs., son
John and John Hawkins
   D. January 8, 1724   R.
Wit. James Montgomery, Grace Minton   Page 171

Monro, Sarah: Of Newport Parish. Leg.- son Robert
Pitt; daughter Henrietta Monro; daughter, Sarah Monro;
daughter Mary Monro. Ex., son John Monro
   D. May 31, 1725   R.
Wit. John House, Edward Weatherly   Page 172

Day, James: Leg.- son James; son Thomas. Exs., wife
and son James Day
   D. September 26, 1725   R.
Wit. W. Bridger, Jr., Melchizadick Webb, John Proctor
Page 172

Norsworthy, George: Leg.- wife Christian; son George;
daughter Elizabeth, a negro at Capt. William Wilkinson's,
in lieu of what her grandmother Elizabeth Bridger left
her; to daughter Martha, what her grandmother Elizabeth
Bridger left her; daughter Christian. Exs., wife and
brother-in-law William Scott
   D. December 4, 1724
Wit. Tristram Norsworthy, Peter Lugg, William Denson
Page 173

Smelly, Lewis: Leg.- son Giles; daughter Elizabeth
Joyner; daughter Ann; daughter Mary; wife Elizabeth
Exs., wife and son Giles Smelly
   D. October 20, 1724   R
Wit. John Dunkley   Page 174

Braswell, Richard: Leg.- son Richard; son Robert; son
Valentine; son Jacob; son John; daughter Martha Murfrey;
daughter Ann Strickland; daughter Jane Williams; granddaughter Susannah Braswell. Ex., wife Sarah

D. July 28, 1724/25   R.
Wit. Edward Powers, Sr., Edward Powers   Page 174

Walsten, Mary: Of ye Lower Parish. Leg.- daughter
Mary Baldwin; daughter Sarah Baldwin; daughter Prudence
Baldwin; son William Baldwin. Exs., grandsons, Mathew
and Arthur Lowry
    D. June 14, 1725   R.
Wit. John Dawson, Theophilus Joiner   Page 175

    Whitley, Arthur. Appraised at the house of Thomas
Allings, by William Noyall, Richard Casey, John Butler
    D. April 23, 1725   Page 175

    Brown, Edward. Appraised at the house of Gyles
Driver, by Christopher Reynolds, John Butler, William
Noyall.   November 23, 1725   Page 176

    Norsworthy, George. Appraised by Henry Pitt,
Arthur Benn, Thomas Copeland   March 12, 1724
                                                  Page 176

    King, Robert, Sr.: Leg.- son Robert; son Henry; son
Samuel; son Arthur. Ex., son Robert. Thomas Moscrop
to divide estate.   D.   (No dates)
    Wit. Thomas Moscrop, Robert Murry, Sarah Pilkington.
                                                  Page 178

    Brantley, John. Appraised by James Pyland, Arthur
Wills (?), James Wilson   April 26, 1725   Page 180

    Forbes, Alexander. Appraised by Elias Hodges, Samuel
Davis, Thomas Mu-----   April 21, 1726   Page 180

    Bridger, Col. Samuel. Account estate. To William
Wilkinson and Elizabeth his wife one-third of her father,
William Webb's estate. We the subscribers, Thomas Walton
and Mathew Jones have settled the accounts of Col Bridger
and Madam Elizabeth Bridger   Page 182

    Driver, Gyles. Appraised by John Council, John

Dawtrey (Daughtrey), Richard Wootten   1725
                                              Page 183

Watts, John. Account estate, settled by Joseph Godwin,
William Wilkinson   Page 184

Norsworthy, Tristram. Appraised by Nathaniel Parker,
Joseph Smith, William Weston, Thomas Parker
March 22, 1725   Page 186

King, Robert. Appraised by Joseph Smith, William
Smith, Tristram Norsworthy, William Weston
November 17, 1725   Page 188

Fulgham, Nicholas. Appraised by Hugh Giles, Richard
Wilkinson, Christopher Dickinson   Page 189

Wilkinson, Richard: Leg.- daughter Rachel; son Richard;
son-in-law Henry Turner; to Elizabeth Turner, who now
lives with me; daughter Elizabeth; daughter Mary; daughter
Ann; if my daughter Elizabeth should die before her hus-
band her part to return to my children. Exs., son
Richard and daughter Rachel.
D. May 27, 1715   R.
Wit. Humphry Higginson, Elizabeth Turner   Page 192

Fulgham, John: Leg.- son John; son Anthony ------
Not completed ----- to be found in Book A   Page 193

Woodley, John: Leg.- son John; daughter Frances; wife
Frances. If my son and daughter die without heirs, be-
quests to Elizabeth Copeland the daughter of Joseph Cope-
land. Wife, Extx.
D. December 9, 1724   R.
Wit. Daniel Elbank, Alexander Forbes, Thomas Woodley
                                                 Page 194

Fiveash, Thomas: Of the Upper Parish. Leg.- cousin
Martha, the daughter of John Fiveash; cousin Francis, the
son of John Fiveash; cousin Mary, daughter of Thomas
Fiveash; brother Peter Fiveash; sister-in-law Martha
Harris, the clothes, which belonged to my wife. Brother
Peter Fiveash, Ex.   D. January 4, 1725/6   R.

26

Wit.   James Pyland, Elizabeth Sparkman   Page 194

Thomas, John: Leg.- wife Hannah, 100 acres; son
Richard, 100 acres adjoining John Clark, John Sherrard,
West and Portis; son Samuel; son Jacob 384 acres. Ex.
Joseph Weston. Son Jacob in the care of Joseph Weston
    D. December 31, 1725   R.
Wit. John Williams, John Johnson   Page 195

Harrison, John. Appraised by Henry White, Thomas
Wrenn.   June 24, 1725   Page 196

Driver, Giles: Leg.- daughter Mary; daughter Sarah;
daughter Prudence; daughter Patience; son William the
plantation on which my brother Thomas Driver now lives;
son Giles; daughter Mary to be satisfied with the bequest left her by her uncle, William Richards. .Exs.,
wife and brother-in-law Robert Richards
    D. January 9, 1724   Robert Richards, John Lawrence,
    Christopher Reynolds, Jr., Giles Driver, Thomas Driver
    or any three of them to divide my estate
Wit. Thomas Loyde, John Lawrence, Thomas Driver
                                                      Page 199

Goodman, Rebeccah: Leg.- son William; daughter Mary
Evans; daughter Ann Bell. Son William, Ex.
    D. October 24, 1727   R.
Wit. Charles Binns, Elizabeth Atkinson   Page 199

Underwood, Thomas: Leg.- wife Mary; son William;
son John; daughter Sarah; daughter Mary; daughter Ann;
daughter Elizabeth; son Thomas. Exs., wife and son
William Underwood.
    D. September 29, 1729   R.
Wit. William Crumpler, John Crumpler   Page 200

WILL BOOK 3

Green, Thomas. Appraised by Richard Wilkinson,
Arthur Benn, Robert Richards, Jr. Signed Mary Green
Ordered May 23, 1726   R. June 27, 1726   Page 1

Day, Captain James. Appraised by Henry Applewhaite,
Joseph Godwin, Thomas Applewhaite. Signed, Ann Day
Ordered April 13, 1726.   R. July 25, 1726   Page 2

Richards, Thomas: Leg.- son Thomas; daughter Ann;
daughter Prudence. Ex., brother Robert Richards, Jr.
D. February 23, 1725/26   R. July 25, 1726
Wit. Robert Richards, Jr., Edward Driver   Page 6

Thomas, John. Appraised by Francis Williamson, John
Johnson, Joseph Price. Signed, Joseph Weston
Ordered June 8, 1726   R. July 25, 1726   Page 6

Copeland, Joseph: Leg.- wife Mary; son John; daugh-
ter Elizabeth; son Thomas. Wife, Extx.
D. February 28, 1725/26   R.
Wit. Richard Webb, John Lupo, Melchizideck Inslie (?)
                                                              Page 8

Bidgood, John, Jr.: Leg.- wife Ann; daughter Mary;
son William; son John; son James; son Josiah; (all under
eighteen) Wife, Extx.
D. March 18, 1715   R. August 22, 1726
Wit. Joseph Copeland, Thomas Wrenn   Page 9

Copeland, Joseph. Appraised by Samuel Davis, Thomas
Murry, Benjamin Hodges.   R. August 22, 1726
                                                              Page 10

Grifing (Griffin), Robert. Appraised by John Hodges,
Philip Wheadon, Benjamin Hodges, Henry White
R. June 26, 1727   Page 11

Grifin (Griffin), Andrew: Leg.- son Ephenetus, 300
acres upon the Black Creek; son Mathew 300 acres on the
Blackwater. Wife Mary, Extx.
D.   June 20, 1726   R. September 26, 1726
Wit. Thomas Joyner, William Jones   Page 11

Bidgood, John. Appraised by Elias Hodges, John
Miller, Peter Woodward, Thomas Murry.
R. October 24, 1726   Signed Ann Bidgood   Page 12

Williams, Richard. Appraised at the house of Joseph
Hall, by John Hurst, Joseph Wright, John Wright, Michael
Fulgham. Ordered September 27, 1726
R. October 24, 1726   Page 12

Prime, John: Leg.- wife Martha, reversion of bequest
at her death to my nephew Thomas Wright; to Nephew
Robert Ruffin.   Wife, Extx.
D. March 4, 1717/18   R. November 28, 1726
Wit. Joseph Chapman, John Screws, Edward Crocker
                                                  Page 12

Day, Ann: Leg.- brother Joseph Allen; brother Arthur
Allen; sister Elizabeth Allen; cousin Mary Bridger; cou-
sin James Bridger; Ann Burnett; Mary Bridger; Katherine
Allen; James Allen; sister Elizabeth Bridger; brother
William Bridger, my diamond ring that was Thomas Day's;
Helena Worden (?); brother John Allen; John Worden, Jr.;
Exs., brothers Arthur and Joseph Allen
D. December 2, 1726   R. January 23, 1726
Wit. Roger Delk, John Bruce, Mourning Thomas
                                                  Page 14

Council, Hodges: Leg.- wife Rebecca; son John; son
Hodges; son James; daughter Sarah. Wife, Extx.
D. October 8, 1720   R. January 23, 1726
Wit. William Daughtry, John Daughtry, Robert Wilkins
                                                  Page 15

Stevenson, John: Leg.- son John; son Abraham; son
Thomas; son Charles; son George; daughter Mary; son
William. Wife Elizabeth, Extx.
D. November 23, 1727   R. February 27, 1727
Wit. Thomas Flowers, Abraham Baggett   Page 16

Everitt, Simon: Of the Lower Parish. Leg.- son

Thomas 225 acres adjoining the land of Richard Mathews;
grandson Simon Everitt, son of my son John; son Samuel,
land on Poplar Swamp; son Simon land on Mill Dam Swamp;
son Joseph; son Thomas; daughter Jannett
    D. September 14, 1726   R. February 27, 1726
    Wit. Jacob Darden, William Thomson, Thomas Dixon
                                                    Page 17

    Exum, Ann: Leg.- daughter Elizabeth; granddaughter
Katoren Godwin; grandson Jeremiah Lawrence; grandson
Exum Scott; granddaughter Ann Murfry; grandson Richard
Exum Outland; daughter Mary Mackquinny; daughter Jane
Outland; daughter Mourning Scott and her children; daugh-
ter Christian Norsworthy; my deceased daughter Sarah's
children. Ex., son-in-law William Scott
    D. February 3, 1726/27   R. March 27, 1727
    Wit. Thomas Sikes, James Denson, Henry Sanders
                                                    Page 19

    Bresey, Hugh: Leg.- son William; grandson Francis,
the land on which his father lived at sixteen; son Hugh;
son Campion; daughter Elizabeth Elsberry; son Michael;
daughter Susannah Britt; to son Thomas' son Hugh
    D. December 30, 1721   R. March 27, 1727
    Wit. Owen Griffin, John Turner, Joshua Turner
                                                    Page 20

    Godwin, Elizabeth: Leg.- son John; son William; my
five daughters. Ex., son John Godwin
    D. February 4, 1726/27   R. March 27, 1727
    Wit. John Chestnutt, Thomas Whitley, John Whitley
                                                    Page 21

    Brock, Susannah: Of the Lower Parish. Leg.- daugh-
ter Elizabeth Reynolds; grandson John Reynolds; son
Thomas Calcote. Ex., son Thomas Calcote
    D. March 7, 1723/24   R. March 27, 1727
    Wit. Arthur Smith, Jr.   Page 22

    Gray, Richard: Leg.- wife Rebecca; daughter Ann;
daughter Rebecca; daughter Mourning; son John; daughter
Martha Brown her mother's chest; my wife and the children
I had by her, viz: James, Ann, Rebecca and Mourning
Exs., wife and son James
    D. November 11, 1724   R. March 27, 1727
    Wit. Thomas Applewhaite, Joseph Wiles   Page 22

    Exum, Ann. Appraised by Thomas Glae, Thomas Sikes,
Robert Eley   R. April 24, 1727   Page 24

Godwin, Elizabeth. Appraised by Benjamin Beale, John Chestnutt, John Whitley.   R. May 22, 1727   Page 26

Hodghes, Elias: Leg.- daughter Sarah Davis; wife Sarah; daughter Mary. Wife, Extx.
D. April 2, 1727   R. May 22, 1727
Wit. John Goodrich, John Hodghes   Page 27

Riddick, George: Leg.- Catherine Moreland to be paid what is due her from her father's estate; to my cousins Charles, Samuel and George Goodrich; I desire that Edward Wood shall be at liberty from all persons, whatsoever; my land to be divided between my sons-in-law, Thomas Moreland and John Goodrich.
D. April 7, 1727   R. May 22, 1727
Wit. Peter Fiveash, John Carroll   Page 29

Garland, John: Of the Lower Parish. Leg.- sons, John, Samuel and Joseph my land in Carolina; son John the plantation bought of John Page; son Peter; daughter Sarah; to my wife; daughter Mary Daughtrey; to my five youngest children, viz: Joseph, Ann, Prudence, Patience and Samuel. Ex., son John Garland
D. March 9, 1726/27   R. May 22, 1727
Wit. Hugh Giles, Anthony Fulgham, George Clarke
                                                Page 30

Wilkinson, Richard, Jr. Appraised at the house of Joseph Smith, by Tristram Norsworthy, William Hawkins, George Norsworthy   R. May 23, 1727   Page 31

Kea, Stephen. Appraised by James Pyland, John Brantley, Peter Fiveash   R. June 26, 1727   Page 32

Webb, William. Appraised by Samuel Davis, Henry White, Thomas Murry. Ordered May 22, 1727
R. June 26, 1727   Page 32

Briggs, Mary: Leg.- daughter Elizabeth Throp, the money in the hands of Col. Bridger; son Benjamin Bell; daughter Ann Crafts. Ex., Samuel Crafts
D. March 21, 1726   R. June 26, 1727
Wit. James Bell, William Cogin, John Grisard
                                                Page 33

Crafts, Thomas: Of the Upper Parish. Leg.- wife
Mary; son Thomas; son John; son Samuel; daughter Mary;
daughter Martha Brantley; daughter Elizabeth Tewell
  D. October 29, 1722   R. July 24, 1727
  Wit. Thomas Hylliard, Michael Harris, Hugh Edwards
Page 34

Maker, Susanna: Leg.- daughter Mary Maker; daughter
Ann; daughter Susannah; to unborn child; to my four eld-
est children. My children in the care of Roger Ingram
Exs., Robert Ingram and William Dixon
  D. June 12, 1727   R. August 28, 1727
  Wit. Susannah Maker, Elizabeth Welch   Page 35

Williams, Thomas. Appraised by John Mangum, Thomas
Ward, William Bell   R. August 28, 1727   Page 36

Williams, Thomas: Of the Upper Parish, Planter.
Leg.- wife Susannah, if she should marry the reversion
of the bequests left her to sons John and Thomas; daugh-
ter Joyce; son Joseph; I desire that my wife's son Thomas
Davis, may be paid, what his father, John Davis left him
Wife, Extx.
  D. March 5, 1726/27   R. May 22, 1727
  Wit. Michael Deloach, Joseph Quantock   Page 37

Deloach, Michael: Planter. Leg.- wife Mary; son
Thomas; son Michael. Wife, Extx.
  D. April 20, 1727   R. August 28, 1727
  Wit. John Williams, Joseph Quantock   Page 38

Richards, Thomas. Appraised by Thomas Copeland, John
Penny, Thomas Gross.   R. October 24, 1726   Page 39

Linsey, John: Of the Upper Parish. Leg.- wife Ann;
son Roger; son William
  D. August 25, 1726   R. Mary Miller
  Wit. John Miller, Mary Miller   Page 40

Kea, Henry: Of the Upper Parish. Leg.- wife Elizabeth;
son William; son Robert; son Thomas; daughter Mary
Wife, Extx.
  D. April 19, 1727   R. August 28, 1727
  Wit. James Pyland, John Welch   Page 40

Clothier, John. Appraised by Thomas Mandew, Thomas
Underwood, Abraham Joyner   R. September 25, 1727
Page 41

Screws, John: Leg.- son William; son Robert; son
Edward; daughter Mary; daughter Elizabeth; son Joseph;
to beloved wife; to my youngest daughter; son John
D. August 27, 1720   R. September 25, 1727
Wit. George Pyland, Benjamin Hodges   Page 42

Boulton, John: Leg.- son Richard; to Ann Hyde; to
Henry Bradley. I desire that Ann Hyde may not be
molested until my son becomes of age. Ex., William
Simmons
D. November 26, 1726   R. September 25, 1727
Wit. William Watkins, Sarah Watkins, Ann Hyde
Page 42

Jones, Joseph: Leg.- wife Elizabeth; son William; to
Francis Ward the land on which he lives, if he pays the
balance due to my son William; daughter Mary. Exs., wife
Elizabeth; friends Francis Williamson and John Dunkley and
brother-in-law William Kinchen, Jr.
D. December 5, 1726   R. September 25, 1727
Wit. John Exum, John Dunkley, William Jones (?)
Page 43

Sugars, John: Leg.- daughter Elizabeth Bynum; daughter
Abigail Jones, the land upon which Edward Jones lives;
daughter Priscilla; grandson Sugars Jones. Wife Elizabeth,
Extx.
D. December 1, 1726   R. September 25, 1727
Wit. Francis Arrington, George Bruton, Mary Walker
Page 45

Garland, John. Appraised by Charles Fulgham, Richard
Wilkinson, William Green, Epaproditus Williams
R. November 26, 1727   Page 47

Hodges, Elias. Appraised by Thomas Hall, John Goodrich,
Thomas Murry   R. November 22, 1727 Page 48

Maker, Susanna. Appraised by James Pyland, Peter Fiveash, James Wilson.   R. November 26, 1727   Page 49

Screws, John. Inventory returned by Mary Screws
R. November 26, 1727   Page 50

Norsworthy, Christian: Leg.- son George; daughter
Christian; daughter-in-law Elizabeth; daughter-in-law
Martha to her uncle Charles Norsworthy; cousin Christian
Outland; cousin Elizabeth Scott; to friend James Turner;
if my children die in their minority, bequests to be
equally divided between the children of brothers-in-law
William Scott and William Outland
    D. November 6, 1727   R. November 26, 1727
    Wit. Edward Mason, George Lawrence   Page 50

Jolleffe, James: Of the Lower Parish. Leg.- wife
Mary; son John; daughter Elizabeth land which adjoins
John Butler and Christopher Reynolds; son James
Wife, Extx.
    D. February 28, 1726   R. November 26, 1727
    Wit. John Roberts, Christopher Reynolds, John Smelly
                            Page 51

Briggs, James. Appraised by James Wilson, Thomas
Skelton, Thomas Shelly. Ordered, August 2, 1727
    R. January 22, 1727   Page 52

Bridger, Elizabeth: Leg.- son Joseph; son John; son
Robert; daughter Hester; daughter Elizabeth. Exs., sons
Robert and John Bridger
    D. December 14, 1727   R. January 22, 1727
    Wit. Mary Whitley, Edward Driver   Page 54

Tiller, Susannah: Leg.- son Major; daughter Judith
Smith; daughter Mary Rives; daughter Elizabeth Reid;
daughter Ann Adams. Ex., son John Reid
    D. January 5, 1724/25   R. January 22, 1727
    Wit. John Edwards, Robert Hicks, Jr.   Page 55

Segraves, Francis: Leg.- daughter Frances the wife
of Jonathan Sanderson; daughter Lucretia, the wife of
Thomas Turner; son William; daughter Elizabeth; son
Francis; daughter Ann; daughter Susanna; daughter Sarah;
wife Lucretia. Exs., wife and son William Segraves
    D. October 9, 1725   R. January 22, 1727
    Wit. Richard Hutchins, Abraham Ricks   Page 56

Dogan, Bryan. Appraised by Richard Wilkinson,
Robert Richards, Joseph Norsworthy, Edward Driver
    R. January 22, 1727   Page 57

Bunkley, Robert. Appraised at the house of Thomas
Newman, by Henry Pitt, Joseph Wright, Thomas Gross
February 26, 1727   Page 57

Hurst, John: Leg.- wife Mary, the plantation bought
of William Price; son James; son William; son John; sons
Philip and Walter to be bound out at 14 to learn a trade;
daughter Alice; daughter Mary; son John a ring given him
by Dorothye Hurst. Wife, Extx.
D. January 1, 1727   R. February 26, 1727
Wit. Joseph Wright, Robert Brown, John Anthonyrue
                                                     Page 58

Fulgham, Michael: Leg.- son John; grandson Henry West,
the son of Henry West; brother Anthony Fulgham; Hardy
Council to have the upbringing of my son John, who is to
be of age at 18. Wife, Extx.
D. January 12, 1727   R. February 26, 1727
Wit. James Benn, John Wright   Page 59

Story, Thomas: Leg.- sister Elizabeth Smith; sister
Mary Story; brother John Story; sister Elizabeth's four
children, to one of them named Mary Smith; to Goddaugh-
ter Mary Driver. Exs., my two sisters
D. December 29, 1727   R. February 26, 1727
Wit. John Giles, Richard Scammell   Page 60

Jolley, James. Of the Lower Parish. Inventory
presented by his Executrix.   February 26, 1727
                                                     Page 61

Copeland, Joseph. His estate which was in the pos-
session of Thomas Copeland, decd., appraised by Samuel
Davis, Henry White, Thomas Murry, Benjamin Hodges
March 25, 1728   Page 62

Andrews, John. Appraised by Thomas Godwin, Jr., John
Saunders, Robert Coging   March 25, 1728
                                                     Page 63

Cooke, Isack: Of Newport Parish. Leg.- brother John
Cooke; sister Bridgett Rogers; sister Mary Stringer; to
Roger Nevill. Ex., Roger Nevill
March 6, 1727/28   R. March 25, 1728
Wit. Jacob Darden, John Murfrey, John Sikes
                                                     Page 63

Mackmial, Thomas. Appraised by James Johnson, John Darden, William Daniel. Signed by Thomas Gale, Jr. March 25, 1728   Page 64

Hurst, John. Appraised by William Noyall, John Wright, Joseph Wright.   March 25, 1728   Page 64

Jones, Mathew: Leg.- son Scervant my tract in Warwick County, devised me by my father; my sister Margaret Jones and cousin Mathew Jones to raise the aforesaid son; daughter Ann the plantation bought of Thomas Briant at Nottoway Swamp; daughter Margaret the land adjoining Dr. Browne's line; daughter Agathy, the tract which was a survey of Thomas Sumerlings on the Notoway River, reversion of bequest to son Albridgeton; son Britton, 144 acres in Warwick County, which I bought of Edward Kippen and the rest of my land on the Nottoway; my land and stock to be sold in Brunswick County; to loving wife. Extx., Elizabeth Jones.   D. January 28, 1727/28   R. March 25, 1728
Wit. Mary Wrenn, Ann Bidgood   Page 66

Kea, Henry. Appraised by James Pyland, James Wilson, Thomas Moreland   March 25, 1728   Page 66

Surginor, John: Leg.- son Robert, with reversion of the bequest to my son John, the younger; son Benjamin; daughter Mary; daughter Ann; son John the elder
Ex., son Robert Surginor
   D. October 3, 1727   R. March 25, 1728
Wit. Edward Chitty, John Stevenson   Page 68

Bridger, Joseph John: Leg.- brother James; uncle Joseph Allen; to my loving father, 350 acres at Round Hill. Exs., father and uncle Joseph Allen
   D. December 3, 1727   R. March 25, 1728
Wit. Reuben Proctor, Elizabeth Brantley, Ann Burnett
Will presented by William Bridger and Joseph Allen
                                                   Page 68

Gent, John: Leg.- eldest son Thomas; youngest son John; to loving wife. Exs., Oliver Woodward, Thomas Allen
   D. December 3, 1727   R. March 25, 1728
Wit. Oliver Woodward, Christopher Reynolds, John Gurley
                                                   Page 68

Jones, Jacob: Leg.- brother William Jones. Ex., bro-
ther Nathan Jones
D. November 21, 1727   R. March 25, 1728
Wit. John Bowen, Mathew Griffin, Elinor English
Page 69

Story, Thomas. Appraised by Robert Richards, Joseph
Norsworthy, Richard Scammell   March 25, 1728
Page 71

Sampson, James: Leg.- son Barcroft; daughter Margaret
100 acres adjoining Isaac Jarrett and Nicholas Derring;
daughter Elizabeth 100 acres on which the widow Madera now
lives, adjoining the land of Edward Brantley and Burwell's
line; daughter Ann Derring, the plantation on which her
husband Nicholas Derring now lives. Trustees, Samuel
Croft and John Floyd
D. November 30, 1727   R. March 25, 1728
Wit. James Ingles, Charles Goodrich, Thomas Jones
Page 71

Whitley, Mary. Appraised by Robert Wright, James
Wright, Christopher Dickinson   April 22, 1728
Page 73

Glover, George. Appraised by Mathew Wills, Roger
Ingram, William Bidgood   April 22, 1728
Page 73

Day, Capt. James. Account estate. Errors accepted
by Joseph Allen, the Ex. of Ann Day, decd. Examined by
Thomas Walton, James Benn   March 25, 1728
Page 74

Surginor, John. Appraised by Thomas Holliman, Joseph
Parnall, William Crocker   April 22, 1728
Page 75

Thomas, William. Appraised by John Davis, Thomas
Davis, Richard Webb   April 22, 1728
Page 75

Miller, John. Appraised by William Harrison, Benjamin
Hodges, William Bamer, Philip Wheadon   April 22, 1728
Page 76

Greshion, James: Leg.- wife Margaret, the rent due me
from Charles Ryall

D. September 20, 1727   R. April 22, 1728
Wit. Nicholas Pyland, John Cortis, Jan Bates Cortis
Administration granted Buller Herbert, his greatest
creditor   Page 76

Hiden, Ephraim: Leg.- daughter Elizabeth; daughter
Sarah. Exs., Captain Wilkinson and my wife Elizabeth
D. January 25, 1727/28   R. April 22, 1728
Wit. William Morgin (?), Daniel Gray   Page 77

Pearce, Philip: Leg.- wife Sarah; son Nathan; son Ar-
thur; son Simon; son Richard; son Thomas. Exs., wife
Sarah and son Richard Pearce
D. March 20, 1727/28   R. April 22, 1728
Wit. Richard Teasley, Peter Mackcone, George Teasley
                                                  Page 78

Pyland, James: Leg.- wife Elizabeth; son James, my box
of doctor's instruments; daughter Ann; son Thomas; son
William; daughter Katherine; son Edward
D. March 20, 1727/28   R. April 22, 1728
Wit. Robert Butler, Ann Fones   Page 78

Watts, Thomas. Of the Lower Parish, Planter. Nuncupative will presented by Rachel Smith, Ar. Smith and
Arthur Smith. Leg.- Arthur Smith; Rachel Smith and her
brother Arthur Smith; to kinsman William Lane
D. March 15, 1727/28   R. April 22, 1728
                                                  Page 80

Driver, Thomas. Appraised by William Noyall, Arthur
Benn, Timothy Tines. Signed John Butler, Adm.
Ordered February 26, 1727   R. May 27, 1728
                                                  Page 79

Wrench, John: Leg.- wife Elizabeth; son Samuel Farmer
Wrench; son John Wrench, the plantation upon which, Thomas
Hail lived; two sons of age at 18
D. February 8, 1727   R. April 22, 1728
Wit. John Hail, Joyce Cambell, John Heard   Page 80

Bragg, James: Of Newport Parish. Leg.- Thomas Story,
who married my daughter Elizabeth; daughter Sarah Driver;
daughter Mary Norsworthy. Extx., wife Mary Bragg
D. April 29, 1727   R. April 22, 1728
Wit. James Giles, Hugh Giles   Page 82

Bradshaw, Nicholas: Leg.- daughter Elizabeth, whom I
leave in the care of my sister, Mary Bradshaw; daughter
Ann; daughter Mary; my two youngest children to be in the
care of John and Mary Corbill. Exs., brothers, John
and George Bradshaw
    D. January   , 1727   R. April 22, 1728
    Wit. Joseph Godwin   Page 82

Watts, Thomas. Appraised by William Brock, Thomas
Brown. Adm., Rachel Smith   May 27, 1728
                                         Page 83

Copeland, Thomas. Appraised by James Giles, Charles
Norsworthy, William Best, Humphrey Marshall
    Ordered April 22, 1728   R. May 27, 1728
                                       Page 84

Ward, Thomas: Planter. Leg.- wife Jane; daughter
Hannah, if without heirs to son John; daughter Mary;
son Benjamin; daughter Olive; son Francis. Exs., wife
and son Benjamin Ward
    D. April 15, 1727   R. May 27, 1728
    Wit. John Williams, Joseph Quantock, Sus. Williams
                                       Page 87

Murrey, William. Appraised by William Harrison, John
Goodrich, Benjamin Hodges   May 27, 1728
                                       Page 89

Pearce, Philip. Appraised by John Teasley, Ralph
Vickers, William Page.   May 27, 1728   Page 89

Bowin, Richard: Leg.- wife Elizabeth; daughter Millicent; daughter Mary; daughter Elizabeth; daughter Rebecca;
between all my children. Extx., wife
    D. September 9, 1727   R. May 27, 1728
    Wit. P. Hackcone, Richard Pierce, Richard Teasley
                                       Page 90

Penny, Ralph: Leg.- wife and unborn child, the land
on which Francis Floyd now lives, reversion of bequest to
my brothers, William and John Penney. Exs., wife and
Christopher Dickinson
    D. February 5, 1727/28   R. May 27, 1728
    Wit. William Hawkins, Joseph Smith, Joseph Williams
                                       Page 91

Wrench, John. Appraised by Joseph Wright, Benjamin
Beale, John Wilkinson. Ordered April 22, 1728
R. May 27, 1728   Page 93

Lilburn, Sarah. Appraised by John Davis, Thomas Davis,
Richard Webb. Signed John Lupo, Adm.
Ordered April 8, 1728   R. May 27, 1728
                                                   Page 94

Farecloth, William: Leg.- son Benjamin; son Moses;
daughter Hannah; daughter Elizabeth Mercer; daughter Sarah
Revell; son William; granddaughter Martha, the daughter of
Samuel Farecloth; to Sarah Pope, the wife of Henry Pope
Exs.,daughter Hannah and sons Moses and Benjamin Farecloth
D. January 9, 1727
Wit. Joseph Cobb, Robert Scott
Codicil: In which Robert Scott is made trustee
Wit. John Revell, Joseph Cobb   R. May 27, 1728
                                                   Page 96

Joyner, Thomas: Leg.- brother Jonathan; brother Mathew;
sister Cherry; sister Patience; sister Elizabeth; brother
Alexander; brother-in-law John Dunkley. Exs., brother
Alexander and John Dunkley
D. April 8, 1728   R. May 27, 1728
Wit. Richard Lewis, Edward Boykin   Page 97

Sampson, James. Appraised by Lawrence Baker, Robert
ffones, Roger Ingram. Signed Nicholas Derring
R. May 27, 1728   Page 98

Bradshaw, Richard. Appraised by James Hunter, William
Williams, Robert Browne. Signed George Bradshaw
R. May 27, 1728   Page 100

Denson, James. Account Estate. Received by Francis
Denson, orphan of James Denson; received by me, Thomas
Gale, Jr., guardian of Joseph, the orphan of James Denson.
Presented by Thomas Walton, Gent., late Sheriff of this
County   R. November 26, 1728   Page 101

Cooke, Isaac. Appraised by John Garner, John Marshall,
Michael Murfree. Signed Roger Nevill
R. June 24, 1728   Page 102

Fulgham, Anthony. Appraised by Francis Gross, John
Rodway, William Rutter, William West
    Ordered May 27, 1728   R. June 24, 1728
                                              Page 103

Askew, Nicholas. Appraised by John Wilkinson, John
Garner, Benjamin Beal. Ordered May 27, 1728
    R. June 24, 1728   Page 104

Hall, Poole. Appraised by John Wright, Joseph Wright,
Richard Casey   R. June 24, 1728   Page 104

Flowers, Henry. Appraised by George Washington, Oliver
Woodward, Benjamin Johnston. Signed Mary Flowers
    Ordered April 22, 1727/28   R. June 24, 1728
                                              Page 106

Richards, Robert: Leg.- loving wife; son William; granddaughter Prudence Driver; granddaughter Prudence Richards;
son Robert; son Thomas. Exs., wife and son Robert Richards
D. August 11, 1724   R. June 24, 1728
    Wit. Edward Driver, Joseph Driver   Page 107

Gray, John: Leg.- wife Ann; son Richard; son Aaron;
daughter Ann West; daughter Mary; daughter Sarah; daughter
Elizabeth. Exs., sons Richard and Aaron Gray
    D. March 29, 1728   R. June 24, 1728
    Wit. Henry Applewhite, John Hawkins   Page 108

Penny, Ralph. Appraised by Nathaniel Parker, Joseph
Smith; John Williams, Joseph West, at the house of Mary
Penny.   R. June 24, 1728   Page 109

Richards, Robert. Inventory presented by Elizabeth
Richards.   R. August 26, 1728   Page 109

Bowin, Richard. Appraised by John Teasley, Ralph
Vickers, William Page.   R. August 26, 1728   Page 111

Hiden, Ephraim. Appraised by Joseph Wright, George

Crudup, John Monro.   R.   August 26, 1728   Page 111

Norsworthy, Christian. Appraised by Joseph Smith,
Henry Pitt, Robert Bridger. Signed William Scott
R.   October 26, 1728   Page 112

Marshall, Joseph. Appraised by Francis Gross,
Thomas Gross, William Richards. Ordered June 24, 1728
R.   August 26, 1728   Page 114

Rigin, Ann: Nuncupative will, proven by Mary Smith .
and Elizabeth Richards. William Noyall to have the care
of her two children, Daniel and Patience Rigin; bequest
to Martha Noyall. (Recorded as Ann Riggin)
D.   June 19, 1728   R.   October 26, 1728
                                                  Page 115

Jordan, Margaret. Appraised by Charles Reynolds,
Joseph Wright, Robert Driver. Signed John Jordan
     Ordered May 27, 1728   R.   August 26, 1728
                                                  Page 115

Howell, John: Leg.- wife Mary; son John; son William;
son Samuel; son James, land adjoining Benjamin Beal; my
three daughters. Exs., wife and son John
D.   January 1, 1727   R.   August 26, 1728
Wit.   John Heard, John Hale, Edward Hale
                                                  Page 116

Jones, Mathew. Appraised by Lawrence Baker, Thomas
Murry, Samuel Davis.   R.   August 26, 1728
                                                  Page 117

Wrenn, Thomas: Leg.- wife Elizabeth, the plantation
called the "Freshet"; son Thomas; son John; son James;
daughter Mary; my estate to be divided among all my children by Samuel and John Davis. Exs., wife and son John
D.   February 14, 1725/26   R.   August 26, 1728
Wit.   Samuel Davis, Benjamin Bidgood, Jer. Proctor
                                                  Page 118

Woodley, John. Account estate. Signed Frances
Woodley. Examined by W. Bridger and Thomas Walton
R.   August 27, 1728   Page 119

Wilson, John. 1720. Account estate. Signed
Frances Woodley. Examined by W. Bridger and Thomas
Walton.   R. August 27, 1728
                                                  Page 121

Williams, Epaphroditus: Leg.- sister Juliana Wright;
sister Mary Hale; to Mary, the daughter of Nathan Bagnall
and his wife Ann; to Rachele, the daughter of Thomas Parker and his wife Rachele; my wife Rachele, at her death to
Susanna and Priscilla Marshall, the daughters of Humphrey
Marshall; to Sarah Pilkington, Jr. Wife, Extx.
    D. July 14, 1728   R. September 23, 1728
    Wit. Thomas Bevan, Hugh Giles   Page 123

Long, John. Appraised by William Noyall, John
Wright, Christopher Reynolds. Ordered August 26, 1728
    R. September 23, 1728   ,   Page 125

Williams, Epaphroditus. Appraised by Hugh Giles
William Green, Charles Dickinson   R. October 28, 1728
                                                  Page 125

Joyner, Abraham: Leg.- son Abraham; son William;
daughter Elizabeth; daughter Sarah; to all my children
    D. July 9, 1727/28   R. October 28, 1728
    Wit. William Joyner, Joseph Joyner, John Joyner
                                                  Page 126

Pope, Henry: Leg.- son William; son Henry; son
Richard; son Jacob; son John; daughter Mary Williams;
daughter Jane Braswell; son Joseph a tract of land on
Blackwater Creek; daughter Mourning a tract on the Meherrin River; son Thomas a tract on the Murrahock River;
son Samuel; to Mary Clothier at her freedom from my
wife; to cousins, Edward and John Pope. Exs., wife
Sarah and son John Pope
    D. May 28, 1728   R. October 28, 1728
    Wit. Epenetus Griffin, John Denson, Jr.
          Martin Cleuse (?)   Page 127

Duck, William: Leg.- wife Margery; son Timothy; son
Robert, land adjoining John Carr; my two eldest sons,
William and John; son Jacob; daughter Bridget; daughter
Dorothy; daughter Isabel. Wife, Extx.
    D. August 4, 1727   R. October 28, 1728
    Wit. Hardy Council, John Johnson, John Duck
                                                  Page 128

Howell, John. Appraised by B. Beal, John Garner,
Robert Driver.   R.   October 28, 1728
                                                      Page 129

House, James: Leg.- son James; son Thomas; to my daughter-in-law, Mary House, the wife of son Thomas; son John;
daughter Ester; to Ann House Wetherall; granddaughter
Cleary House; daughter Hester. William Hawkins and my
son John to divide my estate. Ex., son John House
   D. March 23, 1727/28   R.   October 28, 1728
   Wit. William Hawkins, John Anthony Rue
                                                      Page 129

Ingrum, Roger. Appraised by William Harrison, Benjamin Hodges. Signed Elizabeth Ingram
   Ordered August 26, 1728   R.   November 11, 1728
                                                      Page 130

Ward, Thomas. Appraised by Arthur Jones, John Mangum,
William Bell   R.   November 25, 1728   Page 133

Price, Joseph: Leg.- cousin William Price, Jr.; wife
Martha. Exs., loving father, Francis Williamson and wife
Martha. D. March 7, 1725/26   R.   November 25, 1728
   Wit. Abraham Bagget, Francis Harris   Page 133

Riggan, Ann. Appraised by Robert Richards, Joshua
Whitney, Christopher Reynolds. Signed William Noyall
   R. November 25, 1728   Page 134

Daniel, John: Leg.- wife Elizabeth and my two chil-
dren. Wife, Extx.
   D. January 24, 1727/28   R.   November 25, 1728
   Wit. Joseph Norsworthy, Thomas Norsworthy   Page 134

Lowry, Mathew. Appraised by John Dawson, Timothy
Tines, Thomas Uzzell. Ordered October 25, 1728
   R. November 25, 1728   Page 135

Gent, John. Appraised by George Washington, Benjamin
Johnston, John Barnes, Sr. Signed by Thomas Allen and
Oliver Woodward.   R. March 25, 1728
                                                      Page 136

Benn, Arthur: Leg.- son James (not 21); son Arthur, land on the Nottoway River; daughter Mary; son Christopher land on the Nottoway; wife Frances. Wife, Extx
    D. May 8, 1728   R. December 23, 1728
    Wit. Arthur Smith, John Lowe, James Benn.
                                  Page 137

    Riddick, George. Appraised by Peter Fiveash, James
Piland, John Bunkley   R. December 23, 1728
                                  Page 139

    Coggan, William. Appraised by Richard Price, William
Pope, John Teasley. Ordered November 25, 1728
R. January 27, 1728   Page 140

    Joyner, Abraham. Appraised by Epenetus Griffin, Hodges
Council, Robert Johnson.   R. January 27, 1728
                                  Page 140

    Butler, John. Appraised by Timothy Tynes, Arthur
Benn, Christopher Reynolds. Signed Ann Butler
    Ordered February 26, 1727   R. January 1, 1728
                                  Page 141

    Kerll, Eleanor. Appraised by Benjamin Beal, John
Wilkinson, John Garner, Thomas Gale, Jr.
    Ordered December 23, 1728   R. January 27, 1728
                                  Page 142

    Young, Alexander: Leg.- friend, John Exum, my whole
estate. D. December 25, 1726   R. January 27, 1728
    Wit. John Dunkley   Page 143

    Fullgam, Michell: Of the Upper Parish. Leg.- to my
cousin John Fulfham; to cousin John Williamson; sister
Mary Fulgham; brother John Fulgham. Ex., brother Edman
    D. November 26, 1728   R. January 27, 1728
    Wit. John Johnson, Anthony Fulgham, Mary Johnson
                                  Page 144

    Rutter, William. Nuncupative will, proven by Arthur
Brown and Joshua Hunter. Signed by Mary Rutter
He desired that William Wootten should have what was his,
and that the remainder of his estate should belong to his
wife.   R. January 27, 1728
                                  Page 145

Turner, Joshua. Appraised by Theophilus Joyner,
John Garner, William Godwin. Signed by Christopher
Dickinson. Ordered November 26, 1728
    R. January 27, 1728   Page 145

Townsand, Henry. Appraised by Thomas Pursell, Hugh
Mathis, William Blake. Ordered January 25, 1728/29
    R. January 27, 1728   Page 145

Benn, Arthur. Appraised by Robert Richards, John
Chapman, Christopher Dickinson. R. January 27, 1728
                                        Page 146

Councill, James. Appraised by William Daughtry, John
Lawrence, William Fowler. R. February 24, 1728
                                        Page 148

Daniel, John. Appraised at the house of Elizabeth
Daniel by Christopher Dickinson, Joseph Norsworthy, John
Chapman   R. February 24, 1728   Page 149

Pope, Henry. Appraised by Robert Johnson, Epenetus
Griffin, John Bowin. (Estate in N. C. mentioned.)
    R. February 24, 1728   Page 149

Shelly, John. Account of estate, examined by James
Baker and Joseph Bridger. R. February 24, 1728
                                        Page 150

Pitt, Thomas. Appraised at the house of Henry Pitt
by William Weston, Francis Gross, Robert Murray
    Ordered October 24, 1726   R. February 24, 1728
                                        Page 151

Scott, John. Appraised by Joseph Parke, William
Blake, Francis Sharpe. Signed by Frances Scott
    Ordered February 8, 1728/29   R. February 24, 1728
                                        Page 151

Scott, Robert. Appraised by George Washington, Henry
Applewhite, Benjamin Johnston. Signed Elizabeth Scott
    R. March 24, 1728
                                        Page 152

Johnson, John. Appraised by Thomas Williams, Thomas
Turner, Virgus Smith   R. March 24, 1728
                                              Page 153

Burnett, Ann: Of the Upper Parish. Leg.- cousin
Joseph Williamson. Ex., brother Francis Williamson
   D. April 8, 1729   R. April 28, 1729
   Wit. William Dixon, Elizabeth Brantley   Page 154

Runels, Henry: Leg.- son John; daughter Patience;
daughter Darkes Bowin; daughter Elizabeth Johnson; wife
Elizabeth; son-in-law John Weaid; son-in-law John Bowin,
my Ex.
   D. February 11, 1725/26   R. April 28, 1729
   Wit. Joseph Bradshaw, John Denson, Jr.
                                              Page 155

Pierce, Jeremiah. Appraised by Thomas Murray, Thomas
Hill, Benjamin Hodges.   R. April 28, 1729
                                              Page 156

Lowry, Martha: Of the Lower Parish. Leg.- daughter
Ann; son Henry; daughter Mary; grandchildren, James and
Martha Lowry. Daughter Ann, Extx.
   D. January 21, 1729   R. April 28, 1729
   Wit. William Wiggs, John Garner, John Bunkley
                                              Page 156

Proctor, Reuben: Of the Upper Parish. Leg.- cousin
Reuben Proctor, the son of George Proctor; to cousin
George Proctor's children; to brother Jeremiah Proctor's
children. Ex., brother Jeremiah Proctor
   D. April 11, 1729   R. April 28, 1729
   Wit. William Dixon, Samuel Davis, Joseph Williamson
                                              Page 157

Fulgham, Micael. Inventory, returned by Mary Fulgham
R. May 26, 1729   Page 158

Joyner, Thomas, Jr. Inventory presented by John
Dunkley.   R. May 26, 1729
                                              Page 158

Fulgham, John: Leg.- my estate to all my children.
Ex., son Anthony Fulgham
   D. December 14, 1728   R. May 26, 1729
   Wit. John Westray, Martha Norsworthy, John Johnson
                                              Page 159

Powell, Nathaniel: wife Mary; son Jacob; son Arthur;
son Nathaniel; (sons under 18) daughter Mary daughter
Rachel
D. October 23, 1728   R. May 26, 1729
Wit. Robert Berryman, James Brown   Page 159

Tarleton, Roger: Leg.- son Roger; grandson James, the
son of Thomas Tarleton; granddaughter Ann, the daughter of
Roger Tarleton; daughter Sarah Nolleboy; to granddaughter
Sarah, the daughter of Daniel Nolleboy; son William; son
Thomas; daughter Elizabeth Nash; daughter Mary Jolliff;
son Joseph; wife Margaret. Ex. son Joseph Tarleton
D. December 12, 1726   R. April 28, 1729
Wit. Abraham Ricks   Page 161

Powers, Edward, Sr.: Leg.- son William; to Charles
Powers; wife Elizabeth; to Elizabeth Darden, the wife of
John Darden; son Edward; residue of my estate to be di-
vided among my four sons and three daughters
Ex., son Edward Powers
D. April 7, 1729   R. May 26, 1729
Wit. Davie Hooper, Joseph West, Jacob Johnson
                                            Page 162

Purcell, Arthur: Leg.- son Arthur land on the Blackwater; son Thomas the land I bought of Thomas Joyner;
daughter Isabella, the wife of Arthur Whitehead; loving
wife. Exs., sons Arthur and Thomas Purcell
D. April 21, 1717   R. May 27, 1729
Wit. Arthur Smith, Joshua Turner, Mathew Lowry
Presented by Mary Purcell, widow   Page 163

Goodson, Thomas. Appraised by Thomas Calcote, Thomas
Summerell, Thomas Uzzell. Ordered November 25, 1728
R. May 5, 1729   Page 164

Runnells, Henry. Appraised by Hodges Council, Epenetus Griffin, Joseph Bracher. R. June 23, 1729
                                            Page 166

Kindred, Samuel: Leg.- son John land on Reedy Branch,
and Blunt's Swamp; wife Mary; son Samuel, land adjoining
Charles Porter and James Braswell; the plantation on which
John Williams lives to be sold; to daughters, Sarah and
Faithe, the land in Surry County on which Mathew Delk
lives; daughter Jane; daughter Mary; daughter Catherine

daughter Elizabeth. Ex.,
     D. January 25, 1728/29   R. June 23, 1729
     Wit. Samuel Adkins, James Braswell   Page 166
     Deposition of Robert Berryman, proving that he wished
his wife to have everything he had not given his children.   R. June 23, 1729   Page 168

     Fulgham, John. Appraised by Arthur Pursell, John
Johnson, John Batten.   R. June 23, 1729
                                             Page 169

     Proctor, Rueben. Appraised by Samuel Davis, John
Davis, Thomas Murry   R. July 28, 1729
                                             Page 169

     Scott, John: Leg.- wife Joan; refers to negroes left
his children by their uncle, James Tooke; daughter Mary;
daughter Sarah; to James Tooke Scott; to Thomas Scott; to
my cousin William Hollowell, 200 acres upon Kingsale
Swamp, which was given me by my deceased father William
Scott. Exs., wife Joan and son James Tooke Scott
     D. March 12, 1728/29   R. July 28, 1729
     Wit. William Wilson, William Dixon, Thomas Harris,
          George Bell   Page 171

     Tarleton, Roger. Appraised by Thomas Gale, Jr.,
Jacob Darden, Michael Murphrey.   R. July 28, 1729
                                             Page 172

     Powers, Edward, Sr. Appraised by Samuel Brown, John
Vasser, Arthur Whitehead.   R. July 28, 1729
                                             Page 173

     Benn, Arthur. Appraised by Samuel Browne, John Vasser,
James Garner, William Hickman. Ordered November 28, 1728
     R. August 25, 1729   Page 174

     Barlow, Sarah: Leg.- daughter Mary; son Thomas; grand-
daughter Sarah Carrell. Ex., son Thomas Barlow
     D. March 19, 1728/29   R. August 25, 1729
     Wit. William Dixon, John Brantley, Clay Brantley
                                             Page 175

     Murry, John. Account of estate. To clothing and bring-
ing up the child. Examined by Thomas Walton and James
Baker.   R. August 9, 1729   Page 175

Vasser, Peter. Appraised by Robert Mounger, William
Jones, Richard Atkinson. Ordered May 26, 1729
R. June 14, 1729   Page 176

Pursell, Arthur. Appraised by John Johnson, John
Turner, Daniel Herring   R. August 25, 1729
                                                    Page 177

Williams, Peter. Appraised by John Chapman, John
Monro, Thomas Gross. Signed Mary Williams
Ordered August 25, 1729   R. 22d. of 7ber 1729
                                                    Page 178

Powell, Nathan(iel). Appraised by William Pope,
Robert Crocker, Simon Everett. Signed by Robert and
Mary Berryman.   R. September 22, 1729   Page 179

Crocker, William: Leg.- son Joseph; daughter Patience;
daughter Mary. Wife Mary, Extx.
D.   R. October 27, 1729
Wit. Robert Crocker, Joseph Crocker   Page 179

Richards, Robert. Appraised at the homes of Robert
Richards, Mrs. Elizabeth Richards and William Richards,
by John Chapman, Charles Dickinson, John Clark
R. October 27, 1729   Page 180

Green, William: Leg.- son Bartholomew, the land on
which Christopher Dickinson now lives, also my mill in
the Upper Parish now in the occupation of Henry White,
for Capt. Joseph Bridger's life; son George my land at
the "Freshet", now in the tenure of William Davis; wife
Mary; daughter Sarah Bevan; to Martha Montgomery; to
Mary, Elizabeth and Green Green, the daughters of Mary
Green, widow; daughter Prudence; daughter Rebecca. My
estate to be divided by Samuel Davis, John Davis, Arthur
Smith and Christopher Dickinson. Exs., wife Mary and
Samuel Davis.
D. January 27, 1727/28   R. October 27, 1729
Proved by depositions of Richard West and William
Pilkington, aged 30 years   Page 183

Wiggs, Katherine: Leg.- son William; refers to deceased
husband, Henry Wiggs; son George; son Luke; daughter Sarah,

jugs bought of Benjamin Chapman; daughter Catherine
Stevenson; daughter Mary Britt; daughter Elizabeth
Bressey. Ex., son George
   D. June 4, 1729   R. November 24, 1729
   Wit. William Brock, Thomas Calcote, George Goodson
                                              Page 184

   Webb, William. Account estate. To burying John
Webb, to the said Webb's wife's part; due to Samuel
Webb, orphan. Examined by Thomas Walton and James
Baker.   R. November 24, 1729   Page 186

   Long, Daniel. Appraised by Hugh Giles, Robert
Richards, Robert Murray. Ordered November 24, 1729
   R. December 22, 1729   Page 186

   Kindred, Samuel. Appraised by Martin Middleton, John
Rochel, Samuel Atkinson.   R. December 22, 1729
                                              Page 187

   Rutter, William. Appraised by William Noyall, John
Wright, Joseph Wright. Ordered January 27, 1728
   R. December 22, 1729   Page 188

   Bunkley, John: Leg.- son Robert; daughter Ann; daughter Sarah; son John; daughter Mary Morgan; to my two sons
named John. Ex., wife Bridgett
   D. June 10, 1725   R. December 22, 1729
   Wit. William Green, James Brown, Ann Hail,
         Sarah Bunkley   Page 188

   Chapman, Joseph: Leg.- wife Alice; son Charles, the
land I bought of John Butler and of John Rodaway; to son-
in-law John Applewhite; daughters, Mary, Martha, Elizabeth
and Alice
   D.   R. December 22, 1729
   Wit. Thomas Uzzell   Page 189

   Moreland, Edward. Appraised by William Holliman,
William Richardson, Christopher Holliman
   Signed Unity Moreland   R. December 22, 1729
                                              Page 191

   White, William: Leg.- my mother; to John Lee; to

Francis Lee; to Mary White; to John White; brother John
White; brother Thomas White; to Mary Bell; brother Henry
White; sister Jane Lee
D. October 13, 1722   R. February 23, 1729
Wit. Thomas Rosser, Samuel Williams   Page 191

Long, Daniel. Additional appraisal by Hugh Giles,
Robert Richards.   R. February 23, 1729
                                                 Page 193

Boykin, John. Appraised by Francis Williamson, John
Dunkley, Edward Harris.   R. February 23, 1729
                                                 Page 194

Bunkley, John. Appraised by W. Bridger, Jr., Robert
Brown, George Mynard. Ordered January 17, 1729/30
R. February 23, 1729   ;   Page 194

Bolton, John. Appraised by Benjamin Clements, John
Arrington, Thomas Macey. Signed by William Simmons
R. March 23, 1729   Page 195

Fulgham, Anthony. Additional appraisal by Francis
Gross, John Rodway, William West. R. March 23, 1729
                                                 Page 195

Crocker, William. Appraised by John Pope, Simon
Everett, John Cain. Signed Mary Crocker
Ordered March 14, 1729   R. March 23, 1729
                                                 Page 196

Jolley, James. Appraised by William Noyall, Robert
Driver, Christopher Reynolds, William West.
R. March 23, 1729   Page 197

Tidmash, Giles: Leg.- son Giles, wife Sarah
Wife, Extx.
D. July 30, 1728   R. March 23, 1729
Wit. Sarah Lee, John Lett   Page 198

Pilkington, William. Appraised by Wm. Bridger, Jr.,
John Monro, Robert Browne. Ordered February 28, 1729
R. March 23, 1729   Page 198

White, John: Leg.- son Valentine; wife Elizabeth; to
John Carpenter; daughter Millicent; daughter Jane; daugh-
ter Mary; son William; son Jonathan. Exs., wife and son
Valentine White.
  D. January 23, 1726/27   R. March 23, 1729
  Wit. James Ramsey, John Carpenter, Elizabeth Redish
                                                Page 198

Harris, Thomas: Leg.- son Joshua; daughter Mary; to
my unborn child. Exs., wife Hannah and brother Henry
Harris. D. December 25, 1729 R. March 23, 1729
  Wit. Thomas Harris, Thomas Atkinson   Page 199

Brewer, Thomas: Leg.- daughter Mary; daughter Ann, the
plantation I bought of John Hall on which the widow, Mary
Williams now lives; son John, the tract I bought of Wm.
Thompson on Gray's Creek in Surry County; son Thomas the
tract I bought of Col. Wm. Cole and the one I bought of
Mr. Thomas Swann, called "Quin-Quan"; son John the money
in the hands of Mr. Perry. Ex., son Thomas
  D. March 4, 1729   R. March 23, 1729
  Wit. Humphrey Marshall, Robert Marshall,
        Elizabeth Marshall   Page 200

Chapman, Joseph. Appraised by William Wilson, Ambrose
Hadley, Edward Crocker   R. April 27, 1730
                                                Page 201

Garland, John. Settled by William Wilkinson and
John Chapman.   1727   R. April 27, 1730
                                                Page 204

Hilyard, Thomas: To be buried by my deceased wife.
Leg.- son Edward; son John; daughter Mary. Ex., friend
Samuel Alexander
  D. March 20, 1729   R. May 25, 1730
  Wit. John Jones, Samuel Alexander, Ann Spann (?)
                                                Page 205

Mackmaill, John: Leg.- loving wife; son John; son
Philip, 100 acres at Corrawock, the plantation on which
David Williams lived, also the land on the road from Pursell's mill to the chapel; land called Clark's Posen to
be sold and the money divided among my daughters by this
present wife; to my five married daughters; to my wife
and her seven childre. Ex., son John Mackmaill. Overseers, Jacob Darden and Richard Pope.
  D. December 22, 1728   R. May 25, 1730
  Wit. Jacob Darden, John Mackmiall   Page 205

Brewer, Thomas. Appraised by John Monro, W. Bridger, Jr., Francis Gross.   R.   May 25, 1730   Page 206

Mackmiall, John. Appraised by John Johnson, William Wesuray, John Tomlin, Mathew Tomlin. R. July 27, 1730
                                                    Page 209

Jones, Edward: Leg.- eldest son Edward; son William; son Joseph land on the Blackwater; daughter Jane; daughter Sarah; daughter Deborah; daughter Mary; wife Deborah Exs., wife and sons Joseph and William Jones
    D. January 15, 1722   R. July 27, 1730
    Wit. Thomas Lane, John Brown, Peter Vasser   Page 210

Rickes, James: Leg.- brother Isaac Rickes; brother Abraham Rickes, Mary his wife and their daughter Martha; brother Robert Rickes and his son Robert; sister Jane Sellaway and her son John Sellaway; to Jacob Rickes; to John Rickes, the son of Isaac Rickes; to William, the son of Jacob Rickes. Exs., Abraham and Robert Rickes.
    D. April 7, 1730   R. July 27, 1730
    Wit. William Denson, John Roberts   Page 211

Nevill, John: Leg.- daughter Penelope; daughter Elizabeth; daughter Martha; daughter Elenora; daughter Florence; daughter Mary; daughter Patience; daughter Sarah; daughter Ann. Exs., wife and son John Nevill
    D. September 30, 1726   R. July 27, 1730
    Wit. John Marshall, Mick'l Murfrey, John Garrey.
                                                    Page 213

Hilliard, Thomas. Appraised by William Brock, Thomas Calcote, Edward Davis. Ordered May 25, 1730
                                                    Page 214

Rickes, James. Inventory presented by Abraham and Robert Rickes.   August 24, 1730   Page 215

Hoggard, Patrick. Appraised by Thomas Calcote, William Brock, George Whitley. Ordered January 17, 1729
    R. September 28, 1730   Page 215

Rickes, James. Appraised by Thomas Gale, Jr., Robert Coggan, William Powell.   R. September 28, 1730
                                                    Page 216

Sauls, Abraham: Leg.- William Broom; son John; son
Abraham; daughter Elizabeth; daughter Sarah, a bequest
left her by her grandmother. Extx., loving wife.
D. April 3, 1730   R. September 28, 1730
Wit. Thomas Lumbly, Thomas Brown, Thomas Wood
                                        Page 218

Tidmash, Gyles. Inventory, signed by William Bidgood
and presented by Sarah Tidmash. R. September 28, 1730
                                        Page 218

Pitman, Thomas: Leg.- son Thomas; son Samuel; son
Robert; son Ambrose; son John; son Arthur; son Samson; son
Joseph; to daughters, Ann, Olive, Pratta, Elizabeth, Lucy
and Faith. Trustees, Robert Lancaster, John Dunkley and
Robert Monger, Jr.
D.   R. September 28, 1730
Wit. Joseph Strickling, Thomas Pitman, Edward Hood
Robert Lancaster's deposition in reference to the
location of his land.   Page 220

Goodson, Thomas. Settlement of Estate. To funeral
charges for said Goodson and his wife. Settled by Henry
Applewhaite and Thomas Walton. R. September 28, 1730
                                        Page 220

Boykin, Edward. Appraised by Francis Williamson, John
Dunkley, Mathew Kinchin. Ordered February 24, 1728
R. September 28, 1730   Page 221

Jones, Joseph. Inventory presented by William
Kinchen, Jr.   R. September 28, 1730   Page 223

Strickland, Mathew. Leg.- son John, 100 acres on the
Green Pond; son William; son Sampson; son Mathew; son
Jacob; daughter Sarah; daughter Ann; daughter Elizabeth;
daughter Jane; son Joseph. Exs., wife Ann and son Joseph
D. July 14, 1730   R. October 25, 1730
Wit. Arthur Taylor, Joseph Strickland, Mathew Cooper.
                                        Page 224

Gray, Richard: Leg.- mother Ann Gray; sister Ann West;
sister Mary Willett; sister Elizabeth; sister Sarah
Ex., brother Aaron Gray
D. October 20, 1729   R. October 25, 1730
Wit. Ann Gray, Sarah Gray   Page 225

Parker, Nathaniel: Of Newport Parish. Leg.- eldest
son Nicholas; son Nathaniel, one-half of my lots in the
town of Hampton; wife Ann; daughter Martha; daughter
Mary. Ex., brother Nicholas Parker
   D. June 29, 1730   R. November 23, 1730
   Wit. Thomas Applewhite, Joseph Bridger, Thomas Parker
                                   Page 226

Hampton, Thomas. Appraised by Jacob Darden, Robert
Smelly, John Marshall. Ordered October 26, 1730
   R. November 23, 1730   Page 229

Bridger, William: Leg.- son William; to grandson
Joseph Bridger; to William Dixon; to Mr. Thomas Bray, the
cane, which was his father's; son James the plantation on
which Jonathan Jones now lives, the land which belonged
to his deceased brother Joseph Bridger at Round Hill, I
have sold to Major Benjamin Edwards for 25L, my said son
to be under the guardianship of Arthur Smith, Jr and his
wife Elizabeth, until he is eighteen; to Elizabeth Smith.
Ex., Arthur Smith, Jr.
   D. September 27, 1730   R. November 23, 1730
   Wit. William Crumpler, William Crumpler, Jr.
                                   Page 230

Brown, Edward. Appraised by Benjamin Wilson,
Edward Harris, Abraham Stevenson. R. November 23, 1730
                                   Page 231

Bridger, Col. William. Appraised by Henry Applewhite,
Thomas Applewhite, Thomas Walton. R. December 28, 1730
                                   Page 232

Pitman, Thomas. Appraised by Robert Lancaster, John
Dunkley, Robert Monger, Jr. R. January 25, 1730/31
                                   Page 238

Salmon, James: Leg.- daughter Phillis; to William
Salmon; son James; to Mary Salmon; to Thomas Salmon; to
John Salmon; to Sarah Salmon; to John Bass
Ex., son James Salmon
   D. November 18, 1730   R. March 22, 1730
   Wit. John Bass, John Dortish (?)   Page 240

Gray, Richard. Appraised by William Best, Humphrey
Marshall, John Penny.   R. January 25, 1730
                                   Page 241

Fulgham, Anthony. Appraised by Francis Williamson,
John Little, Joshua Turner. Ordered June 24, 1729
    R. January 25, 1730/31   Page 242

Parker, Nathaniel. Appraised by Hugh Gyles, John
Norsworthy, Tristram Norsworthy. R. January 25, 1730/31
                                                  Page 243

Rutter, William. Appraised at the house of Mary
Rutter, by Joseph Wright, William Noyall, John Wright
    R. February 22, 1730/31   Page 244

Harris, Thomas. Appraised by Edward Brantley, John
Tharp, Thomas Purcell.   R. February 22, 1730/31
                                                  Page 245

Everett, Samuel. Appraised by Michael Murphrey,
Jacob Darden, Thomas Gale, Jr., Benjamin Beal.
    Ordered January 25, 1730   R. February 22, 1730/31
                                                  Page 246

Pilkington, William. Appraised by W. Bridger, John
Monro, Robert Brown   R. February 22, 1730/31
                                                  Page 247

Brantley, John: Leg.- to granddaughters, Elizabeth,
Martha and Mary Loopers (Lupe); to grandson John, the son
of my son Clay Brantley; to grandson Thomas Brantley, the
son of my son Clay; to friend Thomas Walton
Ex., son Clay Brantley
    D. February 1, 1730/31   R. March 22, 1730/31
    Wit. Thomas Walton, Elizabeth Walton   Page 248

Skelton, Thomas: Leg.- grandson William, the son of
John Tuke and Elizabeth his wife; to daughter Ann; daughter Mary, the land on which William Gladhill, formerly
lived; to friends, James Baker, Thomas Shelly, James
Wilson and Lawrence Baker. Extx., daughter Ann Skelton
    D. January 26, 1730   R. March 22, 1730/31
    Wit. Priscilla Fones, Lawrence Baker   Page 249

White, John. Appraised by Thomas Cook, Henry Harris,
William Lee.   R. March 22, 1730
                                                  Page 251

Cobb, Edward: Leg.- son Henry; daughter Susan Rede
(Read ?); to loving wife; my sons have had their share
Ex., son Henry Cobb
   D. November 26, 1729   R. March 22, 1730/31
   Wit. Edward Cobb, Richard Williams, John Johnson
                                             Page 251

Lundy, James. Account of estate returned by Joseph
Perry.   R. March 22, 1730/31   Page 253

Sikes, Thomas: Leg.- son Thomas; son Joseph; son
William; daughter Elizabeth; daughter Jane
Extx., wife Elizabeth Sikes
   D. January 19, 1730   R. March 22, 1730/31
   Wit. Thomas Gale, Jr., Francis Denson, John Denson
                                             Page 254

Boykin, Edward. Account of estate, returned by
Edward Boykin, Jr. Examined by Francis Williamson and
John Dunkley   R. March 22, 1730/31   Page 255

Screws, John: Leg.- son John; son William; son Joseph;
son Arthur; daughter Elizabeth; to loving wife
   D. November 9, 1729   R. April 26, 1731
   Wit. John Britt, Charles Jordan
   Presented by Elizabeth Screws, relict   Page 256

Powell, John: Of the Lower Parish. Leg.- son John;
son Jacob; daughter Sarah Hutchings; granddaughter Mirikia
Hutchins; son Moses; son Henry; daughter Patience; son
Arthur. Extx. wife Deborah Powell
   D. February 18, 1730   R. April 26, 1731
   Wit. Thomas Gale, Jr., Thomas Bullock, Thomas Gale
                                             Page 257

Salmon, James. Appraised by Owen Mirick, Timothy
Thorp, John Thorp.   R. April 26, 1731
                                             Page 258

Dickinson, Christopher. Appraised by Robert Richards,
John Wright, John Chapman. Ordered March 22, 1730
   R. April 26, 1731   Page 261

Sykes, Thomas. Appraised by Jacob Darden, Mick'l
Murfee, Robert Eley. Signed Elizabeth Sykes

Ordered March 22, 1730   R. April 26, 1731

Page 264

Screws, John. Appraised by Richard Blunt, Ambrose
Hadley, Edward Crocker.   R. May 24, 1731

Page 268

Powell, John. Appraised by Jacob Darden, John
Marshall, Mick'l Murphry   R. April 24, 1731

Page 269

Williams, Epaphroditus. Account of estate. Examined
by John Chapman, Christopher Reynolds, William Noyall
   R. May 24, 1731   Page 270

Woodley, John. Appraised by Thomas Murry, John Davis,
Joseph Chapman.   Signed Mrs. Frances Woodley
   Ordered September 18, 1726 R. September 26, 1726
   (Note by Clerk, - omitted in proper place)   Page 273

Proctor, Rueben. Settlement of estate, to money in
the hands of Thomas Davis and William Dixon. Audited by
Thomas Walton and James Ingles. R. June 28, 1731

Page 278

Norsworthy, Thomas. Settlement. Errors accepted by
Thomas Walton, audited by James Ingles, Samuel Davis and
Lawrence Baker.   R. July 26, 1731   Page 278

Strickland, Mathew. Appraised by Robert Crocker, John
Cain, Robert Berryman. Ordered October 26, 1730
   R. July 26, 1731   Page 280

Gutteridge, John. Appraised by William Sellers,
Oliver Woodward, Thomas Carter   R. July 26, 1731

Page 282

Dowles, John: Of the Upper Parish. Leg.- daughter
Alice Dukes, after the death of her mother; daughter Ann;
daughter Mary; daughter Ruth; daughter Susan
Exs., daughters, Ruth and Susannah Dowles
   D. August 23, 1731
   Acknowledged in court by the said John Doles
   R. August 23, 1731   Page 283

Hollyman, Christopher: Leg.- son James; son John
Extx., wife Susannah Hollyman
   D. August 2, 1729   R. October 25, 1731
   Wit. Thomas Hollyman, Sr., Josiah John Hollyman,
        Thomas Hollyman, Jr.   Page 284

Norwood, Richard. Appraised by Thomas Cook, Joseph
Parks, Edward Brantley   R. October 25, 1731
                                      Page 285

Meacum, John. Estate, audited by James Ingles,
Lawrence Baker   R. November 23, 1731   Page 287

Meacum, Susanna. Account estate, signed by Roger
Ingram, William Dixon. Audited by Thomas Walton and
James Ingles   R. November 23, 1731   Page 288

Sanders, Robert: Of the Lower Parish. Leg.- to cousin Robert Sanders, the son of Thomas Saunders, decd.,
land on the Queen's Grave Swamp; cousin Francis Sanders;
the son of Francis Sanders; to cousin Elizabeth Sanders,
daughter of Thomas Sanders, decd., to her brother Thomas;
to cousin Richard Sanders, son of Thomas Sanders decd.,
the land I bought of Elizabeth Thomas; to John Sanders,
the son of Francis Sanders; to Thomas, the son of Thomas
Sanders, decd., land called "Half Moon"; to my cousin
Phebe Winborn. Exs., John Winborn and Robert Sanders
   D. July 12, 1731   R. December 27, 1731
   Wit. Richard Thomas, Lawrence Wolferston, John Thomas
                                      Page 289

Hollyman, Christopher. Inventory, presented by James
Hollyman   R. December 27, 1731   Page 291

Harris, Thomas. Inventory, supplemented by Henry
Harris   R. March 27, 1732   Page 292

Peterson, John: Leg.- to Burrell Brown, 400 acres, if
no issue to return to my son Batt Peterson; to Jeremiah
Brown, 200 acres, being the plantation on which Joseph
Perry lived, if without heirs, to return to my son John;
to John Smith 100 acres on the Fox Branch; to Mathew Par-
ham of Isle of Wight County, 100 acres on the same Branch;
to grandson John Eppes, 100 acres on which Jonathan Carter

lived, also 100 acres on which Robert Ellis lived and 400
acres out of the tract I bought of Edmond Mecarty, on Meherrin River and Jenitoe Creek; to son Batt; to son John;
daughter Mary Spain; daughter Judith Thweatt; daughter Ann
Thweatt. Exs., sons Batt and John Peterson
    D. March 1, 1731   R. January 24, 1731
    Wit. William Thweatt, Miles Thweatt, John Sturdivant
                                           Page 292

    Coggan, William. Appraised by Thomas Gale, Jr., Robert
Eley, Jr., Jacob Darden   R. March 27, 1732
                                           Page 295

    Walters, Walter: Of the Lower Parish. Leg.- grand-
daughter Martha Brown, the plantation on which Robert Owen
lived; to granddaughter Alice Powell, land adjoining John
Powell and William Watkins at Currawoak; to grandsons
Benjamin and Walter Morrell, land on Blackwater,adjoining
Bridgeman Joyner; to George Morrell and Mary his wife,
land adjoining Richard Beal; granddaughter Mary Morrell;
wife Alice
    D. November 26, 1730   R. January 23, 1731/32
    Wit. Jacob Darden, Sarah Darden, John Chapman
    Revocation of certain bequests
    Wit. Jacob Darden, Stephen Darden, John Powell
    R. March 27, 1732   Page 297

    Body, Mary: Widow and late wife of William Body.
Leg.- son-in-law Thomas Drake; daughter Mary Bragg; daugh-
ter Judith Clark; daughter Sarah Joiner
Ex., Thomas Drake
    D. January 17, 1727   R. April 24, 1732
    Wit. George Washington, Richard Drake, Francis Jones
                                         Page 299

    Baten, Richard: Leg.- son Edward, land between King-
sale Swamp and Blackwater; to my daughter; to my wife
Ex., son Richard Baten
    D. January 28, 1731/32   R. April 24, 1732
    Wit. John Williams, Thomas Gawker, Richard Williams
                                         Page 300

    Thornton, Thomas. Appraised by Thomas Hill and John
Goodrich. Ordered February 28, 1731
    R. April 24, 1732   Page 301

    Saunders, Robert. Appraised by John Daughtry, William
Daughtry, Robert Carr, Jr., John Council Signed by
John Winborn, Ex.   R. May 22, 1732   Page 302

Howel, John: Leg.- loving wife; daughter Penelope;
brother William Howell; rest of my estate to be divided
between my wife and James Howell, Samuel Howell and
Martha Howell and my daughter Penelope.
D. March 20, 1731/32   R. June 26, 1732
Wit. Thomas Pinner, Joseph Bullock, Thomas Dixson
Presented by Elizabeth Howell   Page 304

Braswell, Susannah: Leg.- son Richard; son William;
granddaughter Elizabeth Braswell; daughter Ann; grandson
John Riggs; son James. Trustees, Richard Jones and
Richard Jordan
D. October 22, 1714   R. June 26, 1732
Wit. William Allen, Richard Jones, Richard Jordan
                                                 Page 304

Fulgham, Edmond. Appraised by Arthur Purcell, John
Little, Mathew Tomlin. Ordered March 27, 1732
R. July 24, 1732   Page 306

Joyner, Alexander. Appraised by William West, Robert
Monger, Jr., Thomas Warren.   R. July 24, 1732
                                                 Page 307

Howel, John. Appraisal by Robert Driver, Benjamin
Beal, John Garner.   R. July 24, 1732
                                                 Page 308

Bridger, William: Of the Lower Parish. Leg.- brother
James Bridger, land on Blackwater Swamp; to son Joseph,
15L paid yearly to my trusty friend Arthur Smith until he
is 18, I desire that he should live with his grandfather
and grandmother, if his grandmother should die, I wish
him to live with Arthur Smith and his wife Elizabeth
Ex., Arthur Smith
D. April 2, 1732   R. July 24, 1732
Wit. William Smith, John Bruce, W. Simmons
                                                 Page 309

Bridger, William. Appraised by John Monro, Henry
Pitt, Francis Gross   R. August 28, 1732
                                                 Page 311

Richard, William. Nuncupative will, proven by John
Rodway, Gyles Driver, Olive Driver. Of Newport Parish.
He desired that his wife Frances should have the estate of
her deceased husband, Arthur Benn, and for what was his own

he desired, that she should have one third of what he had
and his two children, viz: William and Jane should have
the rest; his deceased wife's clothes to his said daughter. D. July 3, 1732   R. August 28, 1732

Page 314

Fulgham, Michael. Appraised by William Noyall, John
Wright, Christopher Reynolds. Ordered February 26, 1727
   R. August 28, 1732   Page 315

Harrison, John. Settlement of estate by Lawrence
Baker, Thomas Hill and James Ingles. To Nicholas Casey
and Thomas White, who married two of the daughters of the
said John Harrison and Benjamin Hodges, who married his
widow and relict.   R. August 25, 1732

Page 318

Hall, Poole. Additional inventory, presented by
William Todd.   R. August 28, 1732   Page 319

Fulgham, Anthony. Account current, signed by Hugh
Gyles and John Chapman.   R. September 25, 1732

Page 319

Boykin, William: Leg.- wife Margaret, the plantation
I bought of Thomas Boykin; son Simon; son William land at
Roanoke bought of James Spears; son John, land bought of
my brother Thomas Boykin; son Thomas land on Tucker's
Swamp, on which John Phillips lived; daughter Martha; my
four sons my land at Fishing Creek in North Carolina
   D. June 19, 1731   R. September 25, 1732
   Wit. William Carrell, Thomas Moore, Jr., M. Kinchin

Page 321

Wiggs, Sarah: Leg.- my three sisters, Catherine Stevenson, Mary Britt and Elizabeth Brassey; brother Luke Wiggs;
friend Henry Applewhite. Ex., brother George Wiggs
   D. July 26, 1732   R. September 25, 1732
   Wit. Gwin Summerell, Violet Frissell   Page 324

Dickinson, Christopher. Estate settled by Hugh Gyles,
John Chapman.   R. September 25, 1732

Page 324

Brassee, William: Of the Upper Parish. Leg.- son
William; son Thomas; wife Jane. Ex., son William Brassee

D. May 22, 1732   R. January 22, 1732
Wit. Robert Edwards, William Edwards, Henry Edwards
Page 325

Richards, William. Appraised by John Chapman, Hugh
Gyles, Robert Driver   R. October 24, 1732
Page 326

Ingram, Roger. Account current, signed by William
English. Examined by Thomas Hill, John Goodrich
Page 328

Jordan, James: Leg.- son John, if without heirs to
grandson James Jordan; daughter Elizabeth Scott; land
bought of Joseph Bridger to my grandson James Jordan
Scott; son James' children
D. October 8, 1732   R. January 22, 1732
Wit. Mathew Jordan, Mary Jordan, Thomas Parr
Page 328

Applewhite, Thomas: Leg.- wife Martha; son Thomas;
son Henry; son John; daughter Holland Copeland; daughter
Martha Weston; daughter Mary Benn; daughter Ann
Exs., wife and son Henry Applewhite
D. June 15, 1728   R. January 22, 1732
Wit. Everett West, John Hokins (?)
Page 329

Jordan, James. Appraised by B. Beal, Joseph Wright,
Robert Driver. Signed by John Jordan
Page 331

Gale, Thomas: Leg.- wife Alice; daughter Sarah; daugh-
ter Elizabeth Sykes; daughter Mary Bryant; daughter Alice
Eley; son Thomas. Extx., wife Alice
D. November 15, 1732   R. February 26, 1732
Wit. William Scott, Thomas Bullock, John Hampton
Page 331

Osbourne, Edward. Appraised by Thomas Shelly, John
Barlow, John Floide   R. February 26, 1732
Page 333

Brassee, William. Appraised by John Turner, John
Whitley, William Brassee.   R. February 26, 1732
Page 333

Street, Maddison: Of the Lower Parish. Leg.- cousin
George Whitley; cousin Maddison Whitley; cousin Mary, the
daughter of brother George Street, the plantation on which
Thomas Daniels lives; cousin John Whitley; cousin Thomas
Whitley; to Goddaughter Martha Whitley; to Egbell Sawyer
Jones; sister Sarah Turner; cousin Henry Turner; sister
Ann Smith; cousin Sarah Smith, the daughter of John Smith;
Mary the daughter of Thomas Bevan
  Ex., cousin George Whitley
  D. November 19, 1732   R. February 26, 1732
  Wit. Mary Smith, Charles Fulgham, William Lane
                                          Page 334

Street, Maddison. Appraised by Hugh Gyles, John
Wright, George Clark   Page 338

Holyday, Samuel. Settlement of the estate in the
hands of Anthony Covington Holyday, by William Wilkinson,
Benjamin Willett   R. March 26, 1733
                                          Page 338

Fulgham, Anthony: Of the Upper Parish. Leg.- John
Oin (?); son Anthony; wife Sarah
  D. December 18, 1728   R. January 25, 1730
  Wit. John Turner; Joshua Turner, Jr., Joshua Turner, Sr.
                                          Page 349

Benn, James: Leg.- wife Mary; son James (not 21); son
George, land I bought of John Calloway, also the land
formerly belonging to Josiah Harrison; to unborn child;
daughter Mary. Extx., wife Mary
  D. August 30, 1732   R. April 23, 1733
  Wit. George Benn, Elizabeth Copeland, Jane Casey
                                          Page 340

Sherrer, Sarah. Appraised by Charles Chapman; Richard
Blunt, William Clarke. Signed Edward Crocker
  Ordered March 26, 1733   R. April 23, 1733
                                          Page 343

White, Henry: Leg.- wife Sarah; silver which I have
sent for by Captain Turner, to son Baker; daughter Mary.
Friends, Mr. Mathew Wills and William Baker to divide my
estate.
  D. February 17, 1733   R. May 28, 1733
  Wit. William Glover, John White, Lawrence Baker
                                          Page 344

Johnson, Robert: Leg.- son Robert; son James; son
John; son Abraham; son Isaac, land adjoining Thomas
Swann; son Jacob; wife Ann; daughter Catherine Council;
daughter Priscilla Council; daughter Ann Griffin; daugh-
ter Mary; daughter Sarah. Wife, Extx.
D. September 24, 1732   R. May 28, 1733
Wit. Thomas Drake, Jr., Richard Worrell,
      John Dawson, Jr.   Page 345

Clements, Francis. Estate, signed by Joseph Lane
and Lydia Clements, Extx. Ordered December 2, 1718
R. May 28, 1733   Page 347

Sanders, Henry. Inventory, presented by John Sanders
R. June 25, 1733   Page 349

Daniel, John. Estate settled by Hugh Gyles and
George Clarke.   R. June 25, 1733   Page 349

Edwards, Hugh. Appraised by John Chapman, George
Clark, John Wright. Signed Mary Edwards
Ordered April 23, 1733   R. June 25, 1733
                                     Page 350

Boykin, William. Appraised by John Dunkley, Francis
Williamson, M. Kinchin   R. June 25, 1733
                                     Page 351

Benn, Captain James. Appraised by Hugh Giles, George
Clark, William Noyall. R. June 25, 1733   Page 354

Penny, Ralph. Settlement, by John Chapman, Benn
Willett. R. July 23, 1733   Page 356

Richards, William. Appraised by Francis Gross, Benn
Willett, Robert Driver. R. July 23, 1733
                                     Page 356

Westbrook, John: Leg.- daughter Ann; son John; son
Thomas; daughter Sarah; son William; son James; sister
Elizabeth; beloved wife

D. February 13, 1719   R. July 23, 1733
Wit. Edward Simmons, Thomas Perry, Walker Enniss
                                        Page 357

Miller, Edward: Leg.- son Edward; son John; son
William; daughter Sarah; wife Martha. Friends, Mathew
Jordan, Thomas Murry, John Davis and William Harrison to
divide my estate
D. February 12, 1727   R. August 27, 1733
Wit. John Hodges, Benjamin Hodges   Page 358

Terall, Blackabee: Leg.- grandson James Jordan; grand-
son Joseph Jordan; granddaughter Ann Jordan; son-in-law
James Jordan
D. September 7, 1726   R. August 27, 1733
Wit. Thomas Goodson, Edward Davis
Presented by Patience Jordan, the widow of James Jordan
                                        Page 360

Jordan, James. Appraised by William Bidgood, William
Wilson, Joseph Hill. Ordered January 22, 1732
R. September 24, 1733   Page 362

Butler, Ann. Appraised by Timothy Tines, Joseph
Wright, Richard Kersey. Ordered May 28, 1733
R. October 22, 1733   Page 369

Row, John. Appraised by John Johnson, William Pope,
Richard Williams   R. October 22, 1733
                                        Page 370

Gent, John. Appraised by Nicholas Williams, Robert
Rickes, Francis Jones. Signed by Oliver Woodward and
Thomas Allen   R. October 22, 1733
                                        Page 370

Reynolds, Christopher. Appraised by Hugh Giles,
Richard Williams, Joseph Wright. Ordered March 27, 1733
R. October 22, 1733   Page 372

Garland, John. Appraised by John Chapman, John Wright,
Charles Fulghan, Edward Driver. Signed Martha Garland
Ordered April 23, 1733   R. October 22, 1733
                                        Page 375

Richards, Robert: Leg.- daughter Prudence Driver; to
Peter Green; daughter Sarah Croom; to Martha, the daugh-
ter of Patience and Peter Green; daughter Susannah; son
Robert; daughter Sarah; granddaughter Martha Green. Ex.,
son Robert Richards
   D. August 6, 1733   R. November 26, 1733
   Wit. Edward Driver, Edward Croom   Page 377

Pope, Richard: Leg.- son Henry; son Richard; wife
Sarah; daughter Jane; daughter Sarah; daughter Charity
Pope. Exs., wife and son Henry Pope
   D. September 24, 1733   R. November 26, 1733
   Wit. Thomas Gale, John Williams, Jr., Jacob Powell
                                    Page 378

Baten, Richard. Appraised by John Johnston, Richard
Williams, William Daughtrey. R. November 26, 1733
                                    Page 380

Howell, John. Settlement of estate by Abraham Rickes,
and Benjamin Beal   R. November 26, 1733
                                    Page 381

Sampson, James. Estate settled by Lawrence Baker,
Thomas Murry and John Goodrich. R. January 28, 1733
                                    Page 382

Richards, Robert. Appraised by Richard Wilkinson,
Joseph Wright, John Clark, John Chapman
   R. January 28, 1733   Page 383

Gulledge, Edward. Appraised by Edward Lundy, Harmon
Read, William Lee   R. January 28, 1733
                                    Page 386

Norwood, Elizabeth. Appraised by Thomas Cook, Henry
Harris, Thomas Smith. Ordered August 7, 1733
   R. January 28, 1733   Page 386

Special, Samuel. Appraised by Timothy Tynes, Sharp
Reynolds. Ordered November 6, 1733
   R. January 28, 1733   Page 388

Thornton, William. Account current, signed by Abraham
Rickes, Benjamin Beale.   R. February 25, 1733
                                    Page 388

Goodrich, George. Settlement of estate, to balance due
to the widow, to Mary Goodrich, orphan; to Joseph Clinch
in the right of his wife Elizabeth. Signed Hugh Giles
and Thomas Hill   R. February 25, 1733   Page 389
   The receipt of Joseph Clinch was witnessed by
   William Seward.

Parker, Nicholas. Account current, to Nicholas Parker,
orphan, his estate. Signed Ann Parker
R. February 25, 1733   Page 390

Harris, Edward: Of the Upper Parish. Leg.- son Edward,
land adjoining John Johnson and John Turner, being land
which was granted to my father, Thomas Harris; son Jacob,
land on the Flatt Swamp of the Meherrin River; sons Nathan
and West Harris, the land granted me on the north side of
Warwick Branch; son Daniel; daughter Ann; daughter Martha
Williamson; son James; wife Mary. Ex., son Nathan Harris
   D. April 27, 1733   R. March 25, 1734
   Wit. Thomas Atkinson, John Harris   Page 391

Williams, John: Leg.- son Richard; son John; son David
Extx., wife Margaret Williams
   D. December 17, 1733   R. March 25, 1734
   Wit. Thomas Parker, Joseph Weston   Page 393

Marshall, Joseph. Account estate, signed by William
Wilkinson, Charles Fulgham.   R. March 25, 1734
                                              Page 394

Hollyman, Thomas: Of the Upper Parish. Leg.- grand-
son Joseph Hollyman land on Blackwater Swamp; grandson
Arthur Hollyman; to Robert Carrell; wife Elizabeth; to
William Hollyman
   D. December 31, 1732   R. March 25, 1734
   Wit. Thomas Atkinson, John Hollyman, Jr.
                                              Page 395

Carrell, Joseph: Leg.- my two brothers, Benjamin and
Samuel Carrell; cousin Benjamin, son of Benjamin Carrell;
cousin Thomas, son of Samuel Carrell; to Sarah White
Ex., brother Benjamin Carrell
   D. March 1, 1733   R. March 25, 1734
   Wit. William Dixon, William Bonner
                                              Page 397

Will Book Four

Cox, Francis. Appraised by Thomas Jarrell, William
Pope, John Thomas. Ordered February 25, 1733
R. April 22, 1734   Page 1

Bateman, Richard, Sr. Settlement ordered November
26, 1733. Signed Hardy Council, Francis Jones
R. April 22, 1734   Page 1

Pitt, Henry. Appraised by Benn Willett, Humphrey
Marshall, James Hunter   R. April 22, 1734
                                           Page 2

Lucus, Mary: Leg.- son John; son William. Ex. son
William Lucus
D. December 31, 1729   R. May 27, 1734
Wit. John Dunkley, Abigail Waynfield, William Reynolds
                                           Page 3

Pitt, Thomas. Account estate, examined by Joseph
Godwin, William Wilkinson, John Monro
R. May 28, 1734   Page 4

Frizzel, Ralph: Leg.- wife Mary; daughter Ann
Holyday; daughter Mary Reynolds; son Ralph; six children
now with me, viz: James, John, Joshua, Elizabeth, Lucy
and Sarah. Exs.; wife and son James Frizzell
D. January 19, 1733   R. May 27, 1734
Wit. Joseph Wiles, Joseph Weston   Page 6

Glover, Sarah. Appraised by Thomas Moreland, James
Carrell, Thomas Shelly. Ordered February 25, 1733
R. May 27, 1734   Page 8

Mercer, James: Leg.- wife Mary; daughter Mary; son
John; daughter Ann; daughter Martha; son Robert; son
James; son Thomas; to my unnamed son; daughter Elizabeth;
daughter Patience; daughter Sarah; son-in-law Robert
Williamson. Wife Mary, Extx.
D. December 11, 1720   R. June 24, 1734
Wit. William Kinchin, Arthur Purcell
                                           Page 11

Hawkins, William. Appraised by Jospeh Smith, Thomas Parker, Tristram Norsworthy. Ordered July 12, 1734
  R. July 22, 1734   Page 14

Ingram, Roger: Leg.- wife Elizabeth; son John; son Roger; daughter Sarah; daughter Elizabeth; son Richard; son William. Exs., Thomas Shelley and Benjamin Hodges
  D. March 12, 1733/34   R. September 23, 1734
  Wit. William Dixon, Thomas Stark, William Atkinson
  Exs., refused and wife Elizabeth qualified.   Page 18

Carr, John: Yeoman. Leg.- daughter Mary; daughter Elizabeth; daughter Sarah; son William; son Abraham; son Hardy; daughter Grace; son John; son Robert; daughter Eleanor Duck; to my wife and my three young sons Ex., son Robert Carr
  D. May 19, 1734   R. September 23, 1734
  Wit. John Darden, John Duck, John Carr
                                   Page 21

Baker, Mary: **Widow** of Henry Baker, Gent. Leg.- son William land in Nansemond County, called "Wickums"; son Lawrence; son James; son Henry; daughter Mary; daughter Sarah; daughter Katherine. Ex., son Lawrence Baker
  D. March 5, 1732   R. September 23, 1734
  Wit. Nicholas Derring, James Briggs, Robert Davis
                                   Page 22

Davis, Thomas: Leg.- to William, the son of William Davis, deceased; to Elizabeth Gray; to John Davis, the son of Samuel Davis; to my daughter Elizabeth at 18, if she should die without heirs, my estate to the sons of my three brothers and my sister Prudence Wrenn Exs., brother Samuel Davis and friend James Day
  D. August 15, 1734   R. September 23, 1734
  Wit. Samuel Davis, Elizabeth Gray   Page 23

Stark, Thomas. Appraised by Thomas Moreland, James Carrell, Thomas Shelley. Ordered May 27, 1734
  R. October 28, 1734   Page 24

Westbrook, John. Appraised by Nathaniel Ridley, Edward Brantley, Thomas Cook. Signed by John Person
  R. October 28, 1734   Page 25

Row, John. Appraised by Richard Williams, William
Pope, John Johnson.   R. October 28, 1734
                                                    Page 26

Williams, Mary: Leg.- son George; son-in-law Mathew
Jones; daughter Sarah Brown; daughter Mary Williams;
son Peter. Exs., my brother Peter Green and my son
Peter Williams
    D. October 27, 1734   R. November 25, 1734
    Wit. Thomas Gross, Anthony Covington Hollyday
                                                    Page 28

Baker, Mary. Appraised by Samuel Davis, Thomas
Murry, John Goodrich   R. November 25, 1734
                                                    Page 28

Giles, Eleanor: Leg.- son Robert Smelly; grandson
John Smelly; to my son Robert Smelly's wife; to grand-
sons Robert and Thomas, the sons of Robert Smelly; to
Elizabeth Smelly, the wife of my son Lewis Smelly; to
Joshua Whitley, Jr., the son of my granddaughter; to
Lewis, the son of William Joyner. Ex., my grandson
John Smelly
    D. February 17, 1732   R. November 25, 1734
    Wit. Thomas Uzzell, H. Lightfoot   Page 29

Williams, Mary. Appraised by Francis Gross, Thomas
Gross, Thomas Applewhite, Anthony Covington Holyday
    R. December 23, 1734   Page 31

Warren, William. Appraised by Joseph Gray, John
Hodges, John Dunkley. Ordered December 21, 1734
    R. January 27, 1734   Page 32

Smelley, Robert: Leg.- son John; son Thomas; son
Robert. Exs., sons Robert and Thomas Smelley
    D. August 2, 1734   R. January 27, 1734
    Wit. Thomas Gale, John Mackmial   Page 34

Mackmiall, John: Aged 25 years. Leg.- wife
Elizabeth; to my unborn child. Wife, Extx.
    D. October 18, 1734   R. January 27, 1734
    Wit. Mathew Westray, John Batten   Page 35

Carr, John. Appraised by James Johnson, Jr., John
Darden, John Duck   R. January 27, 1734
                                                    Page 36

Murry, George. Appraised by John Miller, Benjamin
Hodges, Peter Woodward. Ordered March 7, 1725
R. January 27, 1734   Page 37

Minyard, William. Appraised by Joseph Wiles, George
Parker, Robert King   R. January 27, 1734
                                                  Page 38

Davis, Thomas. Appraised by Thomas Hill, John Goodrich,
Melchizadeck Deshey.   R. January 27, 1734
                                                  Page 39

Parker, George: Leg.- daughter Mary; son John; to John
Gray; to Sarah Weston; to William Smith, Jr; son Francis;
daughter Elizabeth. Money for the last two children to
be placed in the hands of Mr. Nathaniel Bagnall, William
Smith, Jr. and Henry King, whom I appoint my Exs.
D. January 27, 1734   R. February 24, 1734
Wit. Robert King, John Gray   Page 41

Underwood, Thomas. Inventory, presented by William
Underwood.   R. February 24, 1734
                                                  Page 42

Pitt, John: Leg.- daughter Martha, the land on which
Captain Joseph Bridger now lives; grandson Joseph Bridger,
the land on which John Turner now lives; daughter Rachel,
the land on which Ann Smith now lives, also the land on
which Elizabeth Shaw lives; daughter Esther; daughter
Prudence, the land on which Edward Driver and Robert Smith
live; daughter Ann Godwin, the land on which William
Godwin and Samuel Croom live; grandson William Bridger
Ex., William Godwin
D. December 19, 1729   R. February 24, 1734
Wit. Edward Driver, Richard Pilkington
                                                  Page 43

Boykin, William. Account estate, to Thomas Vaughan,
who married the Extx. Examined by John Dunkley and
Mathew Kinchin.   R. February 24, 1734
                                                  Page 44

Powell, William: Leg.- son William; son Joseph, land
at Corrowaugh, adjoining Robert Carr; son Benjamin; son-
in-law Samuel Redlehusk; daughter Martha; daughter Rebecca
Wilkinson; daughter Mary Holland; daughter Rachel; daugh-

ter Alice; daughter Lydia; wife Mary. Ex., son William
D. October 3, 1734   R. March 24, 1734
Wit. John Darden, Thomas Powell, Daniel Day

Page 46

Pitt, Captain John. Appraised by Hugh Giles, Thomas
Whitfield, George Clark   R. March 24, 1734

Page 47

Parker, George. Appraised by Mathew Jones, Francis
Gross, Giles Driver   R. March 24, 1734

Page 49

Norwood, Richard. Appraised by Nathaniel Ridley,
John Person, J. Edwards. Ordered June 24, 1734
R. March 24, 1734   Page 48

Brown, Joseph. Appraised by John Pitt, Richard
Snowden, Anthony Covington Holyday, John Penny
Ordered February 24, 1734   R. March 24, 1734

Page 50

Mackmiall, John. Estate authorized to be sold by
Jacob Darden   R. March 24, 1734

Page 51

Jordan, Richard. Appraised by Arthur Jones, Joseph
Ward, John Davis. Ordered April 12, 1735
R. April 28, 1735   Page 52

Fulgham, Anthony. Account estate, examined by
William Wilkinson, Benn Willett   R. April 28, 1735

Page 54

Powell, William. Appraised by George English, James
Johnson, Thomas Powell   R. April 28, 1735

Page 55

Ingram, Roger. Appraised by Thomas Hill, Thomas
Moreland, Thomas Murry, Samuel Davis
R. May 26, 1735   Page 57

Carr, Robert: Leg.- wife Mary; son Robert; daughter
Elizabeth Darden. Exs., wife and son Robert Carr

D. May 10, 1734   R. May 26, 1735
Wit. Hardy Council, Michael Council, Charles Council

Briggs, Henry. Appraised by Richard Kirby, Thomas
Macey, Arthur Arrington   R. May 26, 1735

Bunkley, John. Appraised by John Pitt, Richard
Snowden, Robert Brown. Ordered March 24, 1734/35
R. May 26, 1735

Taylor, Edward: Leg.- son Joseph; son Edward; son
George; daughter Elizabeth. Wife, Extx.
D. June 29, 1734   R. May 26, 1735
Wit. Robert Eley, Jr., Ambrose Saunders, Sarah
     Ogbourne

Warren, William. Appraised by Mathew Kinchin, John
Dunkley, Joseph Gray. Ordered April 28, 1735
R. May 26, 1735

Braswell, Sarah: Leg.- grandson John Braswell, Jr.;
daughter Jane; grandson Benjamin Braswell; to the other
children of my son John, viz: Mary, William and Sampson
Exs., son John Braswell and grandson John Braswell
D. March 20, 1733/34   R. May 26, 1735
Wit. Richard Blow, Jr., Samuel Smith, Samuel Willis

Kea, Henry. Account estate, funeral charges for his
daughter Mary Kea. Signed Richard Webb and William
Bidgood. Examined by Thomas Moreland and James Carrell

Briggs, Henry, Jr. Account estate, signed William
Barton. Examined by Joseph Gray and M. Kinchin
R. May 26, 1735

Wood, George. Appraised by William Killebrew, Martin
Middleton, Peter Durdinow. Ordered January 27, 1734
R. June 23, 1734

Driver, Thomas. Appraised by Hugh Giles, Joseph

Wright, Timothy Tynes. Funeral expenses for the said
Driver and his wife and for his son Thomas Driver
  R. June 23, 1735   Page 69

Norsworthy, Charles: Leg. - wife Ann; eldest son
Charles; second son Thomas; son George; daughter Ann;
to my unborn child. Wife, Extx.
  D. November 17, 1734   R. June 23, 1735
  Wit. Benn Willett, Peter Best   Page 69

Dickinson, Christopher. Settlement of estate, to a
third part paid to John Bridger, who married the widow;
to the three orphans. Examined by Lawrence Baker,
Thomas Moreland, Joseph Hill. R. June 23, 1735
                                                 Page 71

Kinchen, William: Leg.- son Mathew; daughter Elizabeth
Exum; grandson William Jones; daughter Martha Jarrell;
daughter Patience Taylor and her husband Etheldred Taylor;
daughter Sarah Godwin; granddaughter Martha Godwin; son
William; wife Elizabeth; grandson William Kinchen; grand-
daughter Mary Jones. Ex., son Mathew Kinchen
  D. August 13, 1734   R. July 28, 1735
  Wit. Arthur Purcell, John Dunkley, Henry Flowers
                                                 Page 72

Norsworthy, Charles. Appraised by Benn Willett,
Thomas Applewhite, Humphrey Marshall. R. July 28, 1735
                                                 Page 75

Bevan, Thomas: Leg.- son Thomas (not 21); son
George; son Robert; son Joseph; daughter Mary; wife
Mary. Exs., wife and son Thomas Bevan
  D. March 22, 1734   R. August 25, 1735
  Wit. Hugh Giles, Rachel Davis   Page 76

Williams, Garret: Leg.- wife Elizabeth; son Daniel
Extx., wife Elizabeth Williams
  D. May 10, 1735   R. August 25, 1735
  Wit. William Watkins, William Jelks, Isaac Winingam
                                                 Page 80

Porter, Charles. Appraised by John Rochel, William
Turner, Martin Middleton
  R. October 27, 1735   Page 81

Rigin, Ann. Account estate, signed by William Noyall
Examined by John Chapman, Hugh Giles
R. October 27, 1735   Page 82

Lilburn, Sarah. Account estate, signed by W. Bidgood
Examined by Jesse Brown and Henry West
R. October 27, 1735   Page 83

Williams, Mary. Account of estate in the hands of
Peter Green. Examined by Thomas Woodley, Thomas Summerell, Thomas Calcote.   R. November 24, 1735
                                                 Page 85

Lowry, Mathew. Joannah Lowry's account against her
husband's estate. Examined by William Brock and Timothy
Tynes. R. November 24, 1735   , Page 86

Jones, Richard. Inventory, presented by Elizabeth
Jones. R. November 24, 1735   Page 87

Wheadon, Philip: Leg.- son James; son Joseph. Ex.,
son Joseph Wheadon. Friends, Lawrence Baker, John
Hodges and John Goodrich to divide estate
D. November 27, 1735   R. January 26, 1735
Wit. John Goodrich, Rachel Miller   Page 88

Vick, Robert: Of Nottoway Parish. Leg.- son Robert;
son Joseph; son Benjamin; son Nathan; wife Sarah; daughter Mary. Exs., wife and son Robert Vick
D. October 25, 1735   R. January 26, 1735
Wit. J. Turner, Richard Vick, Jacob Vick
                                                 Page 88

Penny, John: Leg.- wife Mary; son John; youngest son
William. Wife, Extx.
D. July 20, 1735   R. January 26, 1735
Wit. Anthony Covington Holladay, Benn Willett
                                                 Page 90

Bradshaw, Nicholas. Account estate, to Ralph Frizzell
for Mary Bradshaw; to Elizabeth Bradshaw; to John and
George Bradshaw   R. January 26, 1735
                                                 Page 91

Moxson, Robert. Inventory. R. January 26, 1735
                                                 Page 92

Wheadon, Philip. Appraised by Thomas Murry, William
Harrison, Benjamin Hodges   R. February 23, 1735
                                        Page 92

Applewhaite, John: Leg.- wife Sarah; to my unborn
child; sister Ann; to the heirs of Mary Benn, given them
by my deceased father; brother Thomas; sister Holland
Copeland; sister Martha Weston; friend Thomas Copeland.
Exs., wife and friend Henry West
   R. December 20, 1735   R. February 23, 1735
   Wit. Peter Best, Thomas Copeland   Page 94

Hanpton, John: Of the Lower Parish. Leg.- brother
Francis Hampton; to John, the son of Francis Hampton;
to Martha Hampton; to Mary Hampton; to John, the son of
Michael Murphry; to Elizabeth Dixon, the wife of Thomas
Dixon, Jr.; to Sarah, Mary and Elender, the daughters
of Michael Murphry; to Rachel, the daughter of Thomas
Hampton; to Sarah Simmons, my sister; to John Hole; my
wife Ann and at her death to go to Benjamin Hampton, if
without heirs, reversion to John Hampton.
Wife Ann, Extx.
   D. February 19, 1735   R. March 22, 1735
   Wit. Thomas Gale, Thomas Bullock, Jacob Powell
                                        Page 95

Goodman, William. Appraised by Arthur Jones, William
Crocker, W. Pitman.   R. March 22, 1735
                                        Page 96

Jordan, Richard. Account of estate examined by
Robert Cannon and Joseph Ward. R. March 22, 1735
                                        Page 98

Wrenn, John. Appraised by John Goodrich, William
Harrison. R. April 26, 1736   Page 100

Parker, Thomas: Leg.- eldest son William; son Elias;
daughter Ann; son Thomas; son Wilkinson; daughter Sabre;
daughter Priscilla; grandson Elisha Parker; daughter
Rachel. Wife, Extx.
   D. January 30, 1735   R. April 26, 1736
   Wit. Robert King, George Norsworthy, James Bagnall
                                        Page 101

Bagnall, Nathan: Leg.- wife Ann; son Joseph; son
James; daughter Mary; daughter Easter; daughter Ann;son

Nathan; son Richard; son Joshua; son William; son Samuel
  Exs., Wife Ann and son James Bagnall
  D. February 30, 1735   R. April 26, 1736
  Wit. William Smith, Joseph Weston, William Smith, Jr.
                                             Page 102

  Norwood, William: Leg.- to William, the son of Henry
Harrison; to John, the son of Thomas Clark; sister Rebecca;
sister Elizabeth; sister Mary; sister Hannah; to Elizabeth
Vaughan; my clothes between Henry Harrison and Thomas
Clarke. Exs., brothers Henry Harrison and Thomas Clarke
  D. February 8, 1735   R. April 26, 1736
  Wit. Benjamin Chapman Donaldson, Charles Travers,
       John Gladish   Page 103

  Whitney, Joshua: Leg.- wife Mathon; son David; son
Jeremiah; son Samuel; daughter Kolzing; son Joseph;
daughter Ruth; son Francis; daughter Ketring. Exs.,
sons, David and Jeremiah Whitney
  D. December 26, 1735   R. April 26, 1736
  Wit. John Bentley, Jeremiah Bentley, James Blair
(Will also proven in North Carolina)   Page 104

  Baldwin, William. Appraised by Richard West, John
Wright, John Clark   R. May 24, 1736   Page 106

  Bulls, Martha. Appraised by Robert Driver, B. Beal,
John Garner, Joseph Garner. Ordered April 26, 1736
  R. May 2, 1736   Page 107

  Bevan, Peter. Appraised by Charles Fulgham, John
Gibbs, George Whitley. Signed Bartholomew Green
  R. May 24, 1736   Page 108

  Driver, Robert. Appraised by Francis Gross, John
Rodway, Humphrey Marshall. Ordered April 26, 1736
  R. May 24, 1736   Page 108

  Penny, John. Appraised by Edmond Godwin, Thomas
Applewhaite, Benn Willett   R. May 24, 1736
                                             Page 109

  Richards, Robert. Estate in the hands of Charles
Fulgham. Examined by Joseph Godwin, Thomas Walton,
Thomas Pierce   Page 110

Bradgg, Mary: Leg.- granddaughter Sarah Driver;
granddaughter Hester Driver; grandson Charles, the son
of Edward Driver; grandson Joseph Norsthey (Norsworthy?);
granddaughter Martha Norsthey; granddaughter Mary
Norsthey; grandson Charles Norsthey; son-in-law Edward
Driver and son-in-law Joseph Norsthey; granddaughter
Mary Driver. Exs., son-in-law Edward Driver, friend
Thomas Whitfield, Jr.
   D. July 31, 1735   R. May 24, 1736
   Wit. Henry Applewhaite, William Frizzell
                                          Page 111

Kinchen, Mathew: Leg.- mother Elizabeth; brother
William; my wife Elizabeth; to unborn child, with rever-
sion of bequest to William, the son of Etheldred Taylor
and to William Jones, the son of Elizabeth Exum; to
William Jarrell, if he performs an agreement, which I
had with Gilbert Mackinnie; to William, the son of my
brother William Kinchen; my uncle William Joyner; friend
John Dunkley; sister Elizabeth; sister Martha; sister
Patience; to James Godwin's children, James, Martha and
Mathew Godwin. Exs., brothers-in-law, Thomas Jarrell
and Etheldred Taylor
   D. March 4, 1735/36   R. May 24, 1736
   Wit. John Dunkley, Thomas Joyner, Edward Buxton
                                          Page 113

Warren, Thomas: Leg.- wife Sarah; son Thomas; daugh-
ter Mary; daughter Jane; daughter Martha; daughter
Patience. Wife, Extx.
   D. September 9, 1735   R. May 24, 1736
   Wit. John Dunkley, John Warren   Page 115

Duck, John: Leg.- daughter West; wife Priscilla
Wife, Extx.
   D. March 20, 1735   R. May 24, 1736
   Wit. William Noyall, John Long, John Parmentoe
                                          Page 116

Ferrell, Silvester: Leg.- wife and children
   D. April 10, 1736   R. May 24, 1736
   Wit. Robert Murry, Patrick Sweney   Page 117

Norsworthy, Tristram. Appraised by Samuel Whitfield,
Giles Driver, Joseph Wheston, Robert King
   Ordered June 11, 1736   R. June 28, 1736
                                          Page 117

Carter, George. Inventory presented by Sarah Carter
   R. June 29, 1736   Page 118

80

Ingram, Roger. Settlement of estate. To widow's part,
to John Ingram; to Roger Ingram; to Richard Ingram, to
William Ingram, to Sarah Ingram, to Elizabeth Ingram.
Examined by Samuel Davis, Thomas Murry
R. June 28, 1736   Page 119

Norwood, Elizabeth. An error in appraising negroes
which were her dower in my father's estate. Signed,
Thomas Clarke, Ex. of William Norwood, who was the Adm.
of Elizabeth Norwood   R. June 29, 1736 Page 121

Jones, Mathew. Account estate, examined by Hardy
Council and James Baker   R. June 29, 1736
                                                   Page 121

Carter, Thomas: Of the Lower Parish. Leg.- sons
James and Benjamin, a tract on the south side of the
Nottoway River, adjoining George Gurley and George Carter
and William Edwards; son Samuel; son William; wife Eliza-
beth; daughter Elizabeth; daughter Ann. Wife, Extx.
D. November 10, 1732   R. July 26, 1736
Wit. George Gurley, Augustine Hixson   Page 122

Brown, Samuel. Appraised by John Chesnutt, John
Gibbs, George Whitley   R. July 26, 1736
                                                   Page 123

Applewhite, John. Appraised by Joseph Weston,
Humphrey Marshall, Thomas Applewhite, Edmond Godwin
Ordered March 24, 1735   R. July 26, 1736
                                                   Page 124

Davis, Robert: Leg.- son Thomas, land on the Blackwater; son Arthur Davis; between my wife and all my
children. Exs., wife and son Thomas Davis
D. June 22, 1736   R. July 26, 1736
Wit. John Davis, William Murry, John Wills
                                                   Page 125

Kinchen, Mathew, Gent. Appraised by Francis Williamson,
Thomas Joyner, John Dunkley
R. August 23, 1736   Page 126

Williams, Peter and Mary Williams. Division of their

estates, to the four eldest children, to the youngest
son George Williams, by Samuel Davis and Thomas Woodley
R. August 23, 1736   Page 131

Vasser, John, Jr. Appraised by Arthur Whitehead,
John Pope, Jr., Thomas Davis. Signed Sarah Vasser
Ordered August 13, 1736   R. August 23, 1736
                                                     Page 132

Ducke, John. Appraised by John Darden, John Eley,
William Fowler. Ordered May 24, 1736
R. August 23, 1736   Page 132

Cannon, Robert. Appraised by Joseph Ward, John
Davis, Thomas Shurly. Ordered July 29, 1736
R. August 23, 1736   Page 134

Whitney, Joshua. Appraised by Richard West, Thomas
Summerell, Timothy Tynes   R. August 23, 1736
                                                     Page 134

Moreland, Catherine. Appraised by Richard Hardy,
John Gray, Benjamin Carrell   R. August 23, 1736
                                                     Page 135

Little, Robert: Of the Upper Parish. Leg.- sons
John and Jacob, land which is to be divided between them
by John Person and John Inman; to my two sons and three
daughters now living with me; to Lewis Dupra, the son of
John Dupra; to Sarah Oaks, the daughter of Joseph Oaks;
daughter Elizabeth Oaks; daughter Lucy Dupra. Exs., son
John and daughter Sarah Little. John Person, overseer.
D. March 29, 1736   R. August 23, 1736
Wit. John Inman, Lewis Dupra, Charles Travers
                                                     Page 136

Vasser, John: Leg.- son after his mother's death; to
daughter Sarah; daughter Elizabeth; granddaughter Sarah
Vasser; wife Margaret. My estate to be divided into
three parts, one part to my wife; one to Simon Everett,
and the third to my son Nathan Vasser. Exs., wife
Margaret and Simon Everett
D.   R. August 23, 1736
Wit. John Drake, Thomas Williams, John Marshall
                                                     Page 137

Newsom, William. Appraised by Arthur Whitehead, John
Pope, Jr., Thomas Grangshaw (?). Ordered January 26, 1735
R. September 28, 1736   Page 137

Evans, David. Appraised by Francis Williamson, Thomas
Moore, John Dunkley. Signed, Elizabeth Evans
Ordered July 8, 1736   R. September 13, 1736
                                                        Page 138

Turner, James: Leg.- Martha Pugh; daughter Kizzia;
wife Mary. Exs., Joseph West and Thomas Crinshaw
D. November 7, 1735   R. September 28, 1736
Wit. Samuel Willis, Joseph West   Page 139

Seaboth, William: Leg.- son William; son John; son
Thomas; son Edward; son David; son Samuel; daughter Jane;
daughter Sarah; wife Sarah. Exs., wife and son William
D. November 9, 1735   R. September 28, 1736
Wit. Robert Ricks, William Wood, Richard Bryant,
        John Wood   Page 140

Foster, John: Leg.- eldest son Christopher; son John,
land adjoining Charles Barham and Thomas Phillips; son
Arthur; wife Mary; daughter Elizabeth; daughter Faith;
daughter Mary; daughter Lucy; daughter Sarah. Exs.,
wife and my brother Christopher Foster
D. February 23, 1735   R. September 28, 1736
Wit. Richard Griffith, Christopher Foster,
        Faith Emry, Fortune Foster   Page 141

Fulgham, Nicholas: Leg.- son Nicholas; son Joseph;
son Joshua; daughter Elizabeth; daughter Susanna; daughter Martha. Exs., wife Isabella and son Nicholas Fulgham
D. July 7, 1736   R. September 28, 1736
Wit. Charles Fulgham, Mary Bevan, Elizabeth Smith
                                                        Page 142

Vasser, John. Appraised by John Pope, Samuel Browne,
Richard Price   R. October 25, 1736
                                                        Page 143

Warren, Thomas. Inventory presented by Sarah Warren
                        R. October 25, 1736
                                                        Page 145

Norwood, James. Inventory presented by Thomas Smith
                        R. October 25, 1736
                                                        Page 145

Davis, Robert. Appraised by Samuel Carrell, Thomas
Shelley, James Briggs. Ordered July 26, 1736
                                            Page 146

Davis, John. Appraised by John Pope, Richard Vick.
Signed, Elizabeth Davis. Ordered October 7, 1736
                    R. October 25, 1736   Page 147

Jolley, James. Account of estate, paid John, the
son of the said James Jolly, decd. Examined by John
Monro and Jacob Darden.   R. November 22, 1736
                                            Page 148

Worrell, William: Leg.- son William; son John; to my
honored father; wife Ann. Ex., friend John Dew, Jr.
  D. September 21, 1736   R. November 22, 1736
Wit. H. Edwards, Augustine Nickson .   Page 148

Cook, Thomas, Sr.: Leg.- son Thomas; son Jones;
daughter Sarah; daughter Susannah; son Benjamin; son
John; daughter Rebecca; son Arthur. Exs., son Thomas
and Jones Cook
  D. January 21, 1735/36   R. November 22, 1736
Wit. John Brantley, Valentine White   Page 149

Moreland, Catherine. Account of estate, returned
by Thomas Moreland   R. November 22, 1736
                                            Page 150

Wright, John: Leg.- son James; son John; daughter
Sarah Browne. Exs., wife Martha and son John Wright
  D. August 15, 1736   R. November 22, 1736
Wit. William Noyall, John Long, Priscilla Hall
                                            Page 150

Fly, Jeremiah: Leg.- son-in-law William Bulls; son
John; daughter Rachel; daughter Charity; wife Mary;
daughter Mary. Wife, Extx.
  D. November 19, 1733   R. December 27, 1736
Wit. Arthur Smith, Rachel Smith   Page 151

Foster, John. Appraised by Thomas Hoult, Charles
Barham, Thomas Phillips.   R. December 27, 1736
                                            Page 152

84

Lugg, Peter. Appraised by Robert King, William Smith, Aaron Gray. Ordered September 27, 1736
R. December 27, 1736   Page 153

Vick, Robert. Appraised by Arthur Whitehead, Robert Newsom, Henry Thomas   R. February 28, 1736
                                              Page 154

Carter, Thomas. Appraised by Richard Blow, Jr., Henry Thomas, Robert Newsom. Ordered January 15, 1736
R. February 28, 1736   Page 155

Gay, Henry: Leg.- son Henry; son John; son Thomas; son William; son Joshua; daughter Sarah Babb. Ex., son Thomas Gay
D. February 3, 1735/36   R. April 25, 1737
Wit. James Denson, Joseph Denson   Page 156

Brantley, Edward: Of Nottoway Parish. Leg.- wife Elizabeth; son James; son Lewis; son Joseph; son John. Exs., sons Lewis and James Brantley
D. January 26, 1736   R. April 25, 1737
Wit. Joseph Claud, James Bass, William Spence, Charles Bass   Page 157

Moxson, Robert. Account of estate returned by Robert Pitt, the Adm.   R. April 26, 1737
                                              Page 158

Boykin, Edward. Appraised by James Turner, John Inman, John Jones. Ordered March 21, 1736/37
R. April 26, 1737   Page 159

Copeland, John. Appraised by Thomas Murry, John Hodges, William Glover, Mel'k. Deshey
Ordered November 22, 1736   R. April 25, 1737
                                              Page 159

Wrenn, Elizabeth. Appraised by James Day, John Hodges, William Glover   R. May 23, 1737
                                              Page 160

Crocker, William: Leg.- son Anthony; son Peter; son Arthur; son William; daughter Elizabeth. Wife, Katherine, Extx.

D.   December 4, 1735   R.   May 23, 1737
Wit. John Wombwell, Joseph Wombwell,
      Joseph Grotten (?)   Page 160

Ryall, Thomas. Account estate, among items, paid to
Thomas Ryall, the son of Thomas Ryall, decd. Examined
by James Barlow and Hardy Council. R. May 23, 1737
                                              Page 162

Stevenson, John: Leg.- son John; son Peter; son
William, the land I bought of Edward Boykin; son
Solomon; son George; daughter Mary; daughter Eliza-
beth. Wife Katherine, Extx.
D. February 24, 1728/29   R. May 23, 1737
Wit. Francis Exum, Joseph Ward   Page 162

Boykin, William. Settlement of estate made by John
Dunkley, Thomas Gale   R. May 23, 1737
                                              Page 163

Turner, John. Appraised by Hugh Giles, Charles
Fulgham, Joseph Wright. Ordered November 22, 1736
R. May 23, 1737   Page 164

Gay, Henry. Appraised by Robert Eley, Jr., Eley
Eley, Jonathan Weaver   R. May 23, 1737
                                              Page 165

Stevenson, William. Appraised by Richard Blunt, John
Williams, William Clark. Signed Giles Kelly
R. May 23, 1737   Page 166

Barnes, John: Leg.- son John, land adjoining Nicholas
Williams and Richard Washington; son Thomas; daughter
Elizabeth Flowers; grandson Henry Flowers; son William;
daughter Juda Davis; daughter Best; son Jacob, land ad-
joining on Arthur Washington and Edward Flowers; son
Joshua; daughter Sarah Sumerell land adjoining Robert
Lawrence; to Thomas Crafford; to loving wife. Exs.,
sons Jacob and Joshua Barnes
D. March 27, 1736   R. May 23, 1737
Wit. William Williams, Thomas Allen, Benjamin Flowers
                                              Page 167

Baldwin, William. Account of estate, examined by

Benn Willett and John Chapman   R.   June 27, 1737

Page 169

Bulls, Martha.   Account of estate returned by John
Chesnutt.   R.   June 27, 1737   Page 170

Williamson, Francis: Nuncupative will, proven by
Francis Williamson, Arthur Williamson and Thomas
Williamson. Leg.- son Francis; son James; son Benjamin;
son Joseph; daughter Martha; daughter Sarah; daughter
Mourning; son Hardy; to my wife
    D. March 14, 1736   R.   June 27, 1737
                                                      Page 170

Roberson, Jonathan: Leg.- wife Elizabeth, reversion
at her death, to her daughter Mary Whitfield; to my cousin James Roberson, if he serves out his indenture
    D. March 22, 1736/37   R.   June 27, 1737
    Wit. William Murfee, James Davis   Page 170

Jordan, Elizabeth.   Account of estate, returned by
Mathew Jordan.
    D. December 1, 1733   R.   July 25, 1737
                                                      Page 171

Worrell, William.   Appraised by John Pope, Arthur
Whitehead, Richard Vick   R.   July 25, 1737
                                                      Page 172

Wainwright, William.   Appraised by Timothy Tynes,
Thomas Brock, Thomas Browne. Ordered June 27, 1737
    R. July 25, 1737   Page 172

Bayton, Richard, Jr.   Appraised by John Williams,
William Pope, John Johnston   R.   July 25, 1737
                                                      Page 173

Braddy, Elias; Leg.- daughter Elizabeth, my land in
North Carolina; daughter Mary; son Elias; wife Margaret.
Exs., son Elias and son-in-law Henry Crafford
    D. March 2, 1735   R.   July 25, 1737
    Wit. John Joyner, James Joyner   Page 173

Summerell, Thomas.   Appraised by Joseph Hill, Ambrose
Hadley, W. Bidgood   R.   July 25, 1737   Page 175

Brantley, Edward. Appraised by Simon Turner, Henry
Harris, Thomas Barrow. Signed, Lewis and James
Brantley.   R. July 25, 1737   Page 176

Bragg, Mary. Account estate, returned by Thomas
Whitfield, Jr. and Edward Driver.   R. August 22, 1737
                                                      Page 177

Vasser, John. Additional appraisal by John Pope and
Richard Price   R. September 26, 1737
                                                      Page 178

Williamson, Francis, Jr. Appraised by John Dunkley,
James Atkinson, John Holleman. Ordered September 21,
1737   R. September 26, 1737   Page 178

Applewhaite, John. Appraised by Joseph Hill, Ambrose
Hadley, Edward Crocker. Ordered May 6, 1737
R. September 26, 1737   Page 179

Beach, William: Leg.- Edward Guleg; Ann Guleg; William
Guleg, land in the hands of Henry Adams; to Lucy Guleg.
Exs., Harmon Read, Henry Adams
D. September 7, 1737   R. October 24, 1737
R. Francis Stainback, William Lee, Edward Guleg
                                                      Page 181

Ingraham, Jeremiah: Leg.- my honourable father; my
sister Wardwell, all my wife Elizabeth's clothes; to my
brother John's son Jeremiah; brother Edward; brother
John; brother Joshua and brother Isaac; Captain Samuel
Little in New England, my trustee for my friends, and
he is to send whomever he thinks fitting with a power
of attorney to receive my estate, by the first oppor-
tunity after my executors have made up an account here
in Virginia
D. September 10, 1737   R. October 24, 1737
Wit. William Hurdle, Roger Delk, John Welch,
      Peter Hardin   Page 181

Parnal, Joseph: Of the Lower Parish. Leg.- eldest
son Thomas; son William; daughter Elizabeth; son Joseph;
my youngest son John; wife Elizabeth. Ex., son Thomas
Parnal
D. March 10, 1736   R. November 28, 1737
Wit. Arthur Moore, William Vasser, Jacob Moore
                                                      Page 182

Chapman, John: Of the Lower Parish. Leg.- daughter
Patience Wiles; son John my "Bath Seal"; son Charles;
daughter Mary; son Joseph; sons William and Thomas to
live with their mother until they are 14; wife Mary;
daughter Elizabeth. Exs., wife Mary and son Charles
Chapman
   D. September 10, 1736   R. November 28, 1737
   Wit. Charles Fulgham, Jr., Mary Bevan   Page 183

Westray, Robert. Appraised by John Bowin, John
Lawrence, Virgus Smith. Signed Mary Westray
   R. November 28, 1737   Page 185

Braddy, Elias. Appraised by John Joyner, James
Turner, Chaplin Williams. Ordered August 22, 1737
   R. November 28, 1737   Page 185

Chapman, John. Appraised by Hugh Giles, John
Applewhaite, Thomas Whitfield   R. November 28, 1737
                                    Page 186

Dugan, Bryan. Estate settled by Hugh Giles and
Charles Fulgham.   R. November 28, 1737
                                    Page 187

Ingraham, Jeremiah. Appraised by James Carrell, John
Gray, Thomas Moreland   R. November 28, 1737
                                    Page 187

Mangum, John. Appraised by John Davis, Edward
Brantley, Joseph Ward. Signed Frances Mangum
   Ordered September 26, 1737   R. November 28, 1737
                                    Page 189

Caleclough, Thomas. Appraised by Robert Driver,
Thomas Uzzell, John Smelly. Ordered November 28, 1737
   R. January 23, 1737   Page 190

Sharro, Elizabeth: Of the Lower Parish. Leg.- son
John; daughter Elizabeth Thomas; daughter Eleanor Thomas;
grandson William Screws. Ex., Joseph Parnal
   D. January 8, 1736   R. January 23, 1737
   Wit. Luke Wiggs, Joseph Parnal   Page 192

Williams, Richard: Leg.- son John, land on which
Arthur Edwards now lives; son Solomon, land on which
John Row did live; son Mathew; daughter Mary; wife Sarah;
son Elisha my land in Nansemond County, adjoining William
West; son George land in Nansemond; son Joshua land in
Nansemond; son Daniel land in Nansemond; friend William
Wiggins; to my young childre. Ex., son Daniel Williams.
  D. November 8, 1737   R. February 27, 1737
  Wit. John Johnston, James Garner, Elisha Williams
                                            Page 193

Williams, John: Leg.- wife Sarah; son Richard, when
he is 18; daughter Elizabeth. Ex., brother Elisha
  D. November 21, 1737   R. February 27, 1737
  Wit. John Johnston, Nathan Godwin, George Williams
                                            Page 195

Chapman, Joseph. Settlement of estate by Joseph
Hall and William Ponsonby.   R. February 27, 1737
                                            Page 196

Marriner, John. Appraised by John Goodrich, William
Harrison, John Hodges, Benjamin Hodges
February 27, 1737   Page 196

Green, Mary: Of the Parish of Newport. Leg.- children of my daughter Mary Bevan; son Bartholomew; children of my son Thomas; children of my daughter Montgomery;
daughter Martha; son George; daughter Prudence; daughter
Rachel. Daughter Prudence Green, Extx.
  D. November 19, 1737   R. February 27, 1737
  Wit. John Long, Bartholomew Lightfoot   Page 197

Cook, Thomas. Appraised by Simon Turner, Henry
Harris, Jacob Harris   R. February 27, 1737
                                            Page 198

Applewhaite, Thomas. Settlement of estate and an
account current of the estate of Henry Applewhaite was
presented by Joseph Weston and Samuel Whitfield
  R. February 27, 1737   Page 200

Gray, John: Leg.- son William; son Richard; son John;
son Mathew; son Henry; daughter Margaret; daughter
Patience; wife Elizabeth. Wife, Extx.
  D. December 13, 1737   R. March 27, 1738
  Wit. Richard Hardy, Elias Wills   Page 200

Brown, Joseph. Account estate examined by Joseph
Godwin and John Monro   R. April 24, 1738
Page 201

Caleclough, Thomas. Account estate examined by John
Monro and Jacob Darden   R. April 24, 1738
Page 202

Stephens, William. Additional appraisal by William
Clark, Richard Blunt, John Williams
R. April 24, 1738   Page 202

Sharro, Elizabeth. Inventory returned by Richard
Thomas   R. April 24, 1738   Page 203

Lowry, Joanna: Of the Lower Parish. Widow. Leg.-
son James Lowry; son Mathew Lowry; rest of my estate to
be divided among Francis, Thomas, George and Joseph Floid.
Ex., my son George Floid
D. March 30, 1736   R. May 22, 1738
Wit. Robert Tynes, Elizabeth Driver   Page 203

Williams, John. Appraised by Anthony Lewis, William
Pope, James Edwards   R. May 22, 1738
Page 204

Smith, Thomas. Appraised by James Turner, Simon
Turner, Henry Harris. Signed Samuel Smith
R. May 22, 1738   Page 205

Gray, John. Appraised by James Carrell, Thomas Barlow,
Samuel Carrell. Signed Elizabeth Gray
R. May 22, 1738   Page 206

Lee, Peter. Appraised by Jacob Harris, Valentine
White, Robert Lundy. Signed William Lee
R. June 26, 1738   Page 208

Lowry, Joanna. Appraised by Timothy Tynes, William
Best, Edward Davis   R. June 26, 1738
Page 208

Pearce, Philip. Account estate, signed by Sarah
Pearce and examined by Richard Hardy and Etheldred Taylor
R. July 24, 1738   Page 209

Turner, John. Account estate, among items, paid
John Dugan, the orphan of Bryan Dugan. Examined by Hugh
Giles, Joseph Godwin, William Wilkinson
R. July 24, 1738   Page 209

Meacum, Lewis. Appraised by Thomas Murry, William
Harrison, Benjamin Hodges   R. July 24, 1738
                                                    Page 210

Hollyman, Elizabeth: Leg.- grandson Arthur Hollyman;
grandson Joseph Hollyman; to Sarah Watson; to Susannah
Hollyman; to Thomas Hollyman, Jr., the son of William
Hollyman; to Mary Proctor. Ex., kinsman William Hollyman
D. March 17, 1736/37   R. August 28, 1738
Wit. Thomas Atkinson, John Hollyman   Page 211

Nixon, Augustine. Appraised by Thomas Taylor, Robert
Pitman, Arthur Taylor. Ordered January 23, 1737. Account
of his estate, examined by Thomas Jarrell, Jr. and Richard
Blow, Jr.   R. September 25, 1738   Page 212

Copeland, John. Estate account, paid Thomas Copeland
his part of his father's. Examined by Samuel Davis and
James Baker.   R. October 24, 1738   Page 213

Moreland, Thomas. Appraised by James Carrell,
Samuel Carrell, Thomas Barlow. Signed John Moreland
Ordered March 29, 1738   R. October 23, 1738
                                                    Page 214

Lewis, Zebulon: Leg.- son Benjamin; son Nathan; son
Zebulon; daughter Patience; loving wife.
D. August 6, 1738   R. October 23, 1738
Wit. Christopher Kilbee, John Harris, Benjamin Cooper
                                                    Page 215

Ingraham, Jeremiah. Estate settled by Lawrence Baker
and Nicholas Bourden   R. October 23, 1738
                                                    Page 216

Teasly, John. Appraised by William Page, Ralph
Vickers, Richard Pierce. Signed Richard Teasly
   Ordered June 26, 1738   R. November 27, 1738
                                             Page 217

Coggan, Robert: Of the Lower Parish. Leg.- son
John; son Robert; daughter Elizabeth Stevens; daughter
Ann Stevens; daughter Sarah
Exs., wife Sarah and son John Coggan
   D. January 30, 1737   R. November 27, 1738
   Wit. William Denson, Thomas Gale, John Badgett
                                             Page 218

Barnes, Jacob. Appraised by Robert King, Humphrey
Marshall, William Smith. Signed Francis Floyd
   R. November 27, 1738   . Page 219

Fulgham, Nicholas. Appraised by Hugh Giles, Thomas
Whitfield, Joseph Norsworthy. R. February 26, 1738
                                             Page 219

Bevan, Thomas. Appraised by Hugh Giles, Charles
Fulgham, Thomas Whitfield. Ordered November 24, 1738
   R. February 26, 1738   Page 220

Norsworthy, Christian. Account current, paid John
Norsworthy, guardian of Martha Norsworthy, the things
given her in the will of her father, George Norsworthy;
paid John Monro, the things given his wife in her
father's will. Signed William Scott.
   R. February 26, 1738/39   Page 221

Norsworthy, Tristram. Account estate, examined by
Joseph Godwin, Joseph Weston, Samuel Whitfield
   R. March 26, 1739   Page 222

Braddy, William. Appraised by William Clark, Thomas
Coffer, Joseph Atkinson. Signed Olive Braddy
   Ordered January 22, 1738   R. March 26, 1739
                                             Page 223

Hollyman, Elizabeth. Appraised by Samuel Crafts,
Arthur Crocker, Josiah John Holliman
   R. March 26, 1739   Page 224

Coggan, Robert. Appraised by John Sellaway, William
Bullock, Richard Sellaway.   R.   March 26, 1739
Page 225

Lawrence, John: Of the Parish of Newport. Leg.- son
John, land on the Blackwater on which William Freeman
lives; son William; daughter Margaret; daughter Priscilla;
son-in-law Robert Carr to be paid his wife's part of my
estate; daughter Sarah Moore; daughter Elizabeth.
Exs., wife and son William Lawrence
    D. January 27, 1738   R. April 23, 1739
    Wit. Robert Lawrence, Charles Council, Thomas Brewer
Page 226

Exum, Robert. Appraised by John Dunkley, Francis
Williamson, Joseph Exum, Thomas Joyner
Ordered February 26, 1738   R. April 23, 1739
Page 227

Lewis, Zebulon. Appraised by John Brassell, John
Fort, Christopher Foster. Signed Jane Lewis
    R. April 23, 1739   Page 229

Brantley, Edward. Account estate, examined by James
Ridley and Nathaniel Ridley. Signed James and Lewis
Brantley   R. May 28, 1739   Page 230

Dickinson, Christopher. Account estate, paid John
Bridger in right of his wife, examined by William
Wilkinson, Hugh Giles, Charles Fulgham
    R. June 25, 1739   Page 231

Moore, Tristram. Nuncupative will. May 11, 1739
Deposition of Mr. James Ransom, aged about 35:- that he
had intended disinheriting his son Thomas, but if he lived he would buy land on this side of the river for his
son; and that he designed his land in Gloucester County,
for his son James.
Deposition of Joyce Carrell, aged about 30 years:- heard
him say that his land in Gloucester was to go to his son
James, whom he desired his father to bring up.
Deposition of Roger Stanley, aged about 45 years:- that
he heard him say, that his son Thomas was to have twenty
pounds to buy land etc.   R. July 23, 1739
Page 232

Revell, Randall: Leg.- son Joseph John; son Mathew,
130 acres that I bought of William Thomas; son Holladay.
Ex., son Joseph John Revell
    D. December 30, 1733   R. July 23, 1739
    Wit. John Dunkley, Thomas Warren, John Exum
Page 232

Eley, Robert, Sr. Leg.- son Robert, land on Long
Branch, adjoining John Roberts, Henry Sanders and Mr. John
Lear; son James; son Edward; son John; son Michael; daugh-
ter Christian; daughter Mourning; son William; to Martha,
the daughter of my son James; son Eley; daughter Martha
Williams; daughter Rebecca Williams
Exs., sons, Robert and Michael Eley
    D. April 5, 1738   R. July 23, 1739
    Wit. Joseph White, William Denson, George Armstrong
Page 233

Hunter, James: Of the Parish of Newport. Leg.- granddaughter Mary Allen; granddaughter Elizabeth Allen; daughter Sarah; daughter Mary Allen; son Joshua
Ex., son Joshua Hunter
    D. August 23, 1735   R. July 23, 1739
    Wit. John Monro, ------ Snowden   Page 235

Lewis, Anthony: Leg.- sons Thomas and Anthony my
land on the Blackwater; wife Elizabeth
Exs., my wife and two sons
    D. September 30, 1717   R. July 23, 1739
    Wit. Elias Ballard, William Butler, Mary Butler,
        John Butler   Page 236

Mathews, John. Appraised by Thomas Pursell, Newitt
Drew, William B------   Signed by Martha Mathews
    R. August 27, 1739   Page 237

Smith, Thomas. Account estate, presented by Elizabeth
Parnall. Examined by Nathaniel Ridley and Howell Edmunds
    R. August 27, 1739   Page 237

Lewis, Anthony. Appraised by Samuel Browne, Richard
Price, Lewis Bryan.   R. September 24, 1739
Page 240

Atkinson, James: Leg.- son Thomas; son Timothy; daughter Mary; daughter Drusilla; daughter Sarah Ingram; son

James; wife. Exs., sons Timothy and Thomas Atkinson
   D. September 20, 1737   R. September 24, 1739
  Wit. William Ingram, Elizabeth Evans, Thomas Atkinson
Page 241

Goold, Mary: Of Nottoway Parish. Leg.- daughter
Elizabeth; daughter Mary; son Thomas
Ex., son Thomas Goold
   D. February 22, 1738/39   R. September 24, 1739
  Wit. William Smith, George Smith   Page 242

Benson, William: Leg.- son Samuel; son Bryant; son
Benjamin; daughter Bersheba; daughter Brambly; friend
John Phillips. Ex., son Bryant Benson
   D. August 9, 1739   R. September 24, 1739
  Wit. John Phillips, J. Gray   Page 243

Jordan, James. Account estate, examined by James
Baker, Nicholas Bourden   R. November 26, 1739
Page 244

Stevenson, William. Account estate, examined by
William Hodsden, James Ridley. Signed Giles Kelly
   R. November 26, 1739   Page 248

Moore, Tristram. Appraised by Richard Hardy, James
Carrell, Thomas Barlow   R. November 26, 1739
Page 249

Lawrence, John. Inventory, presented by Margaret
and William Lawrence.   R. January 28, 1739
Page 250

Davis, Samuel: Leg.- wife Amy; son John; son Samuel,
land at Meherrin; daughter Mary; daughter Sarah; daughter Amy; daughter Marcella. Wife, Extx. Brother John
Davis and brother-in-law Nicholas Bourden to collect
all debts
   D. November 16, 1738   R. January 28, 1739
  Wit. John Davis, John Gemmill, N. Bourden,
      Thomas Murry   Page 250

Bradshaw, William: Of Newport Parish. Leg.- brother
Richard Bradshaw; daughter Emey; daughter Mary; my
cousin Richard Bradshaw. Ex., brother Richard Bradshaw

D. October 25, 1739   R. January 28, 1739
Wit. John Britten, Lewis Bryan, Mary Murelle

Page 252

Weston, Benjamin: Leg.- wife Isabella, the estate
which belonged to her, when I Married her; my own estate
to be equally divided between my wife and my children,
Joseph, Mary and Samuel Weston. Wife, Extx.
D. September 27, 1739   R. January 28, 1739
Wit. Charles Fulgham, Joseph Weston

Page 253

Summerell, Thomas: Leg.- son Gwin; daughter Sarah
Wilson; son John; granddaughter Mary Wainwright; grand-
daughter Sarah Wainwright; granddaughter Martha Wilson;
my daughter Mary Wainwright's children; granddaughter
Jane Summerell. Ex., son John Summerell
D.   R. February 25, 1739
Wit. William Brock, William Wainwright

Page 254

Joyner, Theophilus: Leg.- son Joseph; son Theophilus;
son John; son Henry; son Lazarus; daughter Sarah Dawson;
daughter Mary Garland; daughter Mary; daughter Prudence;
wife Henrietta. Exs., wife and son John Joyner
D. January 15, 1724/25   R. February 25, 1739
Wit. Robert Johnson, James Johnson   Page 255

Whitfield, Mary: Leg.- to Benjamin, the son of
Benjamin Beel (Beal); to Richard Beel, the son of Richard
Beel; to William, the son of my cousin William Bradsha;
to Richard Casey, Jr.; to Martha Casey, the daughter of
Richard Casey. Extx., Martha Casey
D. November 21, 1737   R. February 25, 1739
Wit. William Noyall, Martha Noyall   Page 256

Applewhaite, Martha: Of Newport Parish. Leg.- son
Thomas, and to his son John; daughter Holland Copeland;
daughter Martha Weston; granddaughter Mary Benn; grand-
daughter Holland Applewhaite; grandson Thomas Copeland;
grandson James Benn; grandson Henry Applewhaite; daughter
Ann Parker. Ex., son-in-law William Parker
D. July 30, 1739   R. February 25, 1739
Wit. Thomas Copeland   Page 257

Wright, Martha: Leg.- daughter Sarah Browne; son
James; daughter-in-law Mary Wright. Ex., son John Wright
D. January 4, 1738/39   R. February 25, 1739
Wit. William Noyall, Elizabeth West   Page 258

Marshall, Mary: Leg.- son Robert; son John; daugh-
ter Elizabeth Robertson; son Joseph; daughter Mary
Penny; son James; grandson Joseph, son of Humphrey
Marshall, land called "Pines", which is mentioned in
my husband's will. Ex., son Humphrey Marshall
   D. September 30, 1732   R. February 25, 1739
   Wit. Robert Driver, John Penny, Anthony Covington
       Holladay   Page 259

Driver, Edward: Leg.- son Charles; daughter Mary;
daughter Sarah. Exs., friends Robert Driver and
Thomas Whitfield
   D. November 25, 1739   R. February 25, 1739
   Wit. Joseph Bridger, Joseph Wright   Page 260

Richards, William. Account, examined by John
Monro and Joseph Weston   R. February 20, 1739
                                 Page 261

Montgomery, Benjamin. Account estate, among items,
paid for the orphans; examined by Hugh Giles and Thomas
Applewhaite.   R. February 1739   Page 262

Bradshaw, William. Appraised by John Bowin, John
Lawrence, William ffouller (Fowler)
R. February 25, 1739   Page 263

Weston, Benjamin. Appraised by Hugh Giles, Jacob
Dickinson, Joseph Norsworthy   R. February 25, 1739
                                 Page 263

Day, James: Leg.- daughter Mary; daughter Martha;
to unborn child; loving wife
Exs., wife and William Hodsden
   D. October 6, 1739   R. March 24, 1739
   Wit. Thomas Day, Thomas Smith, Elizabeth Jones
                                 Page 264

Macy, Thomas: Leg.- wife Jane, Ester Williams and
Ambrus Williams, the plantation on which I live, at the
death of my wife the said plantation to return to Richard
Kirby and Macy Mary his wife and the plantation on which
they now live to return to Ester Williams and Ambrus
Williams. Exs., Richard Kirby and Ambrus Williams

D. March 12, 1739   R. March 24, 1739
Wit. Ambrus Williams, Moddy Kirby   Page 265

Harris, Robert: Leg.- daughter Ann; son Charles; son
Michael; son Joseph; son James; son Mathew
Ex., son Michael Harris
D. March 22, 1739   R. April 28, 1740
Wit. John Dunkley, Josiah John Holleman
                                                  Page 266

Joyner, Thomas: Leg.- daughter Cherry Harris; son
Jonathan, the land on which William Thomas did live and
on which Arthur Smith now lives; son Mathew; daughter
Patience; daughter Elizabeth; son Thomas; daughter
Catherine Dunkley; granddaughter Catherine Joyner; wife
Patience. Exs., son Mathew and son-in-law John Dunkley
D. April 13, 1740   R. April 28, 1740
Wit. Thomas Williams, Virgus Smith   Page 267

Piland, James. Inventory, presented by Elizabeth
Piland.   R. April 28, 1740   Page 270

Revell, Randall. Appraised by Thomas Williams, John
Washington, William Bailey   R. April 28, 1740
                                                  Page 272

Browne, Samuel: Leg.- son John; grandson Josias, son
of Walter Browne; grandson Jesse Browne, all my books, in-
struments and Medicines; daughter Mary, the wife of John
Drake; grandson Jesse Drake, land on the Nottoway River;
daughter Sarah, wife of John Battel; grandson William
Battel; grandson Jesse Battel; grandson Samuel, son of
John Browne; granddaughter Sarah, the daughter of Walter
Browne; grandson Samuel, the son of Henry King and his
wife Martha; grandson Samuel Nicholas Drake; granddaughter
Penelope, the daughter of William Lawrence and his wife
Penelope; son Jesse Browne, land on Indian Branch in North
Carolina. Ex., son Jesse Browne
D. October 7, 1739   R. June 23, 1740
Wit. Hardy Council, John Gemmill, John Dunkley, John
      Eley   Page 274

Forbes, James. Appraised by Thomas Day, William
Harrison, Benjamin Hodges, George Wilson. Signed James
Baker. Ordered, February 25, 1739/40
R. July 28, 1740   Page 278

Brock, William. Appraised by Timothy Tynes, Thomas Browne, Peter Green. Ordered, June 23, 1740
R. July 28, 1740   Page 280

Harris, Robert. Appraised by Thomas Williamson, Arthur Williamson, Josiah John Holleman
R. July 28, 1740   Page 282

Hawkins, William. Account estate, examined by William Wilkinson, Hugh Giles. R. July 28, 1740
                                                       Page 283

Piland, James. Account estate; among items, paid to James Wilson, for Esther Brantley; to funeral charges for his son. Signed, Elizabeth Briggs. Examined by James Baker, Lawrence Baker, N. Bourden
R. July 28, 1740   Page 284

Kae, Robert Fenn: Leg.- brother Thomas; brother William Kae; to Thomas Casse (Casey); rest of estate to be equally divided between William Brantley, Thomas Rosser and Joseph Floyd. Ex., Thomas Casse
D. February 10, 1739/40   R. July 28, 1740
Wit. Nicholas Casey, William Richards   Page 285

Richards, Thomas: Leg.- brother Simon Ogburn; brother John Ogburn; sister Elizabeth Ogburn; sister Mary Ogburn; sister Prudence Richards; sister Ann Richards; rest of estate to Nicholas Casey. Ex., Nicholas Casey
D. March 9, 1740   R. July 28, 1740
Wit. Robert Fenn Kae, Thomas Casey   Page 286

Wombwell, Thomas: Of Blackwater, Planter. Leg.- son John, the plantation of my father, Thomas Wombwell's; son Joseph; wife Sarah; son Thomas, the land which lies below that of my brother John Wombwell's; daughter Sarah Goodrich; daughter Mary Crocker. Wife, Extx.
D. December 7, 1731   R. April 25, 1740
Wit. Francis Ward, William Allen   Page 287

Carrell, Samuel: Leg.- son Thomas; wife Joice; son John. Wife, Extx.
D. September 28, 1737   R. August 25, 1740
Wit. Richard Hardy, James Piland   Page 288

Applewhaite, Henry. Appraised by William Pope, Edward
Cobb, James Edwards, John Johnson
Signed, Mary Applewhaite.   Ordered March 1739
R. August 25, 1740   Page 290

Best, William. Appraised by John Rodway, Samuel
Whitfield, Thomas Gross. Signed Jane Best
D. August 19, 1740   R. August 25, 1740
                                                   Page 292

Harris, Edward: Leg.- son Edward, land on the Blackwater; son Lewis, land on the Three Creeks, which I
bought of John Dortch; son Joel; son Amos; son Hardy;
daughter Mary; daughter Ann; wife Ann. Timothy Thorpe
and Owen Mirick to divide the land between sons Joel and
Amos. Exs., wife and son Edward Harris
D. August 26, 1739   R. September 22, 1740
Wit. Nathaniel Ridley, Timothy Thorpe   Page 293

Newman, Thomas: Leg.- wife Mary; son John; my wife to
pay to her son Joseph out of her part of my estate; John
Newman to pay Joseph Bunkley, out of his part of my es-
tate. Ex., son John Newman
D. March 9, 1739   R. September 22, 1740
Wit. Richard Jordan, James Jones, Thomas Parr
                                                   Page 295

Pierce, Thomas: Leg.- daughter Mary, my house in
Hampton; daughter Martha; son Thomas; wife Judith
Exs., wife and friend Alexander Hamilton
D. March 19, 1739/40   R. October 27, 1740
Wit. John Summerell, Nicholas Curle
                                                   Page 296

Daughtry, Joseph: Leg.- loving mother; brother John
Daughtry's son Richard; to cousin William, the son of John
Daughtry; to John, the son of my brother John Daughtry;
sister Mary Holland; sister Elizabeth Haslep
Ex., brother John Daughtry
D. September 23, 1740   R. October 27, 1740
Wit. Robert Carr, James Robertson, William Daughtry
                                                   Page 298

Driver, Edward. Appraised by Joseph Wright, Joseph
Bridger, John Applewhaite. Signed, Robert Driver
R. October 27, 1740   Page 299

Miller, John. Appraised by John Hodges, William
Harrison, Benjamin Hodges. Signed, Nicholas Miller
  R. November 24, 1740   Page 300

Smith, Nicholas. Appraised by Joseph Wright, Robert
King, Anthony Fulgham. Signed, Joseph Smith
  Ordered February 25, 1739   R. November 24, 1740
                                    Page 301

Killebrew, William. Appraised by Nathaniel Ridley,
Howell Edmonds, James Ridley. Ordered April 15, 1740
  R. November 24, 1740   Page 302

Exum, Robert. Additional inventory, returned by
Patience Exum.   R. November 24, 1740
                                    Page 304

Matthews, Zeakell: Leg.- son Zeakell; son Edward;
to James Bennett; daughter Martha Hunnicutt; daughter
Priscilla Morgan; daughter Elizabeth; to my wife and
seven childre, viz: Elizabeth, Sarah, Mary, Unity,
Edmond, Moses and Enos. Wife, Extx.
  D. March 21, 1738/39   R. December 22, 1740
  Wit. Nathaniel Ridley   Page 305

Killebrew, William. Appraised by Thomas Barrow,
John Barrow, Martin Middleton. R. December 22, 1740
                                    Page 306

Harris, William. Appraised by John Bowin, John
Dawson, Nicholas Williams. Signed Rebecca Harris.
Ordered October 30, 1740   R. January 26, 1740
                                    Page 308

Pierce, Thomas. Appraised by Joseph Hill, John
Summerell, William Ponsonby. Signed, Judith Pierce
  R. February 23, 1740   Page 309

Jones, James. Appraised by George Parker, John
Newman, William Howell. Ordered January 26, 1740/41
  R. February 23, 1740   Page 313

Murry, Thomas: Leg.- daughter Mary, the wife of

Benjamin Davis; wife Sarah; daughter Sarah; daughter Easter; daughter Elizabeth, the wife of John Lee. Wife, Extx.
   D. August 27, 1740   R. February 23, 1740
   Wit. Thomas Stevens, Benjamin Brantley, Charles
       Fulgham   Page 315

Neaville, John: Leg.- son John; son Thomas; son Joseph; daughter Penellipen. Ex., John Marshall, Jr.
   D. January 1, 1740   R. February 23, 1740
   Wit. Thomas Gale, B. Beale, Thomas Bullock
                            Page 317

Ward, John: Leg.- daughter Mary; wife Sarah. Exs., wife Sarah and Hugh Norvell
   D. January 20, 1739   R. March 23, 1740
   Wit. Hugh Norvell, William Spence, William Broom
                         Page 318

Neaville, John. Appraised by Robert Driver, Joseph Meredith, John Chestnutt. Ex., John Marshall
   R. March 23, 1740   Page 320

Pierce, Jeremiah. Account estate, examined by John Davis, William Hodsden, N. Bourden. Signed Honour
Pierce   R. March 23, 1740
                            Page 323

Bridger, Col. William. Account estate, examined by William Hodsden, James Ridley   R. April 27, 1741
                            Page 324

Boykin, Edward. Account estate, examined by John Person, Howell Edmunds, Benjamin Blunt
   R. April 27, 1741   Page 327

Eley, Ely. Appraised by John Bowin, John Denson, Jr., Joshua Joyner. Ordered August 25, 1740
   R. April 27, 1741   Page 328

Applewhaite, Henry: Leg.- son John, the land I bought of Robert King; son Arthur; daughter Sarah, the land on Nottoway River, on which the widow Mary Applewhaite now lives; son Thomas; granddaughter Ann, the daughter of Thomas

Applewhaite; daughter Amy Davis; daughter Priscilla
Ridley; daughter Ann Godwin; to grandson Henry Apple-
whaite; wife Ann. Wife, Extx.
    D.   R.   April 27, 1741
    Wit. William Ponsonby, Elizabeth Daniel
Page 329

Darden, Jacob: Leg.- son Jacob; son Charles, all my
land in Nansemond, the said son to remain with Samuel
Lawrence until he is 19. Exs., brother-in-law Samuel
Lawrence and son Jacob Darden
    D. March 25, 1739   R. April 27, 1741
    Wit. George Lawrence, John Marshall   Page 332

Allen, Thomas: Leg.- eldest son Arthur; son Thomas;
daughter Ann; daughter Honour, her mother's clothes.
Exs., Rodger Allen and George Bell
    D. April 12, 1741   R. April 27, 1741
    Wit. George Whitley, Roger Woodward, Richard Braswell
Page 333

Smith, Thomas: Of Nottoway Parish. Leg.- son
William, the land I bought of Richard Lundy; son George;
land at the Three Creeks' Bridge; son Thomas; daughter
Rachel; son Joseph; daughter Mary Lundy. Exs., wife
and son Joseph Smith
    D. November 28, 1740   R. April 27, 1741
    Wit. James Ridley, James Sammons
Presented by Elizabeth and Joseph Smith   Page 334

Wilkinson, William: Leg.- son William, land in
Nansemond County; son Willis, land in Isle of Wight
County, on which Robert Smith and William Lain. Over-
seers, John Wills, John Summerell, Thomas Swann, John
Wilkinson. Exs., sons William and Willis Wilkinson
    D. March 6, 1740   R. May 25, 1741
    Wit. Jacob Spicer, Richard Smith, John Pitt
Page 335

Loyd, Thomas: Leg.- son Thomas; son Joseph; son
William; son Moses; daughter Charity; wife Charity; to
Mary Conner. Exs., wife and son Thomas Loyd
    D. February 23, 1740   R. May 25, 1741
    Wit. John Darden, Mary Conner, Susanna Gwinn
Page 337

Woodward, Oliver: Leg.- eldest son Roger; son Oliver;
son Samuel; son Richard; son John; son Joseph; daughter

Patience; daughter Mary. Ex., son Samuel Woodward
   D. February 23, 1740   R. May 25, 1741
   Wit. George Washington, Thomas Alling, Jacob Flowers
                                        Page 338

   Allen, Thomas. Appraised by George Washington,
Benjamin Johnston, Jr., Thomas Drake, Sr.
   R. May 25, 1741   Page 340

   Darden, Jacob. Appraised by John Darden, Thomas
Bullock; Theophilus Joyner. Signed, Jacon Darden
   R. May 25, 1741   Page 342

   Brantley, James. Appraised by Thomas Harris, John
Miller, Edward Miller, Richard Jordan. Signed, Martha
Brantley. Ordered February 23, 1740/41
   R. May 25, 1741   Page 347

   How, Morris. Appraised by John Goodrich, Melchizedeck
Deshey, John Wrenn. Signed Richard Jordan
   Ordered April 27, 1741   R. May 25, 1741
                                        Page 348

   Floyd, Francis. Appraised by John Rodway, Robert
King, Humphrey Marshall, Samuel Whitfield
   Ordered March 23, 1741   R. May 25, 1741
                                        Page 349

   Norsworthy, George. Inventory of estate, presented
by James Tooke Scott. Ordered December 8, 1739
   R. June 22, 1741   Page 351

   Batten, Daniel: Leg.- son John; son Daniel; daughter
Esther; wife Sarah; daughter Jean; daughter Patience;
daughter Priscilla. Wife, Extx.
   D. January 7, 1940   R. June 22, 1741
   Wit. William Eley, Mathew Westray, Thomas Bracey
                                        Page 352

   Jackson, Richard: Of Nottoway Parish. Leg.- wife
Sarah; daughter Mary; daughter Sarah; daughter Katherine;
granddaughter Ann Stuart. Wife, Extx.
   D. October 14, 1740   R. June 22, 1741
   Wit. Benjamin Jenkins, John Jackson, Timothy Atkinson
                                        Page 354

Vaughan, John: Leg.- wife Elliner; to Vaughan
Kilburne, all my land at the death of my wife; to John
Simmons, the minor son of John Simons, Jr. of Surry
County, reversion of the bequest made to John Kilburn
also to him. John Simmons, Sr. to care for the be-
quest made to his grandson. Ex., Vaughan Kilburne
  D. February 9, 1736   R. July 27, 1741
Wit. John Dortch, John Upchurch, John Spence
                                          Page 355

Thomas, William: Leg.- wife Mary; son Richard, land
on the Meherrin River, adjoining Samuel Smith; son
Samuel, the plantation on which I live. Wife, Extx.
  D. May 18, 1741   R. July 27, 1741
Wit. Lewis Brantley, Nathaniel Merrell, Ann Gray
                                          Page 356

Harris, Edward. Inventory, presented by Mary Harris.
  R. July 27, 1741   Page 356

Jordan, James. Appraised by Peter Woodward, Joseph
Hill, Arthur Jones. Signed, Richard Jordan
  Ordered May 25, 1741   R. July 27, 1741
                                          Page 360

Loyd, Thomas. Appraised by John Darden, William
Lawrence, Jeremiah Lawrence. Signed Charity Loyd
  R. July 27, 1741   Page 361

Batten, Daniel. Appraised by Daniel Herring, John
Tomlin, Mathew Tomlin, William Eley
  R. July 27, 1741   Page 363

Norwood, William. Account estate, examined by
John Person, James Ridley, Benjamin Blunt
  R. July 27, 1741   Page 364

Stephens, Edward. Account estate, presented by
Hardy Council. Examined by James Baker
  R. July 27, 1741   Page 366

Applewhaite, Henry. Appraised by William Pope, John
Johnson, Edward Cobb, James Edwards
  R. August 24, 1741   Page 367

Alice Fiveash. Peter Fiveash. Their estates appraised
by N. Bourden and Thomas Murrey. Signed by John Davis
   D. October 18, 1739   R. August 24, 1741
                                            Page 369

Woodward, Oliver. Appraised by Richard Blow, Jr.,
Henry Thomas, George Gurley. Signed Samuel Woodward
   Ordered, May 25, 1741   R. August 24, 1741
                                            Page 371

Applewhaite, Henry. Inventory returned by Ann
Applewhaite   R. August 24, 1741
                                            Page 374

Norsworthy, George. Account estate; to Major Q'Sheal
for discovering and establishing old Col. Norsworthy's
will; to William Scott's trouble in attending the suit
against Martha Norsworthy. The estate was paid in equal
shares to John Monro, the widow Beshier and James Tooke
Scott. Examined by James Baker and N. Bourden
   R. August 24, 1741   Page 375

Fulgham, Edmund. Account estate, returned by
Benjamin Turner   R.   Page 376

Bridger, Captain William. Account estate returned
by Arthur Smith, Jr. Examined by Edmond Godwin and
Jesse Browne   R. October 26, 1741
                                            Page 377

Brantley, James. Account estate, returned by Martha
Brantley. Examined by Charles Travers and William
Washington   R. November 23, 1741
                                            Page 378

Davis, Robert. Account estate, returned by Elizabeth
Davis   R. November 23, 1741   Page 379

Braddy, Elias: Leg.- mother Margaret Braddy, all my
land in Virginia and North Carolina. Mother, Extx.
   D. June 16, 1738   R. November 23, 1741
   Wit. Samuel Taylor, Henry Crafford   Page 380

Wiles, Joseph: Of Newport Parish. Leg.- wife Lucy;

daughter Martha; son Joseph; daughter Mary; to John
Frizzell. Ex., John Frizzell, who is to have the
care of my son Joseph Wiles
    D. August 17, 1741   R. December 28, 1741
    Wit. John Driver, John Ballard   Page 381

    Williams, Margaret: Leg.- son David; grandson John
son of David Williams; granddaughter Mary; the daughter
of Richard Williams; to Mary Altman. Ex., son John
    D. September 10, 1740   R. December 28, 1741
    Wit. William Penny, Mary Altman   Page 382

    Marshall, Humphrey. Estate appraised by John
Rodway, Thomas Grosse and Thomas Whitfield. Signed,
Ann Marshall. Ordered, October 26, 1741
    R. December 28, 1741   Page 383

    Wilkinson, Col. William. Appraised by Hugh Giles,
John Monro, Robert King. Signed, Charles Fulgham, Jr.
    Ordered July 27, 1741   R. December 28, 1741
                                        Page 385

    Gray, John. Estate appraised by Samuel Whitfield,
William Parker, Aaron Gray. Signed, Hannah Gray
    Ordered, August 24, 1741   R. December 28, 1741
                                        Page 387

    Hill; Thomas. Account estate, returned by George
Wilson, examined by William Hodsden, Thomas Smith and
N. Bourden. The above account examined and allowed by
me as guardian to the heir-at-law, signed John Newsum
    R. December 28, 1741   Page 388

    Wiles, Joseph. Estate appraised by John Rodway,
Thomas Whitfield, Anthony Fulgham. Signed John Frizzell
    R. January 25, 1741   Page 389

    Derring, Nicholas: Leg.- son James; son Miles; daugh-
ter Susannah; wife Mary. Exs., sons James and Miles
    D. July 2, 1741   R. January 25, 1741
    Wit. Richard Jordan, Jennings Ingraham, Sarah Meacom
                                        Page 390

Jarrell, Thomas, Sr.: Leg.- grandson Thomas Turner;
daughter Ann Turner; daughter Sarah Parker; to grandson
Thomas Parker, two negroes in the possession of Richard
Parker; son Thomas; grandson Thomas Jarrell. Ex., son
Thomas
    D. April 20, 1741   R. February 22, 1741
    Wit. Richard Blow, Jr., Micajah Edwards,
        Benjamin Flowers   Page 391

Williams, John: Leg.- Robert Jones; to my housekeeper,
Mary Davis; son Jonas. Ex., son Jonas Williams
    D. March 12, 1740/41   R. February 22, 1741
    Wit. Arthur Jones, Thomas Parnall   Page 393

Derring, Nicholas. Estate appraised by Thomas Day,
John Goodrich, Edward Brantley. Signed, James Derring
    R. February 22, 1741   Page 394

Reynolds, Christopher. Account estate, which was
divided between the widow and orphans. Examined by Hardy
Council, Thomas Gale, John Dunkley
    R. February 22, 1741   Page 396

Jordan, James. Account estate, examined by N. Bourden
and Jordan Thomas.   R. February 22, 1741
                          Page 397

Lewis, Zebulon. Account estate, signed by John and
Jane Brassell. Examined by J. Simmons, Timothy Thorpe,
James Ridley   R. February 22, 1741
                          Page 398

Cogan, Robert. Account estate, returned by Sarah
Cogan. Examined by Abram Ricks, Thomas Gale, William
Denson   R. February 22, 1741
                        Page 399

Bradshaw, William. Account estate returned by
Richard Bradshaw. Examined by J. Gray, Ethd. Taylor
    R. March 22, 1741   Page 399

Murfree, Sarah: Leg.- son William; daughter Ann;
daughter Catherine Bryan. Ex., son William Murfree
    D. December 26, 1740   R. April 26, 1742
    Wit. John Daughtry, William Daughtry   Page 400

White, Ann: Leg.- son John; grandson Thomas White; granddaughter Mary White, with the reversion of the bequest to William and Thomas White, the sons of John and Thomas White. Ex.; son George Thomas White
D. September 18, 1739   R. May 24, 1742
Wit. John Goodrich, Edward Brantley   Page 401

Copeland, Thomas: Leg.- sister Mary Whitfield; sister Martha Summerell; sister Sarah; sister Ann; to Samuel Copeland; mother Holland Copeland. Ex., brother Joseph
D. November 22, 1741   R. May 24, 1742
Wit. Henry Pitt, Jr., James Bagnall
                                             Page 402

Goodwin (Godwin?), Samuel. Estate appraised by John Applewhaite, Richard Reynolds, Joseph Wright. Signed by Jacob Dickinson. Ordered March 22, 1741
R. May 24, 1742   Page 403

Benn, Captain James. Account estate returned by Joseph Wright. Examined by Joseph Weston, Joseph Smith, Hugh Giles   R. May 25, 1742
                                             Page 405

Frizzell, Ralph. Estate appraised by John Rodway, Robert King, Anthony Fulgham, Giles Driver. Signed by John Frizzell   Page 406

Whitley, Mary. Estate appraised by Abraham Nicholas, George Minard, Thomas Applewhaite. Signed Samuel Holladay
D. 1741   R. May 24, 1742
                                             Page 407

Wilson, Goodrich: Leg.- mother Honour Pierce, with reversion of bequests to Mary Wilson, the daughter of my brother George Wilson; if she dies under age, to George Wilson; to Sarah White; to Jeremiah Pierce; to Baker White; to brother Samuel Wilson. Ex., George Wilson
D. April 5, 1742   R. June 28, 1742
Wit. Edward Goodrich, James Calcote   Page 408

White, Ann. Thomas White. Estates appraised by Edward Goodrich, N. Bourden, Thomas Day, Edward Brantley
Ordered March 22, 1741   R. July 26, 1742
                                             Page 409

Wilson, Goodrich. Estate appraised by Thomas Day,
John Goodrich; William Miller
 R. July 26, 1742   Page 410

Vaughan, John. Inventory, returned by Vaughan
Kilburn   R. July 26, 1742
               Page 411

Walton; Colonel Thomas. Estate appraised by John
Goodrich, N. Bourden, John Davis. Signed by Charles
Portlock. Ordered, May 24, 1742   R. August 23, 1742
               Page 411

Daniel, Thomas. Estate appraised by Richard West,
George Green, Thomas Wills. Ordered May 24, 1742
 R. August 23, 1742   Page 413

Murfree, Sarah. Inventory returned by William
Murfree   R. August 23, 1742   Page 414

Driver, Edward. Account estate, signed by Robert
Driver. Examined by Thomas Gale, John Jordan
 R. August 23, 1742   Page 415

Warren, Thomas. Account estate, presented by Thomas
Williams, Jr. Examined by John Davis and Edmond Godwin
 R. August 24, 1742   Page 416

Braddy, Elias. Inventory returned by Margaret Braddy
 R. August 23, 1742   Page 417

Wilkinson, Richard: Of Newport Parish. Leg.- granddaughter Mary Holladay, with reversion to granddaughter
Easther Holladay; grandson James Peden; grandson Wilkinson
Parker; granddaughter Ann Peden; granddaughter Mary Holladay; granddaughter Charity Holladay; daughter Mary Peden,
the wife of the Rev. Mr. James Peden; daughter Ann Bagnall;
refers to Nathan Bagnall, my said daughter's deceased
husband; grandson William Bagnall; daughter Rachel Norsworthy; refers to Thomas Parker, my said daughter Rachel's
deceased husband; to granddaughter Elizabeth Godwin, the
wife of Thomas Godwin; grandson William Parker; grandson
Nathan Bagnall; to Ann Giles; grandson Richard Bagnall

Ex., son-in-law Anthony Holladay
 D. April 13, 1741   R. September 27, 1742
 Wit. John Applewhaite, George Reynolds, Lemuel Godwin
                                                Page 418

   Williams, Rachel: Of Newport Parish. Leg.- to Ann,
the daughter of the Rev. James Peden and Mary his wife;
to Mary, the daughter of Anthony Holladay and Easter his
wife; to Easter Holladay, the daughter of aforesaid; to
Charity Holladay, the daughter of aforesaid; to Sabra
Parker; to Mary Scutchins, the wife of Samuel Scutchins;
to Mary Scutchins, the daughter of aforesaid; to William
Parker; to Thomas Parker; to John Wright, the son of
John Wright and Juliana his wife; to Elizabeth Pilkington;
to Ann Chapman, the wife of Charles Chapman; to Ann
Bagnall, relict of Nathan Bagnall; to my kinswoman, the
eldest daughter of Joseph Turner by his first wife; to
Mary Chapmam, the relict of John Chapman; to the Rev.
John Gemmell; to Hugh Giles; to Anthony Holladay, who
married my kinswoman, Easter Wilkinson. Ex., Anthony
Holladay
 D. August 4, 1741   R. September 27, 1742
 Wit. Hugh Giles, Thomas Norsworthy, Ann Marshall
                                                Page 422

   Smith, Arthur: Gentleman. Leg.- wife Mary; son
Arthur, my seal ring; son Thomas, the tract of land which
my father gave to my brother Thomas Smith, where John
Summerell and William Wainwright now live; also land on
the Blackwater, being part of the tract, which I sold to
Henry and Robert Edwards; daughter Mary to be maintained
by my two sons at their discretion, so long as she remains
in the condition, she is now in; daughter Jane Ridley;
daughter Olive Hodsden; daughter Martha Day; grandson
Joseph Bridger; to Sarah Stringer. Wife, Extx.
 D. August 31, 1741   R. September 27, 1742
 Wit. John Summerell, John Smith, George Williams
                                                Page 424

   Gross, Thomas: Leg.- daughter Elizabeth; son Francis;
daughter Mary Covington Hunter; Joshua Hunter to be paid
what I owe him; daughter Angelina. Ex., Christopher
Haines.
 D. August 27, 1742   R. September 27, 1742
 Wit. John Driver, Rebecca Haines   Page 426

   Clark, William: Of the Parish of Newport. Leg.-
wife Ruth; son Joseph; son Benjamin; daughter Elizabeth;
daughter Sarah; daughter Ann. Wife, Extx.
 D. January 17, 1737/8   R. September 27, 1742
 Wit. Thomas Atkinson, Robert Exum, Hugh Hunniford
                                                Page 427

Cobb, Edward: Leg.- son James; son Edward; son-in-law Thomas Summerell; daughter Elinor. Exs., sons James and Edward Cobbs
    D. August 22, 1742   R. September 27, 1742
    Wit. Benjamin Johnson, James Edwards, Jr.,
         James Edwards, Sr.   Page 428

Little, John: Of Newport Parish. Leg.- son John; daughter Rebecca Hynes; son Barnaby; daughter Martha; son John. Wife, Extx.
    D. October 29, 1739   R. September 27, 1742
    Wit. Robert Johnson, Jr., William Page
         Page 430

Inglish, William. Estate appraised by Benjamin Hodges, Thomas Day, William Harrison, Edward Goodrich. Ordered, May 24, 1742. Account of his estate, examined by John Davis, William Hodsden and Edward Goodrich
    R. September 27, 1742   Page 432

Screws, Mary. Appraisal estate by Benjamin Hodges, William Harrison, Thomas Day. R. September 27, 1742
         Page 433

Screws, William. Account estate, to bringing up four small children. Examined by William Hodsden, John Davis and Edward Goodrich
    R. September 27, 1742   Page 434

Bunkley, George. Nuncupative will, proven by Peter Kelly, John Watts and Sarah Alderson, in which he left his whole estate to his sister Sarah Bunkley
    D. August 20, 1742   R. September 27, 1742
         Page 434

Wilkinson, Richard. Estate appraised by Hugh Giles, Joseph Wright, Joseph Weston, Richard Reynolds. Signed by Anthony Holladay.   R. October 25, 1742
         Page 435

Fiveash, Alice. Peter Fiveash. Estates examined by N. Bourden, Thomas Murry. Signed John Davis
    R. October 25, 1742   Page 438

Clark, William. Estate appraised by Joseph Atkinson,

Richard Thomas, Edward Haile. Signed Joseph Clark
     R. October 25, 1742   Page 439

     Gross, Thomas. Estate appraised by John Rodway,
John Clark, Anthony Fulgham. Signed Christopher
Haines.   R. October 25, 1742   Page 440

     Fiveash, Peter. Account estate, examined by Thomas
Smith, William Hodsden, Charles Portlock
     R. October 25, 1742   Page 441

     Wainwright, William. Account estate, to expense of
bringing up Benjamin Wainwright. Examined by John
Wills, William Ponsonby, Joseph Baker
     R. October 25, 1742   Page 443

     Summerell, Thomas, Jr. Estate examined at the
house of John Summerell, by John Wills, Joseph Baker,
William Ponsonby.   R. October 25, 1742
                                                     Page 444

     Basden, Joseph. Inventory presented by James
Basden.   R. October 25, 1742   Page 444

     Hodges, Elias. On the motion of William Harrison,
a clause in his will to be explained in reference to
the gift of a slave and her increase to his daughter
Mary. The depositions of John Goodrich and John Hodges,
filed.   R. October 25, 1742   Page 445

     Williams, Rachel. Inventory presented by Anthony
Holladay.   R. November 22, 1742   Page 446

     Bridger, William. Account of his estate which
belongs to his orphan Joseph Bridger. Signed by Arthur
Smith.   R. November 22, 1742   Page 447

     Holleman, Elizabeth. Account estate, by sale for
Arthur and Joseph Holleman, legacies left them by their
grandfather Thomas Holleman. Signed Thomas Atkinson
     R. November 22, 1742   Page 449

Basden, Joseph. Account estate. R. November 22, 1742   Page 450

Smith, Thomas. Inventory returned by Elizabeth and Joseph Smith   R. November 22, 1742
                                                       Page 451

Norsworthy, Charles. Account estate, examined by Hugh Giles and Robert King.   R. November 22, 1742
                                                       Page 432

Wilkinson, Colonel William. Account estate, expenses for William and Willis Wilkinson; to Charles Fulgham in part toward his wife's claims. Signed, Thomas Swann
R. December 27, 1742   Page 452

Allen, Thomas. Account estate, examined by George Washington, J. Jarrell, Richard Blow, Jr. Signed, George Bell and Roger Allen   R. January 24, 1742
                                                       Page 453

Little, John. Inventory presented by the Extx. R. January 24, 1742   Page 454

Weston, Benjamin. Account estate, examined by Hugh Giles, Thomas Applewhaite, John Applewhaite
R. February 28, 1742   Page 455

Pierce, Thomas: Leg.- Jeremiah Pierce and Honour Pierce
D. November 25, 1742   R. February 28, 1742
Wit. John Miller, Joseph Jones   Page 456

Jordan, Mathew: Leg.- son Mathew; daughter Dorothy; daughter Elizabeth; daughter Martha; unborn child; wife Patience. Exs., wife, Abraham Ricks, Samuel Cornwell
D. November 19, 1742   R. March 20, 1743
Wit. Thomas Deloach, Sampson Flake, Mary Delk
                                                       Page 456

Cobb, Edward. Inventory presented by Edward and James Cobb   R. March 28, 1743
                                                       Page 458

Kinchen, Mathew. Inventory, presented by Thomas
Jarrell and Etl'd. Taylor, Exs. R. March 28, 1743
Page 459

Moreland, John. Estate appraised by Thomas Day,
Thomas Shelly, Thomas Barlow. Signed, Edward Goodrich
Ordered October 25, 1742   R. April 25, 1743
Page 459

Jordan, Mathew. Estate appraised by John Garner,
Francis Ward, Thomas Cofer. Signed, Patience Jordan
R. May 23, 1743   Page 461

Edwards, James: Leg.- friend William Pope; friend
Nathan Godwin; son David; son James; son John; son
William; son Jonas; son Nathan; son Albridgeton. Wife,
Extx. D. April 5, 1743   R. May 23, 1743
Wit. Benjamin Johnston, William Pope   Page 464

Goodwin, Joshua. Estate appraised by Robert King,
Anthony Fulgham, Giles Driver. Signed Thomas Goodwin
R. May 23, 1743   Page 465

Moreland, John. Account estate, examined by Thomas
Smith, N. Bourden, John Mallory.
R. May 23, 1743   Page 467

Walton, Colonel Thomas. Account estate, examined by
N. Bourden, John Davis and Edward Goodrich. Signed by
Charles Portlock   R. May 23, 1743
Page 468

Jordan, Joshua. Estate appraised by Joseph Weston,
Robert King, John Rodway. Signed Sarah Jordan
Ordered June 3, 1743   R. June 27, 1743
Page 469

Miller, John. Account estate, to his daughter
Mourning's funeral expenses. Examined by N. Bourden,
John Davis, Edward Goodrich. R. June 27, 1743
Page 470

Ricks, Robert: Leg.- wife Elizabeth; son Robert, the
land on which William Wood formerly lived; daughter Mary;
daughter Elizabeth; neighbor Nicholas Williams; son

Richard. Exs.; wife and son Robert Ricks
   D. March 25, 1741   R. July 25, 1743
   Wit. William Scott, Jr., John Dendon, Jr., Joseph
        West, Jere'h Lawrence, Jacob Johnson

Page 471

   Edwards, James. Inventory presented by Allinor
Edwards   R. July 25, 1743

Page 474

   Williamson, Francis: Leg.- wife Ann; son Arthur; son
Joseph; son Benjamin; granddaughter Mourning Williamson;
daughter Martha Atkinson; grandson Francis Williamson;
granddaughter Elizabeth -----; grandson Jesse Williamson;
grandson Arthur Williamson; granddaughter Martha
Williamson; grandsons, Burwell, Joseph, Hardy, Absolom,
Benjamin and James Williamson. Exs., sons Arthur and
Benjamin Williamson
   D. May 14, 1743   R. August 22, 1743
   Wit. James Simmons, Thomas Williamson

Page 476

   Ratcliff, John. Inventory presented by Richard
Jordan   R. August 23, 1743

Page 478

   How, Morrice. Account estate, paid for schooling
his children. Signed Richard Jordan. Examined by
N. Bourden and Jordan Thomas. R. September 20, 1743

Page 479

   Jordan, James. Account estate, examined by Jordan
Thomas and N. Bourden. Signed Richard Jordan

Page 479

   Scott, Robert: Leg.- sister Katherine Watkins; cousin
James Tooke Scott; cousin Thomas Scott; cousin Elizabeth
Bacon, the daughter of John Hollowell; to Elizabeth
Denson, the daughter of John Scott; cousin Joseph
Hollowell; cousin Sarah Hollowell; cousin William Scott,
son of my brother William Scott. Ex., brother William
   D. May 24, 1743   R. October 24, 1743
   Wit. Joseph White, William Denson, Henry Saunders

Page 480

   Scott, Robert. Inventory returned by William Scott, Jr.
R. October 24, 1743   Page 482

Kinchen, Mathew. Account estate, signed by Thomas
Jarrell and Eth'd Taylor. Examined by J. Gray and
John Ruffin   R. November 19, 1743
                                             Page 482

Ingram, Roger: Leg.- brother John Ingram; sister
Elizabeth; Goddaughter Ann Shelly; brother John is to
maintain my mother. Ex., brother John Ingram
   D. November 3, 1743   R. February 27, 1743
   Wit. Benjamin Chapman Donaldson, Giles Bowers
                                             Page 486

Britt, William: Leg.- son Alexander; daughter Mary;
to the rest of my children. Wife Elizabeth, Extx.
   D. August 5, 1743   R. March 26, 1744
   Wit. George Goodrich, John Britt   Page 487

Moore, Thomas: Of Nottoway Parish. Leg.- son
Thomas; son William; son Abraham. Ex., son Abraham
Moore
   D. August 12, 1743   R. March 26, 1744
   Wit. Jonathan Joyner, Timothy Atkinson   Page 487

Driver, Giles: Leg.- daughter-in-law Mary Driver;
grandson Robert Driver; granddaughter Sarah Driver;
daughter Ann Garland; son Giles; to my mother; grandson Dempsey Driver; son John; son Charles; son Joseph;
wife Olive. Ex., son John Driver
   D. September 23, 1743   R. March 26, 1744
   Wit. James Frizzell, John Frizzell
                                             Page 490

Parker, William: Leg.- wife Ann; daughter Rachel;
daughter Bathsheba
   D. May 23, 1743   R. April 23, 1744
   Wit. Nathan Bagnall, Thomas Parker   Page 490

Davis, Thomas. Account estate, examined by Richard
Hardy and Thomas Smith   R. June 25, 1744
                                             Page 491

White, George Thomas. Ann White. Account of their
estate, examined by Richard Hardy, N. Bourden. Widow
and orphans referred to. Signed, John Mecum
   R. June 25, 1744   Page 493

Tallaugh, James. Estate appraised by John Johnson, William Fowler, John Lawrence. Ordered February 27, 1743
R. June 25, 1744   Page 493

Jones, William: Leg.- son Joseph; son Jesse; daughter Olive; daughter Honour; daughter Mary; granddaughter Lucy Jones; wife Elizabeth. Exs., sons, Joseph and Jesse
D. December 29, 1742   R. June 25, 1744
Wit. Arthur Sherrod, Nathan Godley
        Elizabeth Sherrod   Page 495

Basden, Joseph. Division of his estate; to Robert Basden; to Martha Basden; to Lilburn Low; to representatives of Ledbetter Low, decd.   Page 496

Riggin, Daniel: Leg.- cousin Rachel Noyall, my plantation on which William Wainwright lives; sister Patience Shivers; to Jonas Shivers; to my uncle William Noyall; to Henry Shivers. Ex., William Noyall
D. March 3, 1743/44   R. July 23, 1744
Wit. Joshua Hunter, John Harrison, William Richards
                                                    Page 497

Pope, William. Estate appraised by Henry Thomas, Arthur Vick, Richard Blow, Jr. June 27, 1743
Signed, Patience Pope   R. April 15, 1744
                                                    Page 499

Davis, Elizabeth. Estate appraised by John Hodges, George Wilson, William Glover R. July 23, 1744
                                                    Page 499

Day, James. Estate appraised by Benjamin Hodges, Melchiz'd Dushee, Thomas Day. Signed, Martha Day and William Hodsden.   R. August 27, 1744
                                                    Page 502

Parker, William. Estate appraised by Joseph Wright, Joseph Weston, Thomas Whitfield, Samuel Whitfield.
Signed, Ann Parker   R. August 27, 1744
                                                    Page 504

English, William. Account estate, examined by James Ridley and Arthur Applewhaite. Signed, William Hodsden
R. August 27, 1744   Page 505

Bevan, Thomas. Account estate settled at the house
of Joseph Baker by John Summerell, Joseph Wright and
Joseph Baker. (First item dated 1735).
R. August 28, 1744 · Page 506

Williamson, Francis, Sr. Inventory presented by
Arthur and Benjamin Williamson R. September 24, 1744
Page 508

Wilkinson, Richard. Account estate, errors accepted
and contents received by agreement the 6th of July, by
John Parker, Nathan Bagnall, George Norsworthy, Rachel
Norsworthy, Ann Bagnall, James Peden, Mary Peden and
Anthony Holladay R. September 24, 1744
Page 509

Beal, Benjamin: Leg.- wife Sarah; daughter Sarah
Godwin; son Benjamin; daughter Mary; daughter Rachel
Dixson; daughter Wilkinson; wife Sarah Beal. Ex., son
Benjamin Beal ·
D. August 7, 1744 R. September 24, 1744
Wit. Thomas Gale, John Chestnutt, John Garner
Page 511

Wrenn, Olive. Nuncupative will, proven by N. Bourden,
William Williams and William Murrey. That she desired
that her child should have everything, which belonged to
her. D. August 1, 1744 R. October 22, 1744
Page 515

Clements, John. Inventory of estate, returned by
George Ellsey (?) R. October 22, 1744
Page 515

Colson, William. Account estate, dated 1741, returned by John Person, Gent., Sheriff
R. October 22, 1744 Page 516

Williams, John: Leg.- daughter Elizabeth Williams.
Ex., friend Benjamin Hodges D. October 4, 1744
Wit. N. Bourden, Philip Pones, Lewis Thomas
Codicil: If my daughter dies without heirs, my estate
to be equalley divided between James Pyland, Jr., the
son of James Pyland and John Carrell, the son of Samuel
Carrell
D. November 2, 1744 R. November 26, 1744
Wit. N. Bourden, Thomas Rosser, Prudence Bourden
Page 517

Proctor, Jeremiah. Estate appraised by John Wrenn, William Glover, Melchizadeck Dushee. Signed Susanna Proctor. Ordered July 21, 1744
R. November 26, 1744   Page 519

Harrison, William. Estate appraised by William Harrison, Benjamin Hodges, Nicholas Casey. Signed Temperance Harrison. Ordered October 6, 1744
R. November 26, 1744   Page 520

Wrenn, Olive. Account sales, signed, Francis Wrenn
R. November 26, 1744   Page 521

Lawrence, Robert: Of Newport Parish. Leg.- son Hardy; son Robert; son George; son Charles; daughter Sarah; daughter Priscilla; wife Ann; brother John Lawrence; son Charles to be placed in the care of his grandfather Hardy Council. Wife Ann, Extx.
D. November 1, 1743   R. January 28, 1744
Wit. William Lawrence, John Lawrence, Hardy Council
                                                        Page 522

Marshall, Humphrey: Of Newport Parish. Leg.- brother Robert; brother John; sister Elizabeth Roberson; to John Marshall the son of my brother Joseph; sister Mary Penny; brother James Marshall; to John Penny, the plantation on which I live; Mary Sikes to have half of the said plantation during her widowhood; if John Penny should die without issue the bequest to my brother James Marshall; to William Penny the son of John. Exs., James Marshall and John Penny
D. January 3, 1744   R. January 28, 1744
Wit. John Driver, Charles Driver   Page 524

Atkinson, Thomas. Estate appraised by Robert Tynes, James Simmons and Richard Thomas. Signed, Joseph Atkinson. Ordered, October 22, 1744   R. January 28, 1744
                                                        Page 525

Jordan, Mathew. Account estate, to cash due Mary Jordan, the orphan of James Jordan. Signed, Lawrence Baker and Jordan Thomas
R. January 28, 1744   Page 527

Wheadon, Joseph: Leg.- John Carrell; to Thomas Carrell; wife Joice; brother James Wheadon; nephew Joseph Wheadon. Extx., wife Joice Wheadon
D. December 1, 174   R. February 25, 1744
Wit. Wil. Salter, Thomas Mean (?), William Balmer, Jr.
                                                        Page 528

Williams, George: Leg.- son George; son Thomas; son
Roland; grandson Thomas Clark land on Nottoway Swamp;
wife Elizabeth and at her death to be divided among all
my children. Exs., wife and son Roland
   D. August 26, 1737   R. February 25, 1744
   Wit. Robert Ricks, William May   Page 529

Long, Edward. Estate appraised by William Wainwright,
John Wright, Joshua Hunter. Signed by Ann Daniel
   Ordered, January 28, 1744   R. February 24, 1744
                                      Page 531

Fulgham, John. Estate appraised by Thomas Whitfield,
Robert King, Nathan Bagnall. Signed, Mich'l Fulgham
   Ordered January 28, 1744   R. February 25, 1744
                                      Page 531

Wiles, Joseph. Estate appraised by John Summerell,
John Wills, Thomas Applewhaite. R. February 25, 1744
                                      Page 532

Gross, Thomas. Account estate, settled at the house
of Christopher Haynes, by John Summerell, John Wills and
Thomas Applewhaite.   R. February 25, 1744
                                      Page 533

Marshall, Humphrey. Estate appraised by John Rodway,
Anthony Fulgham, Thomas Whitfield. Signed by James
Marshall and John Penny   R. March 25, 1745 Page 533

Joyner, John: Of the Lower Parish. Leg.- cousin
Theophilus Joyner, my whole estate. Ex. Theophilus
Joyner. D. January 3, 1741 R. April 22, 1745
   Wit. John Whitley, William Whitley, Thomas Uzzell
                                      Page 535

Williams, John. Inventory of estate returned by
Benjamin Hodges.   R. June 24, 1745   Page 535

Wilson, John. Appraisal of estate by Nelchizadeck
Deshey, William Glover, John Wrenn
   Ordered, April 22, 1745   R. June 24, 1745   Page 536

Gemmill, Rev. Mr. John. Estate appraised by John

Davis, Thomas Day, Benjamin Hodges, William Hodsden.
Signed by Robert Burwell   R. July 22, 1745
Page 538

    Braswell, Richard: Leg.- son William and son Joseph,
my Exs.; daughter Elizabeth; son John; loving wife.
    D. April 21, 1744   R. August 26, 1745
    Wit. Benjamin Johnson, Jr., Joseph Woodward, Arthur
          Edwards   Page 541

    Richards, Thomas. Account estate, examined by John
Summerell, John Applewhaite, Hugh Giles
    R. August 26, 1745   Page 541

    Gardner, William. Estate appraised by Robert Driver,
John Garnes (Garner); Thomas Joiner. Signed, John
Gardner. Ordered January 28, 1744
    R. August 26, 1745   Page 542

    Neaville, John. Division of estate to sons, John,
Thomas and Joseph and daughter Penelope. Examined by
Hardy Council, Abram Ricks and William Denson. Signed
by John Marshall. R. August 26, 1745   Page 544
    Further accounts of the orphans of John Neaville, the
share of Thomas Neaville to be divided among the three
surviving childre.   R. August 26, 1745
Page 545

    Applewhaite, Henry, Jr. Account estate returned by
Philip and Mary Brantley. Examined by Thomas Gray and
Peter Butts.   R. September 23, 1745
Page 547

———————————

WILL BOOK FIVE
———————————

    Lawrence, Robert. Inventory of his estate returned by
Ann Lawrence.   R. October 28, 1745
Page 1

    Joyner, John. Inventory of his estate returned by
Theophilus Joyner.   R. October 28, 1745
Page 1

Meacom, Lewis. Account estate, to the expense of bringing up two small children. Signed, John and Ann Potter. Examined by Thomas Smith and Thomas Day.
R. October 28, 1745 . Page 2

Windham, Reuben. Inventory presented by Edward Windham. R. January 27, 1745 Page 3

Pursell, Arthur: Leg.- son Arthur; son Philip; daughter Sarah Johnson; daughter Mary Fulgham; daughter Patience Exum; daughter Elizabeth Turner; daughter Ann; daughter Jean; daughter Martha. My estate to be divided by Thomas Williamson and Josiah John Holleman. Exs., wife Sarah and son Arthur Pursell
D. July 10, 1745 R. January 27, 1745
Wit. Thomas Williamson, Michael Harris Page 3

Newsum, Thomas: Leg.- son Nathan; son Benjamin; son Jacob; son David; my son Thomas Barham; daughter Sarah Barham; wife Elizabeth. R. January 27, 1745
Wit. Nathaniel Ridley, Jesse Browne Page 5
(Refers to land left his children by their brother)

Bradshaw, John: Leg.- cousin Sarah Bradshaw, the daughter of my brother George; cousin Martha Davis, the wife of Edward Davis. Exs., cousin Edward Davis and Charles Fulgham
D. August 27, 1737 R. January 27, 1745
Wit. Charles Fulgham, Ann Harris Page 7

Johnson, William. Estate appraised by Harris Taylor, Thomas Davis, Simon Everitt. Signed, Peter Johnson
R. January 27, 1745 Page 7

Braswell, Richard. Inventory of his estate returned by William and Joseph Braswell
R. January 27, 1745 Page 9

Bradshaw, John. Estate appraised by Benjamin Hodges, Arthur Applewhaite, Nicholas Miller. Signed by Edward Davis. R. February 24, 1745 Page 9

Weatherall, Aquilla. Estate appraised by Richard
Snowden, Joseph Bridger, John Pitt. Signed, Charity
Weatherall. Ordered June 24, 1745
R. February 24, 1745   Page 11

Morgan, Walter. Estate appraised by John Hodges,
William Miller, Benjamin Hodges, William Harrison.
Signed, W. Bidgood   R. March 24, 1745
                                                       Page 12

Newsum, Thomas. Inventory presented by Elizabeth
and Jacob Newsum   R. March 24, 1745
                                                       Page 13

Moscrop, Susanna: Leg.- grandsons, Adam and Thomas
Murry, the sons of Robert Murry, decd.; daughter Mary
Godwin; granddaughter Jane Applewhaite; granddaughter
Mary Frizzell; sister Elizabeth Driver; to Joseph Weston;
to my five grandchildren, Mary Frizzell, Elizabeth
Godwin, Thomas Godwin, William Godwin and James Godwin.
Ex., Joseph Weston
  D. October 18, 1745   R. March 24, 1745
  Wit. David Williams, Jacob Thomas   Page 14

Morgan, Walter. Account estate, examined by N.
Bourden, James Ridley, A. Jones. R. March 24, 1745
                                                       Page 15

Read, William: Leg.- daughter Ann; son Samuel; son
John; wife Elizabeth
  D. April 21, 1739   R. April 28, 1746
  Wit. John Person, Robert Deane   Page 16

Johnson, Thomas: Leg.- son Joseph; son Moses; lov-
ing wife
  D. April 25, 1744   R. May 8, 1746
  Wit. Thomas Pate, Joseph Johnson   Page 17

Moscrop, Susanna. Estate appraised by Charles
Fulgham, Jr., Joseph Bridger, Jr., Thomas Wills. Signed
Joseph Weston   Page 17

Gardner, William. Account estate, examined by Thomas
Gray and David Hunter   R. May 9, 1746   Page 19

Pitt, Thomas. Estate appraised by Anthony Fulgham, Giles Driver, Christopher Haines. Signed Martha Pitt
Ordered, April 28, 1746   R. June 12, 1746
                                                    Page 20

Minard, George. Estate appraised by James Godwin, John Pitt, Joseph Bridger, Jr. Signed Ann Minard
   Ordered, April 28, 1746   R. June 12, 1746
                                                    Page 21

Snowden, Richard. Estate appraised by John Monro, John Pitt, Edmond Godwin. Signed, Margaret Snowden
   Ordered, May 8, 1746   R. June 12, 1746
                                                    Page 22

Read, William. Estate appraised by Thomas Clarke, Simon Harris, John Jones. Signed, Elizabeth Read
   R. June 12, 1746   Page 23

Pitman, Edward. Estate appraised by Jordan Thomas, Thomas Cole, Arthur Crocker. Signed, Martha Pitman
   R. June 12, 1746   Page 24

Wright, Joseph. Estate appraised by Joseph Weston, Joseph Norsworthy, Richard Reynolds. Signed, Martha
Wright. Ordered, November 25, 1745
   R. June 12, 1746   Page 24

McKenny, Gilbert. Estate appraised by Timothy Thorpe, Henry Rose, James Jones. Signed Sarah McKenny
   R. July 10, 1746   Page 26

Ricks, Abraham: Leg.- daughter Mary Jordan of North Carolina; daughter Elizabeth Pritchard; daughter Lydia Beal; daughter Martha Lawrence, land adjoining that of John Lawrence and Thomas Smelley; daughter Patience Jordan; daughter Ann Marshall; daughter Mourning Jordan; Josiah Jordan and John Lawrence to collect my debts. William Denson, Exum Scott, Joseph White and William Scott to assist in settling my estate. Exs., son-in-law Josiah Jordan and daughter Mourning Jordan
   D. June 24, 1746   R. July 10, 1746
   Wit. James Jordan Scott, John Outland, Jacob Powell
                                                    Page 26

126

Summerell, John: Leg.- wife Lydia; daughter Sarah;
daughter Jean. Wife, Extx.
D. February 14, 1745   R. August 24, 1746
Wit. Hugh Giles, Edmond Godwin, James Fulgham
                                               Page 28

Gibbs, Ralph. Estate appraised by John Rodway,
Christopher Haines; Stephen Smith. Signed, Sarah Gibbs
   Ordered April 28, 1746   R. August 14, 1746
                                               Page 29

Atkinson, Thomas. Account estate, to a negro deliver-
ed to Richard Atkinson. Examined by John Ruffin and
N. Bourden. Signed, Joseph Atkinson
   R. October 9, 1746   Page 31

Ricks, Abraham. Estate appraised by Robert Eley,
Joseph Meredith, Michael Eley. To legacies delivered
to Josiah Jordan; to Patience Jordan, to John Lawrence,
to John Marshall, to Joseph Jordan, to Thomas Pritchard
   R. October 9, 1746   Page 32

Blow, Richard. Estate appraised by Joseph Cobb,
Thomas Crainshaw, George Gurley. Appraisal at
"Contentney", Craven County, North Carolina. Signed
by Henry and Ann Vaughan.   R. October 9, 1746
                                               Page 37

Wombwell, Joseph: Of Nottoway Parish. Leg.- daugh-
ter Elizabeth; daughter Patience; daughter Sarah; son
Jesse; son Mathew. Wife Ann, Extx.
D. August 19, 1746   R. November 13, 1746
Wit. Benjamin Bayley, Arthur Holleman, John Smith
                                               Page 38

Wombwell, Joseph. Estate appraised by Joseph Phillips,
Charles Calthorpe, Thomas Brown. Signed, Ann Wombwell
   R. January 8, 1746   Page 39

Miller, William: Leg.- son James; son William; if sons
should die without heirs, Martha Casey is to inherit
James estate and my brother John Miller's children to in-
herit William's estate. Exs., wife Margaret, friend
George Wilson and friend Edward Goodrich
   D. July 3, 1746   R. January 8, 1746
   Wit. Ann Briggs, Susanna Derring, William Williams
                                               Page 40

Noyall, William: Of Newport Parish. Leg.- daughter
Martha Norsworthy; daughter Ann Harrison; daughter Jane;
daughter Mary Richards; daughter Elizabeth Pitt; wife
Martha; daughter Sarah; daughter Priscilla; daughter
Rachel. Exs., wife and daughter Rachel Noyall
   D. March 28, 1746   R. January 8, 1746
   Wit. William Brock, James Godwin, John Pitt
                                              Page 41

Adkins, Samuel: Leg.- son Moses; son Samuel; son
Michael; son Thomas; wife Elizabeth. Exs., wife and
son Samuel Adkins
   D. May 22, 1746   R. February 12, 1746
   Wit. John Rotchell, John Turner, Howell Edmunds
                                              Page 43

Johnson, William. Account estate, examined by
William Hodsden and Thomas Gray. Signed Peter Johnson
   R. February 12, 1746   Page 44

Williford, John. Appraised by Lawrence Lancaster,
Joseph Lancaster, John Stephenson. Signed Elizabeth
Williford.   R. February 12, 1746   Page 45

Joyner, Lazarus: Leg.- brother Henry; brother
Arthur; rest of my estate to be divided among Henry
Joyner, Arthur Joyner, Prudence Long; sister Mary
Tynes; sister Martha Joyner. Exs., brothers John and
Henry Joyner
   D. December 30, 1746   R. March 12, 1746
   Wit. Richard Norsworthy, Tristram Norsworthy,
        Nathanial Norsworthy   Page 46

Blake, William: Of Nottoway Parish. Leg.- wife
Mary; son Sessums; son Benjamin; son Thomas; son Joseph;
among all my children. Exs., wife Mary; son Joshua
Claud and son Thomas Blake
   D. November 1, 1742   R. March 12, 1746
   Wit. John Barrow, Samuel Smith   Page 47

Page, William: Of Nottoway Parish. Leg.- granddaugh-
ter Mary Page; wife Ann and at her decease to Betty Fort,
if she should die without heirs to Joshua Fort. Exs.,
John and Rebecca Fort
   D. October 16, 1746   R. March 12, 1746
   Wit. John Land, Robert Land   Page 49

Everitt, Simon: Leg.- son Joseph; son Simon; grandson
Amos Williams; to Catherine Due (Dew?); daughter Patience
Turner; daughter Sarah Turner. Exs., sons Joseph and
Simon Turner
    D. November 5, 1743   R. March 12, 1746
    Wit. William Bynum, Elizabeth Bynum, Faith Taylor
Page 49

Dawson, Martin: Leg.- son Henry; daughter Elinor
Jones; daughter Sarah Inman; son Joshua; daughter Martha
Dinkin (?); to my housekeeper, Mary Cocks; daughter
Margaret Warren. Exs., sons-in-law, John Jones and
Robert Warren
    D. September 16, 1745   R. March 12, 1746
    Wit. Henry Crafford, John Pierce, Henry Dawson
Page 51

    Oct. 9, 1746. Henry Dawson entered caveat against the
said will, for a revocation thereof. Rebecca Dawson,
widow and relict refused to accept the provisions made
for her, etc.
Page 51

Jordan, Charles, Sr. Estate appraised at the house
of Mary Jordan, by William Rand and Joseph Baker
    Ordered March 24, 1746/47   R. April 9, 1747
Page 53

Miller, William. Estate appraised by John Mallory,
John Hodges, Benjamin Hodges. Signed by Edward Goodrich
and George Wilson   R. April 9, 1747   Page 54

Noyall, William. Estate appraised by Joseph Bridger,
John Monro, John Pitt. Signed Martha Noyall
    R. May 14, 1747   Page 56

Johnson, Thomas. Estate appraised by Timothy Thorpe,
John Myrick, John Thorpe. Signed, Mary Johnson
    Ordered, May 8, 1746   R. May 14, 1747
Page 58

Gemmill, Rev. Mr. John. Estate examined by Lawrence
Baker, R. Hardy and T. Day. Signed Robert Burwell
    R. May 14, 1747   Page 58

Cocksey, William: Leg.- wife Judith; son John
Ex., son John Cocksey

D. February 21, 1745/46   R. May 14, 1747
Wit. Absalom Atkinson, Peter Vasser, John Nanny
                                              Page 60

Murphry, Michael: Leg.- son John; daughter Elizabeth
Dixon; daughter Mary; daughter Sarah; daughter Elender;
grandson Michael Murphry. Ex., son John Murphry
    D. July 2, 1743   R. May 14, 1747
    Wit. John Garner, B. Beal   Page 61

Wrenn, Mary: Leg.- daughter Ann Potter; daughter
Martha Cary; daughter Patience Bell; my grandchildren,
Mary Meacom, Lewis Meacom, William Cary, Joseph Cary,
Charity Cary, Richard Bell, Benjamin Bell and Mary Bell.
Ex., Mr. John Wrenn
    D. January 27, 1746   R. May 14, 1747
    Wit. Wil. Salter, Benjamin Bell, William Cary
                                              Page 62

Summerell, John. Estate appraised by Edmond Godwin,
Thomas Wills, Charles Fulgham, Jr. Signed Hugh Giles
    R. June 11, 1747   Page 63

Day, Captain James. Account estate, examined by
Edward Goodrich and Charles Portlock. Signed, William
Hodsden and John Mallory.   R. June 11, 1747
                                              Page 65

Johnson, James: Leg.- grandson John Corbett; daughter Mary Corbett; son James; daughter Martha Mayo; daughter Eleanor Ricks; granddaughter Patience Johnson, daughter of son John; son Samuel; son Richard; daughter
Catherine Burn; son Robert; daughter Grace Powell; wife
Mary; son Benjamin; granddaughter Mary Johnson.
Ex., son Benjamin Johnson
    D. January 30, 1745/46   R. June 11, 1747
    Wit. John Darden, John Gwinn, Johnson Corbett
                                              Page 67

Dawson, Martin. Estate appraised by Henry Crafford,
James Turner, Benjamin Blunt. Account of things carried
away by Rebecca Dawson into Carolina
    R. July 9, 1747   Page 70

West, Richard: Of Newport Parish. Leg.- son Everitt;
son Giles; daughter Rebecca Smelley; son Jacamy; son

Robert, land adjoining on Merchant Perry; son James;
daughter Ann; wife Ann. Ex., Hugh Giles
   D. July 3, 1746   R. July 9, 1747
   Wit. Charles Fulgham, Benn Willett; John Wills
Page 71

   Dawson, Martin. Account estate, to paid the follow-
ing legacies, to John Inman, to John Jones, to Robert
Warren, to Henry Dawson, to Joshua Dawson; to Martha
Dickins. Signed, John Jones   R. July 9, 1747
Page 73

   Woodward, Oliver. Account estate, paid Richard
Woodward, paid Joseph Woodward in part of his share.
Signed, Samuel Woodward. Examined by Thomas Gray and
James Holt   R. July 9, 1747
Page 74

   Parker, George: Leg.- wife Martha; daughter Mourning;
son James; daughter Ann; daughter Sarah; eldest daughter
Isabell and her first child. Exs., wife and friend,
Thomas Parker
   D. May 15, 1747   R. August 13, 1747
   Wit. James Jordan, John Wrench   Page 76

   Darden, Jacob. Account estate, among items - to cash
my father received as a legacy to me from my grandfather
George Williamson. Signed Jacob Darden. Examined by
William Hodsden and James Ridley
   R. August 13, 1747   Page 77

   Wiggs, George: Leg.- sister Elizabeth Brassey; bro-
ther Luke Wiggs; cousin Elizabeth Brassey. Sister
Elizabeth Brassey, Extx.
   D. July 30, 1747   R. October 8, 1747
   Wit. Robert Tynes, Arthur Applewhaite   Page 78

   Neaville, Elizabeth: Leg.- daughter-in-law Mary Sikes;
granddaughter Mary Sikes; daughter-in-law Rachel
Wainwright; to Amy and Ann Wainwright; to daughter-in-
law Mary Neaville; granddaughter Rachel Nolleboy; grand-
daughter Elizabeth Garner; granddaughter Sarah Murphry;
granddaughter Elinor Everett; daughter Sarah Carter; son
Francis Hampton; daughter Mary Marshall; son-in-law
James Marshall. Ex., son-in-law James Marshall
   D. September 21, 1747   R. October 8, 1747
   Wit. John Marshall, Jacob Darden, John Everitt
Page 79

Parker, George. Estate appraised by Samuel Godwin, Edmund Godwin, Robert Driver. Signed, Martha Parker
R. November 12, 1747   Page 81

Pitt, Thomas. Account estate examined by Hugh Giles and John Applewhaite   R. November 12, 1747
            Page 84

Powell, William: Leg.- to William Speight, son of John Speigt, with reversion of the bequest to his bro-ther John; to my brother Nathaniel's son Nathaniel; to James Davis; to Elizabeth Speight, the daughter of John and Elizabeth Speight; to Ann, the daughter of James Davis. Exs., John and William Speight
D. September 13, 1747   R. November 12, 1747
Wit. Thomas Gale, Mary Gale, Thomas Outland
            Page 85

Carter, Katherine: Leg.- daughter Kezia; daughter Elizabeth Perry
D. May 28, 1746   R. December 10, 1747
Wit. Thomas Clifton, John Calthorpe   Page 87

Grimmer, Robert. Estate appraised by Benjamin Johnston, Sr., Benjamin Johnston, Jr., Nathan Vasser. Signed by Sarah Grimmer and William Grimmer. Ordered August 13, 1747   R. December 10, 1747
            Page 88

Vickers, Ralph: Leg.- grandsons, Thomas and Simon Boykin, the land which I bought of Benjamin Boykin; granddaughter Martha Boykin; daughter Margaret Vaughan, the wife of Thomas Vaughan. Ex., brother Abraham Carnall
D. February 10, 1741   R. January 14, 1747
Wit. Joseph Powell, Hardy Council, Thomas English. Abraham Carnall, refused executorship and Simon Boykin qualified.   Page 89

Blow, Richard, Jr. Account estate, examined by Edmond Godwin and Thomas Wills. Signed, Henry Vaughan
R. January 14, 1747   Page 92

Goodrich, Benjamin. Estate appraised by Samuel Jones, Richard Jones and John Jordan.

Ordered, October 8, 1747. Signed William Goodrich
R. March 10, 1747   Page 93

Smith, William: Leg.- wife Mary; son William; son
Stephen; son Nathaniel; granddaughter Elizabeth, the
daughter of William Smith; granddaughter Mary, the
daughter of Stephen Smith; daughter Elizabeth Rodes.
Ex., son Stephen Smith
    D. February 20, 1746   R. March 10, 1747
    Wit. Peter Ballard, Joseph Weston   Page 96

Applewhaite, Ann: Widow. Leg.- son Thomas; grand-
daughter Ann Applewhaite the daughter of my son Thomas;
daughter Ann Godwin; daughter Priscilla Ridley; daughter
Amy Jones; son John; grandson Henry, the son of Henry
Applewhaite; granddaughter Amy Applewhaite the daughter
of my son Henry; granddaughter Ann Ridley; granddaughter
Sarah Davis; grandson Henry Applewhaite, son of my son
Arthur; grandson John Lawrence, son of my daughter Sarah
Lawrence. Ex., son Arthur Applewhaite
    D. July 26, 1746   R. March 10, 1747
    Wit. William Ponsonby, Ann Ponsonby, Ann Hunt,
          Elizabeth Daniel   Page 97

Price, Richard. Estate appraised by Francis Wills,
Benjamin Johnston, William Hickman. Ordered November
25, 1745. Sarah Grimmer and William Grimmer returned
the estate of Robert Grimmer, who was the administrator
of the estate of said Richard Price
    R. March 10, 1747   Page 99

Butler, Christopher. Estate appraised by James
Godwin, John Smelley, Christopher Reynolds. Signed
John Butler
    Ordered, March 10, 1747   R. April 14, 1748
                                                  Page 100

Hollowell, Sarah: Leg.- sister Judith; to Mourning,
the daughter of my brother Joseph Hollowell; brother
William. Ex., brother William Hollowell
    D. February 16, 1745   R. April 14, 1748
    Wit. John Murry, Sarah Murry, Benjamin Hodges,
          Benjamin Davis   Page 102

Driver, Robert: Leg.- daughter Prudence Jordan; daugh-
ter Juliana; daughter Elizabeth; daughter Mary; daughter
Patience; grandson William Jordan; son Robert at nineteen.
Ex., Giles Driver

D. March 1, 1747   R. May 12, 1748
Wit. John Chestnutt, Joshua Chestnutt, Thomas
     Pledger   Page 103

Carrell, James. Estate appraised by John Hodges,
William Harrison, James Piland. Signed, Mary Carrell
R. May 12, 1748   Page 105

Richards, Robert. Estate appraised by Richard
Reynolds, Joseph Norsworthy, John Scammell. Signed,
Mary Richards. Ordered March 10, 1747
R. May 12, 1748   Page 107

Hollowell, Sarah. Inventory of her estate presented
by William Hollowell.   R. June 9, 1748
                                   Page 108

Smith, Lawrence: Leg.- daughter Faithy Harris; son
Joseph; son Absalom; son Flood; daughter Jane; daughter
Hannah; daughter Sarah; wife Jane; son Lawrence.
Wife, Extx.
D. June 10, 1746   R. June 9, 1748
Wit. Richard Holleman, James Turner, Jr.
     Jacob Little   Page 110

Casey, Richard: Leg.- wife Jane; daughter Ann; daugh-
ter Sarah; daughter Patience; daughter Martha; son
Richard; grandson John S. Wills; daughter Ann Applewhaite;
friend John Wills; daughter Martha Wills; daughter Sarah
Smelley. Ex., friend John Wills
D. March 8, 1745/46   R. June 9, 1748
Wit. Barth'w Lightfoot, William Wills
                                   Page 112

Deshey, John: Leg.- loving mother; cousin John Wrenn;
cousin Mary Brantley; cousin James Wrenn; cousin Joseph
Wrenn; cousin William Wrenn; cousin Elizabeth Brantley;
cousin Martha Bidgood's children; cousin Francis Wrenn,
in case he should not return the legacy to be given John
Wrenn; cousin Joseph Webb. Mother Mary Deshey, Extx.
D. October 24, 1747   R. June 9, 1748
Wit. Thomas Smith; William Glover, Elizabeth Smith
                                   Page 114

Rew, John Anthony: Of Newport Parish. Leg.- Jane

Brown, the daughter of Samuel Brown, decd.; to Elizabeth
Brown, the daughter of aforesaid; to Martha Pitt; to
Sarah Pitt, the wife of Joseph Pitt; to Mary Brown, the
daughter of Joseph Brown; to John Brown, the son of
William Brown
 D. March 21, 1746/47   R. June 9, 1748
 Wit. William Brown, Jane Brown, Elizabeth Brown,
    Joseph Bridger, Jr.   Page 115

Deloach, Thomas: Leg.- son Samuel; son Thomas; son
Solomon; grandson Richard Deloach. Exs., sons William
and Solomon Deloach
 D. October 26, 1747   R. June 9, 1748
 Wit. Robert Booth, J. Gray   Page 117

Page, William. Estate appraised by Charles Barham,
Thomas Holt, Peter Butts. Signed, John Fort
 R. June 9, 1748   Page 118

Braddy, William. Account estate, to maintaining
four small children. Signed, Olive Braddy. Examined
by Jordan Thomas, James Bridger   R. June 9, 1748
              Page 120

Edwards, John: Leg.- son John; daughter Ann, the
cattle bought at the widow Hart's and widow Culpeper's
sale; daughter Mary; wife Ann. Exs., son John and
Henry Harris. Brother Nathaniel Edwards, trustee
 D. April 27, 1748   R. April 27, 1748
 Wit. Chaplain Williams, Thomas Taylor, Harris Taylor
              Page 121

Bidgood, William, Sr.: Leg.- wife Hester; son William;
daughter Ann Miller; son Josiah; son John; son Richard;
daughter Elizabeth. Exs., friends, Nicholas Miller, Sr.
and Edward Davis, Sr.   D. May 14, 1748
 Wit. John Bidgood, John Miller, Benjamin Davis
 Codicil: son Josiah to be bound to Samuel Person; son
 John to Robert Williams; son Richard to James Derring;
 and the church-wardens to place Elizabeth, where she
 will not suffer too much.   D. August 11, 1748
 Wit. Joseph Hill, Blake Baker, Mathew Jones
              Page 123

Smith, William. Appraised by Joseph Weston, Robert
King, Robert Brown   R. August 11, 1748
              Page 127

Rew, John Anthony. Estate appraised by John Pitt,
Samuel Godwin, James Godwin. Signed, William Brown
R. August 11, 1748   Page 129

Davis, William. Estate appraised by Benjamin
Clements, William Andrews, John Brown. Ordered,
July 6, 1745   R. August 11, 1748
                                                 Page 130

Fulgham, Charles. Estate appraised by Charles
Chapman, John Godwin, Jonathan Godwin. Signed, Charles
Fulgham   R. August 11, 1748   Page 131

Driver, Robert. Estate appraised by John Marshall,
Jr., Joseph Bridger, Jr., John Smelley. Signed, Giles
Driver   R. August 11, 1748   Page 133

Pitt, Henry: Leg.- son William; son Joseph Major
Pitt; son Thomas; daughter Elizabeth Bagnall; daughter
Ann Driver; granddaughter Lydia Benn; son Henry; daughter Patience Fulgham. Exs., son Henry Pitt and daughter Patience Fulgham
    D. December 9, 1747   R. August 12, 1748
    Wit. David Williams, William Bagnall, Richard
          Bagnall   Page 135

Jordan, Mathew: Leg.- wife Dorothy; son Josiah; son
Matthias, the land which I bought of my cousin Mathew
Jordan; daughter Charity; daughter Comfort. Friends,
William Harrison, George Wilson and William Hodsden to
divide my estate. Wife, Extx.
    D. September 27, 1747   R. October 13, 1748
    Wit. William Hodsden, William Harrison, George Wilson
                                               Page 137

Simmons, James. Estate appraised by Robert Johnson,
William Davis, Augustine King. Ordered, August 11, 1748
R. October 13, 1748   Page 139

Dixon, Thomas: Leg.- son William, the land which I
bought of Godfrey Hunt, it being the land on which my son
Thomas lived; son Nicholas; daughter Martha, now the wife
of Thomas Pearse; grandson Thomas Dixon; wife Penelope;
daughter Penelope, the wife of Joseph Bullock; daughter
Mourning, wife of Joshua Crudup; daughter Patience, the
wife of Jonas Shivers. Exs., wife and son Nicholas

D. April 26, 1746   R. January 12, 1748
Wit. Joseph Meredith, Robert Walker, Henry Bullard,
     Florence Bullard, Mary Simmonds   Page 141

Lee, John: Planter. Leg.- son Thomas; daughter
Jane. To be buried in the Bay Church Yard. Exs.,
Peter Fiveash, Henry Harrison
D. January 9, 1748   R. January 12, 1748
Wit. William Harrison, Wil. Salter, Thomas Rosser
                                                Page 143

Garner, James: Leg.- son John; son Jesse; son Joseph;
son James; daughter Sarah; daughter Olive; daughter
Patience Crooms; cousin Benjamin Garner. Exs., brother
Joseph Garner and son Joseph Garner
D. July 22, 1748   R. January 12, 1748
Wit. John Smelley, Joseph Garner, William Godwin
                                                Page 144

Smith, Hannah: Leg.- brother Joseph Smith; cousin
William Smith; cousin Nicholas Smith; to John Weston;
to Joseph Wiles; cousin Nathaniel Parker; cousin
Martha Smith; the estate of my deceased sister Martha
Smith is to be divided between Nathanial Parker and
Martha Smith. Ex., Nicholas Parker
D. December 9, 1748   R. January 12, 1748
Wit. Joseph Weston, Edward Ballard   Page 146

Smith, Lawrence. Estate appraised by John Jones,
John Harris, Simon Harris. Signed Jane Smith and
Absalom Smith   R. January 12, 1748
                                                Page 147

Ballard, Peter. Estate appraised by Samuel Whitfield,
Robert King, Nicholas Parker, Joseph Weston. Signed,
Edward Ballard. Ordered, August 12, 1748
R. January 12, 1748   Page 148

Powell, John: Leg.- son Joshua; son John; son William;
son Joseph; daughter Patience Norsworthy; daughter Ann
Pierce; daughter Elizabeth Johnson; wife Sarah. Exs.,
wife and John Darden
D. September 3, 1748   R. January 12, 1748
Wit. John Darden, William Watkins, William Watkins, Jr.
                                                Page 149

Webb, Richard: Of Newport Parish. Leg.- wife Mary;

to my children, who now live with me; refers to daughter
Martha. Exs., wife and Joseph Webb
    D. February 6, 1745/46   R. February 9, 1748
    Wit. John Carey, William Glover, Samuel Webb
    Will presented by Mary Pollard, late widow and relict
    of the decedent   Page 152

Bidgood, William. Estate appraised by John Smith,
John Chapman, Charles Chapman. Signed, Nicholas Miller
    R. February 9, 1748   Page 153

Pitt, Henry. Estate appraised by Charles Fulgham,
Thomas Whitfield, Sr., Robert King, Samuel Whitfield.
Signed, Henry Pitt   R. February 9, 1748
                                     Page 156

Powell, John. Estate appraised by William Watkins,
William Spivey, Thomas English. Signed, John Darden
    R. March 9, 1748   Page 158

Garner, James. Estate appraised by Theophilus
Joyner, John Garner, John Chesnutt. Signed, Sarah
Garner   R. March 9, 1748   Page 159 -

Deshey, Mary: Leg.- cousin James Wrenn; James Wrenn
to pay a bequest to the two daughters of Ann Bracy, the
wife of Francis Bracy; also to pay John, Joseph and
William Wrenn, Mary and Elizabeth Brantley and Martha
Bidgood's children; cousins, James and Joseph Jordan.
Exs., cousins, James and Joseph Jordan
    D. October 20, 1748   R. March 9, 1748
    Wit. Thomas Smith, William Glover, John Chesnutt
                                  Page 162

Joyner, John: Of Nottoway Parish. Leg.- son
Solomon; daughter Elizabeth Lott (?); daughter Martha
Clark; daughter Esther Beal. Ex., son Absalom
    D. September 2, 1748   R. March 9, 1748
    Wit. Chaplain Williams, Henry Crafford, William
          Grizard   Page 163

Pitt, John: Leg.- son John; son Edmond; daughter
Elizabeth; daughter Mary; daughter Lidia; son Joseph
Exs., brother Joseph Pitt and brother-in-law Thomas
Godwin

D. November 17, 1748   R. March 9, 1748
Wit. Charles Fulgham, Joseph Bridger, Jr., John
     House   Page 164

Adams, David. Estate appraised by Harmon Read, William
Lee, William Wommack. Signed, Robert Adams
Ordered May 19, 1748   Page 166

Pitt, Thomas. Estate appraised by Anthony Fulgham,
Giles Driver, Christopher Haines   R. March 9, 1748
                                             Page 167

Brock, Robert. Estate appraised by Thomas Davis,
Samuel Blow, Nathaniel Davis. Signed, Lucy Brock
Ordered, February 9, 1748   R. March 9, 1748
                                           , Page 168

Smith, Hannah. Estate appraised by Samuel Whitfield,
Robert King, Joseph Copeland. Signed, Nicholas Parker
Ordered, January 12, 1748   R. April 18, 1749
                                             Page 169

Westbrook, James: Leg.- wife Elizabeth; son Benjamin;
son Jesse; brother Thomas Westbrook; friend Joshua Claud;
brother-in-law, William Vaughan; to Helica, daughter of
Thomas Westbrook; son Dempsey. Exs., brother John
Westbrook and brother-in-law William Vaughan
D. February 24, 1748/49   R. April 13, 1749
Wit. James Ramsey, Thomas Westbrook, Helica Westbrook
                                             Page 170

Whitehead, Arthur, Jr.: Of Nottoway Parish. Leg.-
son Arthur, land on Blunt's Swamp; brother Lewis
Whitehead; son Lazarus; son William; son Jesse; daughter
Edith; daughter Seallah; wife Patience. Exs., wife and
brother Lewis Whitehead
D. January 6, 1748   R. April 13, 1749
Wit. Arthur Whitehead, Sr., Joseph Cobb, Jr.,
     Mary Whitehead   Page 172

Deshey, John. Estate appraised by Edward Goodrich,
George Wilson, William Harrison, John Hodges. Signed,
John Wrenn. Ordered, June 9, 1748
R. April 13, 1749   Page 174

Rochester, William: Of Nottoway Parish. Leg.- son
Joshua; daughter Ann; daughter Charity; wife Catherine.
Ex., Nicholas Gurley
D. January 1, 1748/49   R. April 13, 1749
Wit. George Gurley, James Carter, George Gurley, Jr.
Page 176

Pope, Joseph: Leg.- son Hardy; son John; son Joseph;
son Samuel; wife Sarah and my five children. Exs.,
wife and Henry Crafford
D. January 27, 1748/49   R. April 13, 1749
Wit. John Bowen, William Harris, Joseph Braches (?),
Henry Pope   Page 177

Wrenn, James. Estate appraised by Edward Goodrich,
George Wilson, William Harrison. Signed, John Wrenn.
Ordered, March 9, 1748   R. April 13, 1749
Page 178

House, James. Estate appraised by Joseph Bridger,
Robert Bridger, James Godwin. Ordered, April 13, 1749
R. May 11, 1749   Page 178

Smith, Martha. Estate appraised by Joseph Copeland,
Samuel Whitfield, Robert King. Signed, Joseph Smith
Ordered, January 12, 1748   R. May 11, 1749
Page 179

Hawkins, Mary. Estate appraised by Joseph Weston,
Thomas Whitfield, Robert King. Signed, William Hawkins.
Ordered, April 13, 1749   R. May 11, 1749
Page 180

Pope, Joseph. Estate appraised by Joseph Bowen,
M. Griffin, William Bulls. Signed, Henry Crafford
R. May 11, 1749   Page 182

Jones, Elizabeth. Estate appraised by Edward
Goodrich, William Harrison, John Hodges. Signed,
Nathaniel Ridley   R. May 11, 1749
Page 184

Brock, Richard: Leg.- daughter Mary; loving wife.
D. January 17, 1748/49   R. May 11, 1749
Wit. Thomas Atkinson, Benjamin Britt, Richard Willis
Page 186

Joyner, John. Estate appraised by Henry Dawson,
Joshua Dawson, James Turner. Signed, Absalom Joyner
R. June 1, 1749   Page 187

Webb, Richard. Estate appraised by John Mallory,
John Wrenn, William Glover. Ordered, February 9, 1748
R. June 1, 1749   Page 188

Harrison, John. Estate appraised by Joseph Bridger,
James Godwin, Edmond Godwin. Signed, Ann Harrison
Ordered, July 8, 1748   R. June 1, 1749
                                                   Page 189

Goodrich, John: Leg.- son Edward; son John; son
George; daughter Mary Davis; to Samuel, the son of
John Davis; daughter Ann Gray; daughter Honour; son
George, the money in the hands of William Harrison;
to wife. Exs., sons, Edward and John Goodrich.
Friends, William Harrison and Samuel Wilson, overseers.
D. February 6, 1746/47   R. June 1, 1749
Wit. George Wilson, Thomas Morgan   Page 191

Deloach, Thomas. Inventory, returned by William and
Solomon Deloach.   R. July 6, 1749   Page 193

Haines, Edward. Estate appraised by Philip Moody,
Daniel Batten, John Batten. Ordered, March 9, 1748
R. July 6, 1749   Page 194

Scott, Thomas: Of Newport Parish. Leg.- My mother,
reversion at her death to Thomas, the son of my brother
James Tooke Scott; to Ann, the daughter of James Tooke
Scott; to sister-in-law Christian Scott; to George
Norseworthy Scott, the son of my brother, James Tooke
Scott. Exs., mother Joan Scott and brother James Tooke
Scott. D. January 7, 1748   R. August 3, 1749
Wit. James Baker, William Hollowell   Page 195

Barlow, Thomas: Leg.- nephew William Carrell; wife
Martha; daughter Ann; son Jesse; daughter Mary. Exs.,
Wife and nephew William Carrell
D. December 3, 1748   R. August 3, 1749
Wit. R. Hardy, Peter Fiveash, James Piland
                                                   Page 196

Pedin, James: My body to be buried in or at the "Brick Church" of Isle of Wight County. Leg.- wife Mary, during her good behaviour; daughter Ann, which was given to her, by her aunt, Mrs. Williams; son James; daughter Mary. Extx., wife Mary, if she fails to conduct herself wisely, my children to be placed in the care of the Rev. Mr. John Reid, Minister in Newport Parish. To bother John Pedin, Merchant in Mauchtine (?)
D. April 15, 1746   R. August 3, 1749
Wit. John Applewhaite, William Hawkins
Page 198

Miller, John. Estate appraised by Benjamin Hodges, John Gibbs, John Murry.   R. August 3, 1749
Page 200

Pitt, John. Estate appraised by James, Godwin, Samuel Godwin, Charles Fulgham. Signed, Joseph Pitt
R. August 3, 1749   Page 200

Lee, John. Estate appraised by William Hodsden, George Wilson, Robert Hodges. Signed, Peter Fiveash and Henry Harrison. Ordered, January 12, 1748
R. August 3, 1749   Page 202

Deshey, Mary. Estate appraised by John Mallory, John Davis, Joseph Jones. Signed, James Jordan
R. August 3, 1749   Page 204

Fowler, William: Of the Parish of Newport. Leg.- grandson William Fowler; son Samuel; son Joseph; daughter Ann Bryant; son James; granddaughter Ann Fowler, daughter of Arthur Fowler; son Edmond; wife Rebeccah
Ex., son Arthur Fowler
D. December 31, 1748   R. August 3, 1749
Wit. John Darden, Hardy Darden, James Holland
Page 205

Fowler, William. Estate appraised by John Lawrence, William Lawrence, William Edmonds. Signed, Arthur Fowler
R. September 9, 1749   Page 206

Robinson, James. Inventory of estate, returned by Jonathan Robinson.   R. September 7, 1749   Page 208

Davis, Samuel, Gent. Estate appraised by John Goodrich, J. Day, Peter Woodward. Signed, Henry Harrison, Lawrence Smith, John Inman. Ordered, February 28, 1739
R. September 7, 1749   Page 209

Davis, Samuel. Account estate - paid legacy to Samuel Davis, to cash, being the property of Amy Jones, raised out of the stock, for the payment of a legacy to John Davis. Signed, Joseph and Amy Jones. Examined by Robert Burwell and William Hodsden.
R. September 7, 1749   Page 211

Daughtry, John: Leg.- wife Margaret; to my lawful heir. Extx., wife Margaret Daughtry
D. April 28, 1742   R. October 5, 1749
Wit. Jesse Browne, William Moore, William Lawrence
                                                       Page 213

Lucks, John. Estate appraised by Charles Portlock, Nicholas Casev. Robert Hodges. Signed, John Hodges
    Ordered, June 9, 1748   R. October 5, 1749
                                                       Page 214

Brewer, William, Sr.: Of Newport Parish. Leg.- wife Catherine; son George; daughter Mary; daughter Sarah; daughter Elizabeth; daughter Christian; son Michael; son William; son John. Exs., wife and son George Brewer
D. February 24, 1748/49   R. October 5, 1749
Wit. Robert Whitfield, Johnson Corbett, Samuel Corbett
                                                       Page 216

Gibbs, Ralph. Account estate, examined by Hugh Giles and Richard Reynolds   R. December 7, 1749
                                                       Page 217

Giles, Hugh, Sr. Estate appraised by Richard Reynolds; Joseph Norsworthy, Lemuel Godwin. Ordered, August 3, 1749. Signed, Mary Pedin
R. December 7, 1749   Page 218

Brewer, William. Estate appraised by William Lawrence, John Lawrence, William Edmonds. Signed, George Brewer
    Ordered, October 5, 1749   R. December 7, 1749
                                                       Page 220

Driver, Robert. Account estate, examined by Richard

Reynolds and Richard Jordan.   R.   December 7, 1749

Harrison, William. Account estate, examined by
Nicholas Parker and Robert King. R. December 7, 1749

Bidgood, William. Account estate. Nicholas Miller
and Edward Davis, Exs. To paid Reuben Proctor, the
balance of his uncle's estate in Bidgood's possession;
paid John Bidgood, the balance to Ann Proctor; to
Ambrose Proctor; to the orphans of Walter Morgan
R. January 4, 1749

Johnson, James. Estate appraised by Hardy Council,
John Darden, Hardy Darden. Signed, Rebecca Johnson
R. January 4, 1749

Williford, John, Jr. Account estate, signed by
Elizabeth Williford. R. January 4, 1749

Barlow, Thomas. Estate appraised by William
Harrison, Henry Harrison, George Wilson. Signed by
Martha Barlow.   R. January 4, 1749

Garner, James. Account estate, examined by Thomas
Gale, Bartholomew Lightfoot, John Marshall
R. January 4, 1749

Jordan, Mathew, Jr. Account estate, examined by
James Baker, Lawrence Baker, Jordan Thomas
R. February 1, 1749

Carrell, James. Account estate, examined by Lawrence
Baker and R. Hardy.   R. February 1, 1749

Wrenn, John. Account estate, examined by James
Baker. Signed by N. Bourden and Prudence, his wife.
R. March 1, 1749

Miller, Nicholas. Estate appraised by Joseph Hill, Charles Chapman, John Gibbs. Ordered, January 4, 1749 Signed, Alice Miller   R. March 1, 1749
Page 234

Chapman, Charles: Leg.- daughter Rachel; daughter Ann; daughter Reodia: Ex., Thomas Parker
   D. August 10, 1749   R. March 1, 1749
   Wit. Timothy Low, West Gross. Thomas Parker refused to be executor, Joseph Chapman qualified   Page 235

Carrell, Mary: Leg.- son Thomas; my children, Mary, James and Richard to live with their brother Thomas Carrell. Lawrence Baker and Richard Hardy, trustees.
   D. November 6, 1749   R. March 1, 1749
   Wit. Richard Carter, Martha Barlow, Elizabeth Gray
                                                  , Page 236

Daughtry, John. Inventory, returned by Margaret Daughtry.   R. March 1, 1749
Page 237

Jones, Thomas: Of the Parish of Newport. Leg.- son Thomas; son William; daughter Mary Inglish; daughter Ann Johnson, the estate which I have brought to my son-in-law, Abraham Johnson; daughter Catherine Griffin; daughter Sarah Johnson; daughter Martha Johnson; son Philip. Ex., son Philip Jones
   D. November 15, 1748   R. March 1, 1749
   Wit. John Darden, James Johnson, Jr., Henry Hedgepath
                                                  Page 238

Jordan, Joshua. Account estate, examined by Edmond Godwin and John Monro   R. March 1, 1749
Page 239

Thomas Gale, John Eley and James Bridger were appointed to set apart the dower of Rebecca Johnson, in the estate of her husband, James Johnson. R. March 1, 1749
Page 240

Macy, Thomas. Estate appraised by Benjamin Clements, John Brown, Henry Simmons. Ordered, April 28, 1740
   R. April 5, 1750   Page 240

Brown, Charles. Estate appraised by Charles Simmons,

William Andrews, John Brown. Signed, Richard Kirby, Jr.
Ordered, February 12, 1746   R. April 5, 1750

Page 242

Whitfield, William. Nuncupative will, proven by
Holland Copeland. That he left his whole estate to his
eldest son, Isham Whitfield   R. April 5, 1750

Page 244

Carrell, Mary. Estate appraised by James Piland,
Henry Harrison, Samuel Wilson. Signed, T. Carrell
R. April 4, 1750   Page 245

Mundell, Frances: Of Nottoway Parish. Leg.- son
John Scott; son William Scott; son John Mundell, the
negro left me by my brother. Ex., son William Scott
D. May 20, 1747   R. April 5, 1750
Wit. Charles Travers, Amos Garris, William Carrell

Page 246

Chapman, Charles. Estate appraised by Richard
Reynolds, John Godwin, Jonathan Godwin. Signed,
Joseph Chapman   R. June 7, 1750

Page 247

Gregory, Robert. Estate appraised by John Gibbs,
Edward Davis, Joseph Hill. Signed, Charles Chapman
Ordered, December 7, 1749   R. June 7, 1750

Page 248

Eley, Eley. Account estate, signed by William and
Ann Joiner. Examined by William Hodsden and R. Hardy
R. June 7, 1750   Page 249

Jones, Thomas. Estate appraised by John Darden,
Robert Eley, John Roberts. Signed, Philip Jones
R. July 5, 1750   Page 250

Wainwright, William. Estate appraised by Richard
Reynolds, Thomas Wills, Joseph Norsworthy. Signed,
Elizabeth Wainwright. Ordered, October 5, 1749
R. July 5, 1750   Page 252

Williams, William. Estate appraised by Benjamin

Beal, Needham Nolley, Samuel Mathews. Signed, John
Mariner. Ordered, June 7, 1750   R. July 5, 1750
                                             Page 252

Simmons, James. Account estate, examined by Thomas
Gale, John Eley, James Bridger. Signed, Philip Moody
R. July 5, 1750   Page 253

Applewhaite, Henry, Jr. Account estate; returned by
Philip and Mary Brantley   R. July 5, 1750
                                             Page 255

James Baker and Jordan Thomas were appointed to set a-
part the dower of Patience Jordan, the widow of Mathew
Jordan, Jr.   R. July 5, 1750
                                           , Page 255

Pitt, Henry. Account estate, examined by Edmond
Godwin, Charles Fulgham, Thomas Whitfield
R. July 5, 1750   Page 256

Whitfield, William. Estate appraised by George
Norsworthy, Nicholas Parker, Robert King
R. July 5, 1750   .   Page 257

Westbrook, James. Account estate, examined by Joshua
Claud, Thomas Clifton, John Person, Jr. Signed by
John Westbrook and William Vaughan
R. July 5, 1750   Page 258

Weston, Joseph: Leg.- daughter Mary; daughter Tabitha;
wife Mary; daughter Ann Smith. Wife, Extx.
D. September 24, 1748   R. September 6, 1750
Wit. Charles Fulgham, Moses Wiles   Page 259

Davis, John: Leg.- son Samuel; nephew William Goodrich
Ex., John Goodrich
D. July 2, 1750   R. September 6, 1750
Wit. Edward Goodrich, John Davis, William Davis
                                             Page 260

Harding, Sarah: Leg.- son Benjamin; grandson John
Harding son of Benjamin Harding; grandson Abraham Harding,
son of James Harding; daughter Martha Jordan, the wife of

John Jordan; daughter Sarah Gray, the wife of Henry
Gray. Ex., son Solomon Harding
   D. January 6, 1747   R. September 6, 1750
Wit. Arthur Crocker, Thomas Cole, William Cofer
Page 261

Jolly, John. Estate appraised by John Smelly, Thomas
Norsworthy, Christopher Reynolds. Signed, Ann Jolly
Ordered, June 7, 1750   R. September 6, 1750
Page 262

Darden, Jacob. Estate appraised by John Baldwin,
Christopher Reynolds, John Butler. Signed, Elizabeth
Darden. Ordered, July 5, 1750 R. September 6, 1750
Page 264

Davis, William. Account estate, examined by Edmond
Godwin, Jordan Thomas. Signed, J. Simmons
   R. September 6, 1750
Page 267

Chesnutt, John. Estate appraised by Christopher
Reynolds, John Powell, Bartholomew Lightfoot. Signed,
Martha Chesnutt. Ordered, July 5, 1750
   R. September 6 1750
Page 268

Dickinson, Jacob: Leg.- wife Mary; son Christopher;
daughter Chasity; daughter Celia, provision for unborn
child. D. February 7, 1749/50 R. September 6, 1750
   Wit. Thomas Willis, John Godwin, Robert Bevan
Page 269

Dering, Nicholas. Account estate, - to James Samson's
orphans, their legacies, paid to William Miller; to Ann
Diamond for schooling my sister; legacies paid to son
James, son Miles and daughter Susanna. Signed James
Dering. Examined by James Baker and Lawrence Baker
   R. October 4, 1750
Page 272

William Hodsden, Robert Tynes and William Hollowell
appointed to set aside the dower of Alice Miller, widow
of Nicholas Miller.   R. October 4, 1750
Page 274

John Eley, James Bridger and John Marshall, appointed
to set aside the dower of Ann Simmons, the widow of
James Simmons   R. October 4, 1750   Page 274

Denson, William: Leg.- daughter Elizabeth Eley; son
Edmond; son William, negroes, whom I leave in the care
of my friend William Eley; granddaughter Amy Eley; friend
Hannah Best; son John; grandson Benjamin Eley; wife Ann.
Friend Exum Scott to have the care of my son William.
Wife Ann, Extx.
   D. July 2, 1750   R. October 4, 1750
   Wit. William Eley, James Arthur, Miles Wills
                                         Page 274

Day, Daniel: Leg.- wife Mary. Exs., wife and George
Taylor. D. May 19, 1750   R. November 1, 1750
   Wit. Robert Eley, George Taylor, Edward Taylor,
      Joseph Taylor   Page 275

Eley, Robert, Sr.: Leg.- son Gale, the land I bought
of Mary Parker; son Robert; wife Allis; daughter Amy;
daughter Martha; daughter Rebecca; daughter Allis
Darden. Exs., wife and son Gale Eley
   D. March 29, 1750   R. November 1, 1750
   Wit. John Roberts, Thomas Roberts, Henry Saunders
                                     Page 276

Weston, Joseph. Inventory, presented by Mary Weston
R. November 1, 1750   Page 278

Goodwin, Sarah: Leg.- loving aunt Mary Dickinson;
to Chastity Dickinson; to Sally Dickinson. Ex., aunt
Mary Dickinson
   D. August 23, 1750   R. November 1, 1750
   Wit. Richard Reynolds, John Godwin, Wilkinson Parker
                                     Page 279

Williams, Richard. Estate appraised by Joseph Cobb,
Thomas Cranshaw, Nathan Vasser. R. December 6, 1750
   Account estate of Richard Williams, which is divided
into eight parts, "due to each child", examined by
J. Baker and Isaac Fleming   R. December 6, 1750
                                     Page 281

Gay, Thomas: Leg.- son Thomas; son John; son Charles;
daughter Mary; son William; son Edmond; son Jonathan.
The "Monthly Meeting" to settle my children.
Ex., William Eley
   D. October 26, 1750   R. December 6, 1750
   Wit. John Williams, Richard Pope, Mary Coggan
                                     Page 282

Davis, John. Estate appraised by John Mallory,
William Glover, George Wilson. Signed, John Goodrich
Ordered, September 6, 1750   R. December 6, 1750
Page 284

Deloach, Thomas. Estate appraised by Francis Ward,
Benjamin Ward, Thomas Copher. Ordered, September 6, 1750
   R. February 7, 1750   Account estate, to searching
for the said Thomas Deloach in Blackwater Swamp. To paid
John Bryant for diving for him. Signed, John Deloach
   R. February 7, 1750   Page 285

Whitehead, Arthur, Jr. Estate appraised by Joseph
Cobb, Jr., John Pope, Thomas Crenshaw. Signed by Lewis
Whitehead, Patience Jones, T. Jones. Estate account
in North Carolina, signed Lewis Whitehead, Patience
Jones and Thomas Jones.   R. February 7, 1750
Page 288

Denson, William. Estate appraised by Henry Saunders,
Josiah Jordan, James Hough. Signed, Ann Denson
   R. February 7, 1750   Page 291

Westray, Elizabeth: Widow. Leg.- son William the
plantation devised to me by the will of John Mackmial;
daughter Eunice; daughter Martha; son Robert; son
Benjamin, to be placed with John Westray, Jr.; son
William with Thomas Harris; daughter Eunice with my
mother, Elizabeth Nelms; daughter Martha, with my sister
Mary Corbett. Ex., John Westray, Jr.
   D. November 28, 1750   R. February 7, 1750
   Wit. William Eley, John Westray, Patience Westray
Page 293

Pope, William. Estate appraised by Ratclif Boon, Jr.,
John Wheeler, William Segrave. Signed, John Pope
Ordered, December 6, 1750   R. February 7, 1750
Page 295

Lawrence, Margaret: Leg.- son John; son William;
granddaughter Penelope Lawrence; daughter Priscilla;
daughter Elizabeth; grandson Robert Carr; daughter
Margaret Daughtry; daughter Sarah Moore; son William.
Ex., son John Lawrence
   D. September 26, 1746   R. February 7, 1750
   Wit. William Driver, John Loyd, Giles Smelly.
Page 296

Crocker, Arthur. Estate appraised by Peter Woodward, Thomas Copher, William Copher. Ordered, December 6, 1750
R. February 7, 1750   Page 298

Godwin, James: Leg.- son Joseph; son James; daughter Martha. Exs., wife Elizabeth and brother Samuel Godwin
D. October 1, 1750   R. February 7, 1750
Wit. Thomas Willis, James Pitt   Page 300

Dickinson, Jacob. Estate appraised by Jonathan Godwin, John Godwin, Joseph Norsworthy. Signed, Mary Dickinson
R. February 7, 1750   Page 301

Chapman, Charles. Account estate, examined by Richard Reynolds and Joseph Norsworthy. Signed, Joseph Chapman
R. February 7, 1750   , Page 302

Whiehead, Arthur, Jr. Account estate, examined by Thomas Jarrell, Jesse Browne and A. Jones
R. March 7, 1750   Page 303

Edwards, John. Estate appraised by Arthur Whitehead, Chaplain Williams, John Edwards. Signed, John Edwards and Henry Harris. Inventory of estate in North Carolina filed. Ordered, August 11, 1748   R. March 7, 1750
                                                       Page 304

Croom, Edward. Estate appraised by Thomas Norsworthy, John Smelly, John Newman. Signed, Patience Croom
Ordered, January 7, 1750   R. March 7, 1750
                                                       Page 306

Crocker, Katherine. Estate appraised by Peter Woodward, Thomas Copher, Francis Ward. Signed Anthony Crocker. Ordered, February 7, 1750   R. March 7, 1750
                                                       Page 308

Eley, Robert. Estate appraised by James Hough, Robert Cogan, John Cogan. Signed, Alice Eley
R. March 7, 1750   Page 309

Miller, Alice: Leg.- son George; daughter Martha; son Thomas. Ex.; son George Miller
D. January 16, 1750   R. March 7, 1750
Wit. William Hollowell, James Tooke Scott, John Gibbs
                                                       Page 312

Day, Daniel. Estate appraised by Abraham Johnson,
James Johnson, John Roberts. Signed, Mary Day and
George Taylor   R. March 7, 1750   Page 313

Daniel, William: Leg.- son Peter; son William; son
John; daughter Mary Rite; daughter Sarah Barrett;
daughter Deberry Lucas; daughter Ann; daughter Garland;
son James. Wife, Deborah, Extx.
  D. September 10, 1738   R. March 7, 1750
Wit. John Darden, Mary Darden   Page 315

Inglish, John: Leg.- daughter Ann; daughter Mary;
daughter Charity. Wife Mary, Extx.
  D. November 13, 1750   R. March 7, 1750
Wit. William Watkins, Jr., Jesse Watkins, Jacob
     Spivey   Page 318

Council, Hardy: Of Newport Parish. Leg.- wife
Susannah; daughter Mary; daughter Ann; daughter Martha;
daughter Lucy; son Hardy, 100 acres on which John
Sherard, Jr., now lives; son Charles; son Michael, land
in North Carolina; daughter Susannah; daughter Christian;
son Joshua. Exs., wife Susannah and son Charles Council
  D. February 22, 1748/49   R. March 7, 1750
Wit. Jacob Dickinson, Robert Johnson, Hardy Lawrence
                                             Page 319

Jones, Mathew. Settlement of estate; - to James
Ridley, his part of his father's estate; to Dr. Browne,
for his wife's share; to Mr. Portlock for his wife's
share; to Francis Jones for his wife's share
  R. March 7, 1750   Page 322

Jarrell, Thomas. Inventory presented by Thomas
Jarrell.   R. April 4, 1751   Page 322

Brown, Charles. Account estate, examined by Benjamin
Simmons and Charles Simmons. Signed, Richard Kirby, Jr.
  R. April 4, 1751   Page 323

Gay, Thomas. Estate appraised by Robert Coggan,
John Coggan, Richard Sellaway. Signed, William Eley
  R. April 4, 1751   Page 324

Wills, Thomas: Of Newport Parish. Leg.- son Miles;
son John; son Josiah; wife Martha. Extx., wife
   D. October 18, 1750   R. April 4, 1751
   Wit. John Wills, Miles Milner, Mary Milner

Page 326

Dickinson, Jacob. Account estate, examined by
Thomas Gale, Charles Fulgham, and Richard Reynolds
   R. April 4, 1751   Page 328

Inglish, John. Estate appraised by William Watkins,
Hardy Darden, Jesse Watkins. Signed, Mary Inglish
   R. April 4, 1751   Page 330

Miller, Alice. Estate appraised by William Harrison,
Benjamin Hodges, John Gibbs. Signed, George Miller
   R. April 4, 1751   Page 332

Minard, George. Account estate, examined by Charles
Fulgham. Signed, Ann Minard   R. April 4, 1751
                                               Page 333

Rew, John Anthony. Account estate, examined by
John Rodway, Charles Fulgham. Signed William Brown
   R. May 2, 1751   Page 335

Shelley, Thomas: Leg.- wife Jane; daughter Elizabeth;
son James; daughter Martha; daughter Ann; son Thomas, the
plantation on which James Briggs formerly lived. Exs.,
wife and son James Shelley
   D. March 8, 1750   R. May 2, 1751
   Wit. Lawrence Baker, Joseph Figg, Katherine Baker,
        Ann Baker   Page 336

Gay, Thomas. Account estate, examined by Thomas Gale
and John Marshall. Signed, William Eley   R. May 2, 1751
                                               Page 337

Richards, Robert. Account estate, examined by Richard
Reynolds and John Applewhaite   R. May 2, 1751
                                               Page 339

Miller, George: Leg.- brother Thomas; sister Martha

Ex., brother Thomas Miller
 D. April 14, 1751   R. May 2, 1751
 Wit. William Brown, Reuben Proctor, Mary Pate

Page 340

Holleman, John: Leg.- son Jesse; son Jeddia; son
Christopher; daughter Mary. Wife Elizabeth Extx.
 D. October 12, 1750   R. June 6, 1751
 Wit. William Gwaltney, Thomas Gwaltney

Page 341

Shelley, Thomas. Estate appraised by James Dering,
Arthur Davis, Thomas Carrell. R. June 6, 1751

Page 342

Uzzell, Thomas: Of Newport Parish. Leg.- daughter
Martha; son James; son Thomas; wife Sarah; daughter
Elizabeth Newman; daughter Mary Lowry. Exs., wife
and sons, Thomas and James Uzzell
 D. April 14, 1748   R. June 6, 1751
 Wit. John Smelly, Theophilus Joiner, Bartholomew
       Lightfoot   Page 345

Lane, William. Estate appraised by Samson West,
George Smith, George Whitley. R. June 6, 1751

Page 346

Davis, Samuel: Leg.- my mother Amey Jones, my planta-
tion at Meherrin; sister Mary White; cousin Ann White;
cousin Mary White; sister Sarah; sister Amey; sister
Marcella. Ex., my father-in-law
 D. November 28, 1750   R. June 6, 1751
 Wit. John Davis, Sarah Davis, Amy Davis

Page 348

Williams, Mathew. Estate appraised by Thomas
Parker, Joseph Copeland, Giles Driver. Signed, Nicholas
Parker. Ordered, March 7, 1750   R. June 6, 1751

Page 349

King, Robert. Estate appraised by Nicholas Parker,
Samuel Whitfield, Thomas Parker. Signed, Elizabeth King
Ordered, April 4, 1751   R. June 6, 1751

Page 350

Holleman, John. Estate appraised by Peter Woodward,
Thomas Copher, Thomas Cole. Signed, Elizabeth Holleman
 R. August 1, 1751   Page 352

Uzzell, Thomas. Estate appraised by Bartholomew Lightfoot, Christopher Reynolds, John Joyner. Signed, James Uzzell and Thomas Uzzell   R. August 1, 1751
Page 354

Cook, Reuben: Leg.- son John; son Benjamin; son Joel; son Nathan; daughter Ann Whitehead; daughter Hannah; daughter Thamer; wife Hannah; son William. Ex., son Joel Cook
  D. November 19, 1750   R. August 1, 1751
  Wit. Lawrence Lancaster, Thomas Betts   Page 355

Goodwin, Lemuel. Estate appraised by Nicholas Parker, Joseph Copeland, Anthony Fulgham, Charles Fulgham. Signed, Mary Goodwin.
Ordered, April 4, 1751   R. August 1, 1751
, Page 357

Westray, Elizabeth. Estate appraised by Arthur Turner, Daniel Batten, John Batten. Signed, John Westray, Jr.
  R. September 5, 1751   Page 359

Summerell, John. Account estate, examined by William Hodsden, John Applewhaite, Charles Fulgham. Signed, Catherine Giles, administrator of Hugh Giles, who was the executor of the said John Summerell
  R. September 5, 1751   Page 361

Day, Thomas: Leg.- wife Mary; son Thomas; son John Exs., wife, Mr. William Hodsden and Major Benjamin Cocke
  D. July 24, 1750   R. October 3, 1752
  Wit. William Harrison, James Wheadon   Page 363

Gross, Francis: Of Newport Parish. Leg.- daughter Patience; son Joshua; daughter Hannah; son Thomas Davis Gross; son Jonathan; daughter Sarah Bevan, the wife of Robert Bevan. Exs., son Joshua Gross and daughter Patience Gross
  D. September 18, 1750   R. October 3, 1751
  Wit. Hugh Giles, West Gross   Page 365

Wills, Thomas. Estate appraised by Arthur Applewhaite, Richard Reynolds, John Smelly. Signed, Martha Wills
  R. October 3, 1751   Page 367

West, Richard. Estate appraised by Richard Reynolds,

John Clark, Augustine King. Signed, Robert West
Ordered, September 5, 1751   R. October 3, 1751
Page 369

Miller, Nicholas. Account estate, examined by James
Tooke Scott, William Hodsden and William Hollowell
R. October 3, 1751   Page 371

Rochester, William. Estate appraised by Micajah
Edwards, Henry Thomas, Arthur Williams. Signed,
Nicholas Gurley   R. October 3, 1751
Page 372

Bridger, Joseph: Leg.- grandson John Davis Bridger;
son James; brother Robert Bridger; son William; grand-
daughter Mary, the daughter of my son Joseph Bridger;
granddaughter Keziah Bridger; granddaughter Sarah
Bridger; granddaughter Ann Bridger; granddaughter
Hester Bridger; daughter Martha Jones; daughter
Margaret Goodrich; daughter Mary; daughter Agatha;
daughter Katherine. Exs., sons-in-law, John Goodrich
and Joseph Jones
D. September 5, 1751   R. October 4, 1751 .
Wit. George Reynolds, Hester Whitfield, Ann Giles
Page 373

Mackoy, Caleb. Estate appraised by Richard Reynolds,
Samson West, John Clark. Signed, Martha Mc Koy
Ordered, August 1, 1751   R. October 4, 1751
Page 374

Bullock, Joseph: Leg.- wife Penelope; son Willis;
son Thomas. Wife, Extx.
D. March 10, 1750/51   R. November 7, 1751
Wit. William Howell, John Newman   Page 377

Cook, Reuben. Estate appraised by Peter Woodward,
Thomas Coffer, Anthony Crocker   R. November 7, 1751
Page 377

Gross, Francis. Estate appraised by Richard Reynolds,
Jonathan Godwin, John Godwin. Signed, Joshua Gross
R. November 7, 1751   Page 380

Giles, Captain Hugh. Estate appraised by Jonathan
Godwin, John Godwin, Samson West. Signed by Katherine
Giles. Ordered, April 4, 1751   R. November 7, 1751
Page 381

Haines, Edward. Account estate, - to cash received in Gloucester County. Signed, Sarah Haines   Page 383

Whitley, Thomas. Estate appraised by John Clark, John Goodrich, Joseph Norsworthy. Ordered, April 4, 1751
    R. November 7, 1751   Page 383

Gray, Aaron. Estate appraised by Nicholas Parker, Joseph Hawkins, Henry King. Signed, Sarah Gray
    R. November 7, 1751   Page 384

Wombwell, Joseph. Account estate, examined by R. Kello, Samuel Blow, Etel'd Taylor
    R. November 7, 1751   Page 387

Miller, George. Estate appraised by Benjamin Hodges, John Gibbs, Charles Chapman
    R. November 7, 1751   Page 388

Carrell, Mary. Account estate, examined by Richard Hardy and Henry Harrison. Among items, the amount of Mr. James Carrell's personal estate. Signed, Thomas Carrell
    R. December 4, 1751   Page 389

Bullock, Joseph. Estate appraised by William Bullock, Benjamin Beal, Thomas Pledger. Signed Penelope Bullock
    R. December 5, 1751   Page 390

Allen, Joseph. Estate appraised by Benjamin Crocker, Henry Vaughan, John Jones. Signed Mary Booth, late Allen and William Bynum, who was security for due administration on the estate. Account estate, among items, - to James Allen, to Thomas Tabour, to Judy Tabour, late Allen.
    R. December 5, 1751   Page 392

Turner, Thomas. Estate appraised by Daniel Herring, Henry Johnson, Robert Johnson. Signed, Martha Turner Ordered, September 5, 1751   R. February 6, 1752
    Page 393

Norsworthy, George: Leg.- wife Rachel; reversion of

bequest to nephew William Norsworthy, the son of my bro-
ther Tristram Norsworthy. Ex., my son-in-law Thomas
Parker.
D. October 14, 1751   R. February 6, 1752
Wit. Mary Norsworthy, Nicholas Parker
                                                    Page 397

Sellaway, John: Leg.- granddaughter Martha Sellaway;
Ex., son John Sellaway
D. December 10, 1751   R. February 6, 1752
Wit. Jesses Watkins, William Eley, Edmund Westry
                                                    Page 398

Tomlin, John, Sr.: Leg.- son John; son Joseph; my
mother. Exs., wife Martha and son James Tomlin
D. August 6, 1750   R. February 6, 1752
Wit. Daniel Herring, John Harris, Martha Tomlin
                                                    Page 399

Pedin, Mary: Of Newport Parish. Leg.- daughter
Ann; son James; daughter Mary. Friend Anthony
Holladay of Nansemond County to have the care of
my children and to be my executor
D. October 24, 1751   R. February 6, 1752
Wit. Sarah Bridger, Samson West, Ann Giles
                                                    Page 401

Powell, Thomas: Leg.- son Godfrey; wife Sarah; daugh-
ter Ann Cogan. Ex., son Godfrey Powell
D. February 28, 1750   R. February 6, 1752
Wit. John Marshall, Ann Marshall, Martha Howell
                                                    Page 402

West, Ann: Leg.- daughter Ann; son James; son
Robert. Ex., son Robert West
D. December 19, 1750   R. February 6, 1752
Wit. John Wills, Jr., Priscilla Hall
                                                    Page 403

Westray, Elizabeth. Account estate, examined by
Philip Moody, William Eley, John Marshall. Among items,
paid Patience Westray. Signed, John Westray, Jr.
R. February 16, 1752   Page 404

Applewhaite, John. Account estate, examined by
William Ponsonby and Arthur Applewhaite. To paid
Edward Cruise and Thomas Pope for schooling
R. February 6, 1752   Page 405

West, Robert: Leg.- son Richard, land adjoining
Merchant Perry; son Ralph; sister Ann West; brother
James West. Ex., brother Giles West
D. September 19, 1751   R. February 6, 1752
Wit. Joshua Hunter, Jacemy West, Sarah Gibbs
Page 405

Day, Thomas. Estate appraised by George Wilson,
William Harrison; Joseph Jones
R. February 6, 1752
Page 407

Whitley, Thomas. Account estate, examined by Richard
Reynolds and Joseph Norsworthy. R. February 6, 1752
Page 409

Powell, Thomas. Estate appraised by Benjamin Beale,
John Garner, John Burt. Signed, Godfrey Powell
R. February 6, 1752
Page 410

Sellaway, John. Estate appraised by Daniel Herring,
John Saunders; Henry Saunders
R. March 5, 1752
Page 413

West, Everett. Estate appraised by Joshua Hunter,
William Brown, Bartholomew Lightfoot
Ordered, August 1, 1751   R. March 5, 1752
Page 416

Ward, Benjamin. Estate appraised by Peter Woodward,
Thomas Coffer, Richard Jones. Signed, Sarah Ward
Ordered February 6, 1752   R. March 5, 1752
Page 417

Pledger, Thomas: Leg.- son Thomas; wife Mary; daugh-
ter Martha; daughter Ann; daughter Mourning. Exs., wife
and son Thomas Pledger
D. January 26, 1752   R. March 5, 1752
Wit. Charles Chesnutt, Thomas Norsworthy, Benjamin
     Hampton
Page 418

McKoy, Caleb. Account estate, examined by Richard
Reynolds, John Clark, Thomas Miller
R. March 5, 1752
Page 419

Smith, Thomas: Leg.- wife Elizabeth; son Thomas; daughter Sarah; son Arthur, land including that on which John

Summerell and William Wainwright formerly lived. Exs.,
wife and brother Arthur Smith
  D. March 31, 1748   R. March 5, 1752
  Wit. William Hodsden, John Wrenn, Jeremiah Proctor
                                      Page 422

King, Captain Robert. Estate examined by Samuel
Whitfield, Nicholas Parker
  R. March 5, 1752   Page 423

  Brassie, William: Of the Parish of Newport. Leg.-
son John; son William; son Nathan; son Jesse; wife
Susannah.
  D. December 14, 1751   R. June 4, 1752
  Wit. William Edwards, Robert Edwards   Page 424

  Pursell, Phillip: Leg.- brother-in-law John Fulgham;
to his son John Fulgham; sister Mary Fulgham; to her
daughter Patience Fulgham; sister Sarah Johnson; sister
Patience Exum; sister Elizabeth Turner; sister Ann;
sister Joan; sister Martha. Ex., brother Arthur Pursell
  D. January 3, 1752   R. June 4, 1752
  Wit. John Fulgham, Anthony Fulgham   Page 425

Rodway, John: Leg.- daughter Patience Brown; wife
Susannah; daughter Mary; daughter Susannah. Wife, Extx.
  D. March 11, 1750/51   R. June 4, 1752
  Wit. Charles Fulgham, Nathaniel Hunt, Richard House
                                    Page 427

West, Robert. Estate appraised by Augustine King,
Richard Reynolds, George Whitley. Signed, Giles West
Ordered, February 6, 1752   R. June 4, 1752
                                    Page 428

Driver, Edward. Additional account estate, examined
by Richard Reynolds and Joseph Norsworthy
  D. June 4, 1752   Page 430

Willis, Thomas: Leg.- brother Robert Willis; brother
John Willis in Scotland; wife Martha; to George, the son
of Robert Willis, attorney at law. Exs., friends, John
Woodrop, James Arthur, William Hodsden
  D. December 6, 1750   R. June 4, 1752
  Wit. Samuel Wentworth, Joseph Baker, P. Billings,
      Edward Archer   Page 430

Smith, Thomas. Estate appraised by Edward Goodrich,
William Harrison, William Glover
R. June 4, 1752   Page 432

Benn, Captain James. Estate account, examined by
Thomas Applewhaite and Charles Fulgham
R. June 4, 1752   Page 435

Daughtry, William, Sr.: Leg.- son John; with reversion
of bequest to his son Moses, if without heirs to his bro-
ther Benjamin; daughter Priscilla Hedgepeth; daughter Mary
Holland; grandson William Holland; daughter Elizabeth
Parker; grandson John Daughtry, Jr. Ex., grandson John
Daughtry, Jr.
D. December 24, 1751   R. July 2, 1752
Wit. Robert Whitfield, Charles Darden, Richard Daughtry
                                                   Page 436

Portlock, Charles: Leg.- son Nathaniel; son Charles;
loving wife
D. February 15,1750   R. July 2, 1752
Wit.   Page 439

Pierce, John: Of Newport Parish. Leg.- daughter
Elizabeth; daughter Mourning; John Segraves, the son of
Susanna Seagraves; wife Esther. Exs., friends, William
Pierce and Charles Norsworthy
D. December 19, 1751   R. July 2, 1752
Wit. James Bridger, Robert Coggan, Amy Pierce
                                                   Page 440

House, James. Estate appraised by Samuel Holladay,
Joseph Wail, William Brown.   R. July 2, 1752
                                                   Page 441

Crocker, Edward: Leg.- son William; daughter Martha
Hadley; grandson Joseph Crocker. Ex., son Thomas Crocker
D. September 24, 1751   R. July 2, 1752
Wit. Henry Mitchel, Charles Chapman   Page 442

Pope, Joseph. Account estate, examined by R. Kello
and Jordan Thomas. Among items, expense for Samuel and
John Pope. Signed, Henry Crafford
R. July 2, 1752   Page 443

Tynes, Timothy: Leg.- son Robert; grandson Timothy,
the son of Robert Tynes; wife Elizabeth. Exs., wife
and son Thomas Tynes

D. August 26, 1747   R. August 6, 1752
Wit. William Ponsonby, Joseph Hill, Robert Tynes
Page 446

Willis, Doctor Thomas. Estate appraised by Nicholas
Parker, Anthony Fulgham, Charles Fulgham. Signed,
Martha Willis
R. August 6, 1752   Page 447

Bridger, Joseph, Jr. Estate appraised by Richard
Reynolds, Thomas Miller, Joseph Norsworthy.
Ordered, June 4, 1752   R. August 6, 1752
Page 449

Exum, Mary: Leg.- son Francis; daughter Elizabeth
Smith; daughter Olive Williamson; daughter Ann William-
son. Daughter Mary Exum, Extx.
D. June 1, 1749   R. August 6, 1752
Wit. James Sampson Clark, Samuel Cornwell,
Jordan Thomas   Page 451

Gross, Francis. Account estate, examined by Richard
Reynolds, Jonathan Godwin, John Godwin
R. August 6, 1752   Page 453

Daughtry, William. Estate appraised by James Bryant,
Jacob Butler, John Lawrence
R. August 6, 1752   Page 455

Brasey, Elizabeth: Leg.- cousin Henry Wiggs; cousin
John Wiggs; cousin Mary Everitt; grandson Richard Jordan;
grandson Mathew Jordan; granddaughter Hannah Jordan;
daughter Mary Jordan; son Francis; granddaughter Mary
Outland, my estate in the hands of John Outland;
daughter Elizabeth Outland. Exs., Mathew Jordan and
Francis Bracey
D. July 23, 1751   R. August 6, 1752
Wit. Thomas Gale, Charles Chesnutt, Godfrey Powell
Page 456

Ward, Benjamin. Account estate, examined by Jordan
Thomas and Charles Fulgham. Signed, Sarah Ward
R. August 6, 1752   Page 458

WILL BOOK SIX

Webb, Richard. Account estate, examined by Edward Goodrich and William Harrison.
R. September 14, 1752   Page 1

Burt, John. Estate appraised by Benjamin Beal, John Garner, Godfrey Powell. Signed, Sarah Burt
Ordered, August 6, 1752   R. September 14, 1752
                                                        Page 2

Pope, John, Sr.: Leg.- son John; grandson Joseph, the plantation on which his father William Pope lived; daughter Mary Beal. Extx., daughter Priscilla Pope
D. March 1, 1750   R. September 14, 1752
Wit. John Eley, Ratcliff Boone, Jr., Sarah Eley
                                                        Page 3

Allen, Joseph. Account estate, examined by Joseph Gray, Thomas Jarrell, Howell Edmunds. Signed Mary Buthe. Among items, a negro in the possession of William Bynum, guardian to the heir at law
R. May 15, 1752   Page 5

Pope, John. Estate app raised by Ratcliff Boone, Jr., Henry Johnson, John Stephens. Signed, Priscilla Pope
R. October 5, 1752   Page 6

West, Richard. Account estate, examined by Thomas Gale, Charles Fulgham, Richard Reynolds
R. October 5, 1752   Page 7

Driver, Edward. Estate appraised by David Williams, James Frizzell, Nicholas Parker. Signed, Ann Driver
Ordered, June 4, 1752   R. October 5, 1752
                                                        Page 8

Bracey, Elizabeth. Estate appraised by John Baldwin, John Murfrey, John Garner. Signed, Mathew Jordan
R. October 5, 1752   Page 10

Day, Thomas. Codicil to his will presented by Benjamin Cocke, with a survey of his land. Bequest to his wife to

be used for the schooling of his sons, John and Thomas
Day   R. October 5, 1752   Page 12

Lawrence Baker, John Hodges and William Harrison, appointed to allot the dower of Margaret Wilson, late
widow of William Miller
    R. November 2, 1752   Page 13

    Pierce, John. Estate appraised by Thomas Inglish,
John Segrave and William Gay. Signed, Hester Pierce
    R. November 2, 1752   Page 14

    West, Robert. Account estate examined by Richard
Reynolds, Augustine King and John Goodrich
    R. December 7, 1752   Page 17

Frizzell, John: Leg.- wife Mary; son Ralph; daughter
Mary. Exs., wife and James Frizzell
    D. March 27, 1752   R. December 7, 1752
    Wit. Robert Lawrence, Joseph Driver   Page 18

    Wheadon, Joyce: Leg.- Susannah Hardiman; Sarah
Wheadon; son-in-law John Carrell; Thomas Hardiman; Mary
Wheadon; son-in-law Thomas Carrell; Patience Wheadon;
Martha Wheadon, daughter of James Wheadon; John Jennings
Wheadon; Martha Fiveash and John Tann (?). Ex., Thomas
Carrell
    D. October 28, 1752   R. December 8, 1752
    Wit. Peter Fiveash, John Fiveash   Page 19

    Wrenn, John: Of Newport Parish. Leg.- son John;
daughter Elizabeth; daughter Sally; daughter Martha;
wife Mary. Exs., son John Renn and his uncle Joseph
Wrenn
    D. April 14, 1752   R. December 8, 1752
    Wit. Arthur Pollard, William Glover, John Cary
                                                   Page 21

    Woodward, John. Estate appraised by Edmund Westray,
John Westray and John Selleway. Signed Daniel Herring
    Ordered December 7, 1752   R. January 4, 1753
                                                   Page 22

    Brassie, William. Estate appraised by George Hall,

Thomas Woodley and William Davis   R. January 4, 1753

Page 24

Fulgham, Jesse. Estate appraised by Henry Pitt, Samuel Garland and Anthony Fulgham. Signed, William Hodsden. Ordered June 4, 1752

R. January 4, 1753   Page 26

Moscrop, Susanna. Estate examined by William Hodsden, and Charles Fulgham. Among items, to cash paid Arthur Applewhite by decree of Isle of Wight County Court, being the moiety of a balance due to Thomas Moscrop's estate

R. January 4, 1753   Page 26

Exum, Mary. Inventory of estate, signed by William and Mary Jordan   R. January 4, 1753

Page 27

Shaw, Elizabeth: Of the Parish of Newport. Leg.- grandson Hansford Whitley; Samuel Jones; sons-in-law John Smith and Timothy Lane; Joseph Whitley and Mary his wife. Exs., Joseph Whitley and wife Mary

D. February 12, 1752   R. January 4, 1753
Wit. Richard Reynolds, Joshua Gross   Page 28

Wheadon, Joyce. Estate appraised by James Piland, John Bennett, William Cary.   R. February 1, 1753

Page 29

Williamson, Ann: Leg.- sister Sarah Exum; Moses Exum; brother John Exum; brother William Exum; brother Joseph Exum; cousin Ann Westray; cousin Susannah Atkinson; sister Sarah Exum; Eliza Exum. Exs., friend Thomas Williamson and brother John Exum

D. March 14, 1752   R. February 1, 1753
Wit. Charles Binns, Jacob Williamson, Daniel Mackey

Page 32

Joiner, Theophilus. Estate appraised in Carolina by Benjamin Williams, John Tine, Joseph Boon. Appraised in Isle of Wight by James Uzzell, Bartholomew Lightfoot, John Smelly. Signed John Joiner. Ordered March 5, 1752

R. February 1, 1753   Page 33

Croom, Edward. Estate account examined by John Marshall, John Smelly. Among items, coffin for his son Joseph Croom. Signed Patience Croom

R. February 1, 1753   Page 36

Lane, William. Account estate examined by Richard
Reynolds and Charles Fulgham
    R. February 1, 1753   Page 38

Tomlin, Joseph. Estate appraised by Daniel Herring,
Jr., John Westray, Edward Westray. Signed, Lucretia
Tomlin. Ordered, November 2, 1752
    R. March 1, 1753   Page 39

Gray, Elizabeth. Estate appraised by Richard H-----,
William -----; Henry ----- (torn)
    R. March 1, 1753   Page 40

Brock, Robert. Account estate, examined by Dolphin
Drew. Signed, Lucy Brock   R. March 1, 1753
                                       Page 41

Crocker, Katherine. Account estate, examined by
Jordan Thomas. Signed Anthony Crocker
    R. March 1, 1753   Page 43

Crocker, Arthur. Account estate, examined by Jordan
Thomas   R. March 1, 1753   Page 43

Wilson, John. Account estate, examined by Edward
Goodrich, John Mallory, George Wilson. Signed, William
Carrell   R. March 1, 1753   Page 44

Driver, Giles. Inventory of estate, presented by
John Driver   R. April 5, 1753   Page 45

Hodges, Benjamin: Leg.- daughter Hartwell Davis;
cousins, Elizabeth, Ann and John Hodges, the children
of John Hodges. Ex., Cousin John Hodges
    D. February 28, 1752   R. April 5, 1753
    Wit. James Tooke Scott, Nicholas Miller, ----- Jordan
                                       Page 47

Haines, Edward. Estate account, examined by John
Eley and John Marshall. Signed, Sarah Haines. Four
children mentioned.   R. April 5, 1753   Page 49

Portlock, Charles. Estate appraised by Edward
Goodrich, Nicholas Casey, Thomas Casey
    R. April 5, 1753   Page 50

Driver, Giles. Account estate, examined by Robert
Barry and James Arthur. To paid Giles Driver a legacy,
paid Charles Driver, a legacy; paid Joseph Driver, a
legacy. Signed, John Driver
   R. April 6, 1753   Page 52

Driver, Olive. Inventory of estate, presented by
John Driver   R. April 6, 1753   Page 54

Calcote, Thomas: Leg.- son Joseph; son James; daugh-
ter Mary Wentworth; grandson Henry Calcote; granddaughter
Ann Bevan, her mother has had her full part of my estate.
Exs., sons, James and Joseph Calcote
   D.   R. April 6, 1753
   Wit.   Page 55

Goodrich, Samuel. Estate appraised by Richard Jones,
John Jordan, Francis Wrenn. Ordered, August 6, 1752
   R. April 6, 1753   Page 56

Braddy, Olive. Estate appraised by Francis Ward,
Thomas Copher, Mason Braddy. Signed, James Sampson
Clark. Ordered, March 1, 1753   R. May 3, 1753
                                            Page 56

Gray, John. Account estate, examined by James Baker,
Lawrence Baker and Richard Hardy. Among items, expense
for maintaining six children.   R. May 3, 1753
                                        Page 58

Pedin, Mary. Estate appraised by Richard Reynolds,
Joseph Norsworthy, Sampson West. Signed, Anthony
Holladay. Account estate, examined by John Hyndman
and James Sheddon. Expense listed for three children
   R. May 3, 1753   Page 59

Driver, Olive. Account estate, examined by James
Arthur and Robert Barry. Signed, John Driver
   R. July 5, 1753   Page 63

Goodrich, Samuel. Account estate, examined by Jordan
Thomas and Richard Jones.   R. July 5, 1753
                                          Page 64

Forbes, James. Account estate, examined by Jordan
Thomas and Richard Jones   R.   July 5, 1753

Page 65

House, John. Estate appraised by John Monro, Samuel
Godwin and Joseph Wail. Signed, Jonathan Godwin
Ordered, June 7, 1753   R.   July 5, 1753

Page 66

Davis, John. Account estate, examined by John Wills,
Thomas Applewhaite, Charles Fulgham
R.   July 5, 1753   Page 67

Shelly, Thomas. Account estate, examined by
William Hodsden and Lawrence Baker
R.   August 2, 1753   ·   Page 69

Gray, Mrs. Elizabeth. Account estate, examined by
Lawrence Baker, Richard Hardy and James Baker
R.   September 6, 1753   Page 69

Smith, William: Leg.- daughter-in-law Mary Williams;
daughter Patience; son Joseph; daughter Elizabeth; wife
Elizabeth.
D. December 28, 1752   R. September 6, 1753
Wit. William Hawkins, Stephen Smith   Page 71

Williamson, Ann. Inventory presented by John Exum
R.   November , 1753   Page 71

Delk, John: Leg.- sister Elizabeth Screws; to Lucy
Owen, the daughter of Elizabeth Screws; Elizabeth Delk;
Scelton Delk; wife Mary, with reversion of bequest to
all my brothers and sisters
D. September 29, 1753   R. November 1, 1753
Wit. R. Hardy, William Burt, William Cary   Page 72

Woodward, John. Account estate, examined by John
Eley, James Bridger and John Westray. Signed, Daniel
Herring, Jr. Ordered, November 1, 1753
R.   January 3, 1754   Page 74

Frizzell, John. Estate appraised by Giles Driver,

Samuel Whitfield, Henry Pitt. Signed, James Frizzell
Ordered, December 7, 1752   R. January 3, 1754
                                              Page 75

  Turner, Thomas, Jr. Account estate, examined by
James Bridger, John Eley, Daniel Herring, Jr. Signed,
Martha Turner
  R. January 3, 1754   Page 76

  Braddy, Olive. Account estate examined by Jordan
Thomas and Dolphin Drew. Signed, James Sampson Clark
  R. January 3, 1754   Page 77

  Dickinson, Jacob. Account estate, examined by John
Applewhite and Richard Reynolds
  R. January 4, 1754   Page 78

  House, John. Account estate, examined by John Monro,
Willis Wilkinson
  R. February 7, 1754   Page 80

  Browne, John: Leg.- sister Mary. Ex., father Thomas
Browne.
  D. January 10, 1754   R. February 7, 1754
  Wit. Philip Moody, Edward Haile, William Turner
                                              Page 81

  Delk, John. Estate appraised by James Piland, R.
Hardy, Jeremiah Pierce.   R. February 7, 1754 · Page 82

  Denson, John: Leg.- son John; son-in-law Thomas
Dreaper; son Francis; son William; daughter Ann; son
James; daughter Sarah; daughter Ellenor; daughter
Patience. Ex., daughter Ann Denson
  D. July 1, 1748   R. February 7, 1754
  Wit. William Scott, Samuel Sebrell, Jr., Alse Page,
        Thomas Gay   Page 83

  Gregory, Robert. Account estate, examined by Joseph
Hill, Robert Tynes. Signed, Charles Chapman
  R. March 7, 1753   Page 85

Howell, James. Estate appraised by John Rampson,
Joseph Bullard, Benjamin Beale. Signed, Jonas Shivers
Ordered, February 7, 1754   R. March 7, 1754
Account estate, examined by William Hodsden and Joseph
Hill   R. March 7, 1754   Page 85

Gay, Thomas: Leg.- son Jethro; daughter Mary; son Thomas; son William; daughter Fereby; son John. Ex., William Gay
D. March 18, 1754   R. April 4, 1754
Wit. John Outland, Thomas Outland, Jesse Hutchins

Day, Thomas. Account estate, examined by Joseph Bridger and William Harrison. Signed, John Mallory
R. April 4, 1754

White, John: Leg.- son William; daughter Mary, whom I place in the care of Francis Wrenn and his wife Mary. Exs., John Murry and Francis Wrenn
D. December 7, 1753   R. May 2, 1754
Wit. James Baker, James Baker, Jr.

Bracy, Michael: Leg.- cousin Sarah, the daughter of brother Hugh Bracy; cousin William Bracy; to brother Hugh's daughters, Martha and Emma Bracy; rest of estate among the children of my brothers and sisters
D. January 17, 1748/49   R. May 2, 1754
Wit. Caspar Mintz, William Crocker, William Blunt

Williams, David: Leg.- daughter Rebecca Driver; wife Ann; son James; son John; son David; son Richard. Exs., wife and son James Williams
D. October 20, 1753   R. May 2, 1754
Wit. Richard Jordan, Anthony Fulgham, John Williams

Giles, Hugh. Account estate, examined by John Applewhite and Charles Fulgham
R. May 2, 1754

Bridger, Major Joseph. Account estate, examined by William Hodsden and Joseph Bridger. Signed, Joseph Jones and John Goodrich
R. May 2, 1754

Brantley, Edward. Inventory presented by Willliam Harrison   R. May 2, 1754

White, John. Estate appraised by Samuel Wilson, John Barlow, Jr., James Dering
R. June 6, 1754

Gay, Thomas. Estate appraised by Henry Saunders,
James Hough, John Coggan. Signed, William Gay
R. June 6, 1754   Page 98

Lightfoot, Henry. Estate appraised by William
Hodsden, William Rand; Arthur Applewhite. Ordered,
May 29, 1754   R. June 6, 1754
                                                   Page 99

Wills, Thomas. Account estate, examined by John
Applewhite, Giles Driver. Signed, William Richards
R. June 6. 1754   Page 101

Weatherall, Aquilla. Account estate, examined by
John Pitt, Samuel Godwin, Willis Wilkinson. Signed
Charity Weatherall
R. July 4, 1754   Page 102

Delk, John. Account estate, examined by R. Hardy,
William Carrell, Dolphin Drew
R. July 4, 1754   Page 102

Lightfoot, Henry. Estate appraised by Robert Tynes,
Arthur Applewhaite and James Calcote.
R. July 4, 1754   Page 104

Walton, Thomas. Estate appraised by John Hyndman,
Jordan Thomas, George Wilson
R. July 4, 1754   Page 105

Calcote, Joseph. Estate appraised by Arthur
Applewhite, Bartholomew Lightfoot, Benjamin -----
R. July 5, 1754   Page 105

Scott, Thomas. Aug. 3, 1749. Appraised by John Gibbs,
Joseph Hill.   R. August 1, 1754   Page 107
Account estate, examined by James Baker   Page 109

Smith, Arthur. Appraisal estate, by James Calcote,
Christopher Reynolds, Benjamin Brock.
Ordered, June 6, 1754   R. August 1, 1754
                                                   Page 108

Williams, David. Estate appraised by Henry King,

Lightfoot, Henry, Sr. Account estate, examined by John Wills and Charles Fulgham. To paid the widow, to Bartholomew Lightfoot, to Henry Lightfoot, Jr., to Thomas Lightfoot, to Mary Reynolds, to Patience Reynolds
R. October 3, 1754   Page 122

Person, Samuel: Leg.- cousin Samuel, son of Francis Person; cousin Jesse, son of Francis Person; cousin George, son of John Glover; cousin Benjamin, son of Jesse Hargrave; Samuel Pretlow; John Pretlow; cousin Joseph, son of Francis Person; cousin John, son of Henry Person; cousin Samuel, son of Lemuel Hargrave; sister Mary Glover; cousin Mary, daughter of Francis Person; cousin Henry, son of Francis Person; cousins, William, James and Jacob, the sons of Francis Person; to my cousin Absalom Hollowell's daughter; cousins, Elizabeth and Sarah Glover; cousin Sarah Person, cousin John, the son of Francis Person. Exs., Jordan Thomas and Thomas Pretlow
D. February 17, 1753   R. October 3, 1754
Wit. Joseph Mangum, Henry Mangum, Samuel Person,
     Constant Mangum   Page 123

Woodley, Thomas: Of Newport Parish. Leg.- son John; son Thomas; daughter Martha; grandson Willis Wilson; grandson John Wilson; granddaughter Mary Milner; grandson Samuel Milner. Ex., son John Woodley
D. April 24, 1754   R. October 3, 1754
Wit. Ambrose Hadley, Joseph Hill, Mathew Jones,
     Arthur Davis, Jordan Thomas   Page 125

Woodley, Henry: Of Newport Parish. Leg.- brother Thomas; brother John; sister Martha. Ex., brother John
D. April 11, 1754   R. October 4, 1754
Wit. Ambrose Hadley, Mathew Jones, John Fiveash
                                                         Page 127

Barlow, John: Leg.- son Benjamin; son John; son James; son Thomas; son William; grandson John, son of John Barlow; grandson Nathaniel Barlow. Exs., wife and son Thomas
D. November 15, 1752   R. November 7, 1754
Wit. Jordan Thomas, John Deloach, John Wombwell
                                                         Page 128

Bracy, Michael. Estate appraised by William Davis, John Morris, George Hall
R. November 7, 1754   Page 129

Bagnall, Ann: Leg.- daughter Ann; daughter Easter
Norsworthy; son Richard; son James; son Nathan; son
William; son Samuel; daughter Mary Pitt
Ex., son William Bagnall
D. March 30, 1754   R. November 7, 1754
                                        Page 130

Williams, John: Leg.- sons Joseph; daughter Ann
Pope; son-in-law Nathan Pope; son-in-law Joseph
Hollowell; son-in-law Richard Pope; son John Williams
Exs., son John and son-in-law Richard Pope
D. September 22, 1754   R. November 7, 1754
Wit. William Scott, John Pinner, Thomas Gay
                                        Page 131

Harris, Thomas. Estate appraised by Edward Haile,
William Turner, Arthur Turner. Signed, John Harris
R. January 2, 1755   Page 132

Minard, Ann. Estate account, examined by Charles
Fulgham. Signed, Joseph Minard
R. January 2, 1755   Page 134

Thomas Gale, James Hough, John Marshall, Jr. in the
presence of William Eley, William Pass and John Baldwin,
assigned the dower of Rebecca, the widow of John
Williams   R. January 2, 1755   Page 135

Williams, John. Estate appraised by Thomas Gale,
John Marshall, Jr., William Pass
R. January 2, 1755   Page 137

Barlow, John. Estate appraised by Richard Jones,
Seth Hunter, Francis Wrenn.
R. January 2, 1755   Page 140

Briggs, Edmund. Estate appraised by Richard Jones,
Thomas Copher, Francis Ward. Signed, Hannah Briggs
                                        Page 142

Smith, Arthur. Estate appraised in Surry County by
Wil. Seward, John Ruffin, William Seward, Jr.
Appraised in Isle of Wight County by Samuel Wentworth,
Bartholomew Lightfoot, Arthur Applewhaite, James Easson
R. February 6, 1755   Page 152

Howell, William: Leg.- daughter Elizabeth Rodes; son
Thomas; wife; daughter Mary; daughter Sarah; daughter
Rachel; daughter Mourning; daughter Martha; son John
    D. November 24, 1754   R. February 6, 1755
    Wit. James Jordan, Thomas Jones   Page 154

Tomlin, Joseph. Account estate, examined by John
Eley, Daniel Herring, Edmund Westray. Signed, Lucretia
Tomlin   R. February 6, 1755   Page 155

Reynolds, Rebecca: Leg.- daughter Tabitha; son
Richard; son George; son Christopher; grandson Richard,
the son of Richard Reynolds. Exs., son Richard and
daughter Tabitha Reynolds
    D. May 4, 1745   R. March 6, 1755
    Wit. Robert Tynes, Peter Green, Ann Green
                             , Page 156

Gray, Aaron. Account estate, examined by Charles
Fulgham and Richard Reynolds
    R. April 4, 1755   Page 157

Howell, William. Estate appraised by Thomas Bullock,
William Bullock, John Newman. Signed, Elizabeth Howell
    R. April 4, 1755   Page 158

Thomas, John. Account estate, examined by Joseph Gray
and Richard Kello. Among items, to my wife's distribu-
tive slaves of the balance. (Not signed)
    D. February 3, 1735   R. April 3, 1755
                             Page 160

Godwin, James. Account estate, examined by John Monro
and Willis Wilkinson. To Henry Best and Elizabeth his
wife, Extx.
    R. April 2, 1755   Page 161
    Account of his estate in the hands of Samuel Godwin,
examined by John Monro and Willis Wilkinson   Page 162

Barlow, John. Account estate, examined by James
Baker and Richard Baker. Signed, Thomas Barlow
    R. April 3, 1755   Page 163

Reynolds, Rebecca. Estate appraised by Bartholomew
Lightfoot, William McConnell, Robert Tynes   Page 164

Mac Claren, James: The son of Alexander Mac Claren of
Mc Christown in the Parish of Kilmadock, Pertheshire,
North Britain. Leg.- wife Martha, all my portion of the
Laird ship, of the aforesaid place. Extx., wife Martha
   D. September 8, 1754   R. April 4, 1755
   Wit. John Reid, James Benn   Page 167

Smith; Thomas. Account estate, examined by John
Hyndman, Andrew Mackie, James Sheddon. Signed,
Elizabeth Smith
   R. April 4, 1755   Page 168

Mathews, Richard: Leg.- daughter Mary Pope; grand-
daughter Mary Meriday; son Richard; son John; son Abraham;
granddaughter Martha Bayley; son Joshua; daughter Susannah
Hail. Exs., sons Samuel and Joseph Mathews
   D. December 21, 1754   R. May 1, 1755
   Wit. William Pope, Samuel Everitt, John Everitt
                                                  Page 173

Gay, Thomas. Estate appraised by John Eley, John
Darden, Robert Coggan
   R. February 6, 1755   Page 174

Bell, Benjamin. Estate appraised by James Dering,
Samuel Wilson, John Bennett. Ordered, April 26, 1755
   R. May 1, 1755   Page 175

Daughtry, John. Estate appraised by John Darden,
William Lawrence, John Lawrence. Signed, Elizabeth
Daughtry. Ordered, October 3, 1754
   R. June 5, 1755   Page 176

Brantley, Clay: Leg.- son John; granddaughter
Elizabeth, daughter of Thomas Brantley; grandsons,
James and Thomas, the sons of my son Thomas Brantley;
daughter-in-law Lucy Brantley; to John, Benjamin and
Thomas, the sons of Benjamin Brantley. Ex., son
Thomas Brantley
   D. March 25, 1753   R. June 5, 1755
   Wit. Roger Delk, Jacob Bruce   Page 178

Carrell, Thomas. Estate appraised by Edward Goodrich,
John Miller, John Hodges. Ordered, June 4, 1752
   R. June 5, 1755   Page 180

Walker, John. Estate appraised by James Easton,
William Rand; William Hodsden. Ordered, May 1, 1755
   R. June 5, 1755   Page 182

Mathews, Richard. Estate appraised by Benjamin Beal,
Jonas Shivers, John Garner. Signed, Samuel and Joseph
Mathews.   R. July 3, 1755   Page 183

Wheadon, Joice. Account estate, examined by Richard
Hardy and Dolphin Drew. To a legacy paid to James
Wheadon for John Jennings Wheadon; to Peter Fiveash for
Martha Fiveash, to John Carrell for Mary his wife, to
John Carrell; to Thomas Hardyman
   R. July 3, 1755   Page 184

Holleman, Susannah: Leg.- brother James Holleman;
sister Mary; sister Sarah; sister Rachel; to Susanna
Holleman; to Deudatus Boykib; to Jesse, the son of John
Holleman; to Jeddia and Christopher the sons of John
Holleman; Mary the daughter of John Holleman; Susanna
Vasser; to brother John Holleman's children and Joseph,
John, Elijah, Susanna and Mary, the childrem of brother
Joseph Vasser. Ex., brother Joseph Vasser
   D. June 3, 1755   R. July 3, 1755
   Wit. William Crocker, Joseph Crocker, Thomas Gwaltney
                                          Page 186

How, Benjamin. Estate appraised by William Bidgood,
Edward Dews, William Carrell
Ordered, December 5, 1754   R. August 7, 1755
                                      Page 188

Person, Samuel. Estate appraised by Samuel Jones,
Joseph Mangum, Richard Jones
   R. September 4, 1755   Page 190

Garland, Samuel. Estate appraised by Nicholas Parker,
Thomas Parker, Henry King. Signed, Ann Garland
Ordered, August 7, 1755   R. September 4, 1755
                                      Page 195

How, Benjamin. Account estate examined by Edward
Goodrich and John Mallory
   R. October 2, 1758   Page 196

 Charles Fulgham and Richard Reynolds, appointed to

assign the dower of Sarah, the widow of Aaron Gray;
paid to Bignall Tuel as dower in the right of his
wife, Sarah, the widow of Aaron Gray
 R. October 2, 1758   Page 197

Sanders, Solomon. Account estate, examined by
Charles Fulgham and Richard Reynolds
 R. November 7, 1755   Page 204

Westray, John: Leg.- son John; son Edmund; son
Benjamin; daughter Martha; daughter Mary; wife Ann;
daughter Ann Pierce. Exs., sons, John and Edmund
 D. December 23, 1755   R. January , 1756
                                                Page 205

Goodwin, Samuel. Account estate, examined by Jesse
Browne, William Haynes and James Jordan Scott. Paid,
their share of estate: - Thomas, William, Lemuel and
Joshua Goodwin, paid to Albridgton Jones the share of
Jacob Dickinson
 R. January 1, 1755   Page 207

Murry, Sarah. Estate appraised by John Hodges,
George Wilson, Edward Goodrich and William Harrison
 R. January 1, 1756   Page 208

Driver, Robert. Estate appraised by Richard Reynolds,
George Whitley, Giles West.
Ordered, December 4, 1755   R. February 5, 1756
                                                Page 209

Sanders, Solomon. Additional estate, appraised by
Richard Reynolds, Jonathan Godwin, George Whitley
Signed, Thomas Lile   R. February 5, 1756
                                                Page 211

Deloach, Mary. Estate appraised by Francis Ward,
John Stallings, Thomas Copher. Signed, Michael Deloach
Ordered, January 1, 1756   R. March 4, 1756
                                                Page 212

Hardy, Richard: Leg.- son Richard; daughter Sarah;
wife Mary. Exs., wife and son Richard Hardy
 D. December 6, 1755   R. March 4, 1756
Wit. Hugh Vance, James Piland, Patience Gray
                                                Page 213

Calcote, Joseph. Account estate examined by
Bartholomew Lightfoot and William Rand. Paid the
widow and two orphans
R. March 4, 1756   Page 214

Piland, James. Estate appraised by Peter Fiveash,
John Bennett, John Carrell. Signed, Elizabeth Piland
R. June 3, 1756   Page 216

Hardy, Richard. Estate appraised by Peter Fiveash,
Jeremiah Pierce, John Bennett. Signed, Mary Hardy
R. June 3, 1756   Page 218

Walton, Thomas. Account estate, signed by William
Hodsden. By balance in the hands of Jesse Browne and
Albridgeton Jones, administrators of the estate, of
Charles Portlock, who was the administrator of Thomas
Walton. Paid the widow her share and the heir-at-law
R. June 3, 1756   Page 221

Williams, Joseph: Leg.- son John; daughter Rebecca;
wife Mary. Exs.; wife and Jethro Gale
D. January 26, 1756   R. June 3, 1756
Wit. Thomas Gale, John Richards, John Gay
                                                   Page 222

Wheadon, Joyce. Account estate, examined by Peter
Fiveash and Richard Hardy. Signed, Thomas Carrell
R. June 3, 1756   Page 224

Brantley, James. Estate appraised by Francis Exum,
Simon Turner, Thomas Clark. Signed, Ruth Brantley
Ordered, April 1, 1742   R. July 1, 1756
                                                   Page 224

Vance, Hugh: Leg.- wife Lydia; son James; Charles
Portlock; Nathaniel Portlock. Power of attorney given
Captain Samuel Wentworth to recover a negro in Jamaica
Exs., wife and friend James easson
D. April 2, 1756   R. July 1, 1756
Wit. William Hodsden, Nicholas Casey   Page 226

Haile, Edward: Of Newport Parish. Leg.- son William

son Thomas; wife Elizabeth; daughter Hannah; daughter
Mary; daughter Sarah; son John; son Edward
Ex., son Edward Haile
    D. May 29, 1755   R. August 5, 1756
    Wit. Benjamin Pynes, William Pynes, Jane Pynes,
        Richard Johnson   Page 227

Westray, John. Estate appraised by Robert Johnson,
Arthur Turner, Daniel Batten
    R. August 5, 1756   Page 229

Benn, Captain James. Additional account estate, examined by John Wills and Charles Fulgham
    R. August 5, 1756   Page 231

Scott, Joannah: Leg.- granddaughter Ann Scott; to
Ann Coffield; to Sarah Coffield; to Christian Coffiled;
to Courtney Coffiled; to George Norsworthy Scott; son
James Tooke Scott
    D. July 17, 1756   R. September 2, 1756
    Wit. Edward Goodson, Mary Harris   Page 232

Tomlin, Mathew: Leg.- son Mathew; son Nathan; son
Robert; daughter Martha. Ex., son Robert Tomlin
    D. December 1, 1751   R. September 2, 1756
    Wit. James Bridger, Daniel Herring, Edmund Fulgham
                                  Page 233

Lee, John. Account estate, examined by Dolphin
Drew and Richard Hardy
    R. September 2, 1756   Page 234

Smith, Arthur. Account estate, examined by John
Hyndman, James Easson, James Sheddon. Signed,
Elizabeth Smith.
    R. September 2, 1756   Page 235

Smith, Thomas. Additional account with the estate
of Arthur Smith. Signed Elizabeth Smith. Examined
by James Easson, James Sheddon and John Hyndman
    R. September 2, 1756   Page 241

Cary, William. Estate appraised by John Welch,
John Carrell, Richard Hardy. Signed, William Cary
    R. November 4, 1756   Page 243

Brantley, James. Account estate, examined by H. Edmonds, John Person and David Edmonds. Among items, to Lewis Brantley, judgement recovered by Francis Myrick against them as surviving executors of Edward Brantley, decd.   R. December 2, 1756   Page 244

Lawrence, Jeremiah: Leg.- to George and Charles, the sons of my brother Robert Lawrence, land in Southampton County; to Sarah Lawrence, if she pays a bequest to her brothers, Hardy, Robert, George and Charles Lawrence; to Charles, the son of Jacob Darden; to brother Samuel; to sister Ann Joiner and her husband, William Joiner and her children; brother John; to Samuel, the son of brother John Lawrence. Ex., brother John Lawrence
     D. November 30, 1755   R. December 2, 1756
     Wit. Josiah Jordan, Joseph Scott, Joseph Meredith
                                        Page 246

Godwin, Joshua. Account estate, examined by Joseph Bridger and Dolphin Drew. Estate paid to William Godwin; to Jacob Dickinson in right of his wife, one of the sister of Lemuel Godwin and Thomas Godwin
     D. April 27, 1743   R. December 2, 1756
                                        Page 247

White, John. Account estate examined by Richard Baker and Dolphin Drew. Signed, Francis Wrenn and John Murry.   R. December 6, 1756   Page 249

Baker, James: Leg.- to Henry, the son of my brother Henry Baker, decd., of North Carolina; to my kinswoman, Mary, the wife of James Calcote; to John Glover, the son of William Glover; to Katherine, Richard, Ann and James Baker, the children of my brother Lawrence Baker. Exs., brother Lawrence and Richard Baker
     D. September 14, 1754   R. December 2, 1756
     Wit. R. Kello, William Goodrich, William Marlow
                                        Page 250

Garland, Samuel. Estate appraised by Thomas Parker, Nicholas Parker, Henry King. Ordered, August 7, 1755 Signed, Ann Garland   R. September 4, 1755
                                        Page 251

Goodwin, Lemuel. Account estate, examined by John Applewhaite and Richard Reynolds
     R. January 6, 1757   Page 252

Haile, Edward. Estate appraised by William Jordan,
Anthony Crocker; Andrew Sikes
R. January 6, 1757   Page 253

Scott, Joanna. Estate appraised by Thomas Whitfield,
John Gibbs, John Murry, Nicholas Miller
R. February 3, 1757   Page 256

Best, Thomas. Estate appraised by Richard Bagnall,
Samuel Whitfield; Joseph Copeland. Signed, Nicholas
Parker. Ordered; October 7, 1756
R. February 3, 1757   Page 258

Wrenn, Joseph. Estate appraised by John Mallory,
John Cary, William Glover. Ordered, January 6, 1757
R. February 3, 1757   ,   Page 259

Goodrich, Benjamin. Account estate, examined by
Dolphin Drew, James Dering and Richard Jones. Signed,
William Goodrich   R. February 3, 1757
                                            Page 260

Driver, Robert. Account estate, examined by Thomas
Miller and Richard Reynolds
R. February 3, 1757   Page 262

Holleman, Susanna. Account estate, examined by
Joseph Gray and Richard Kello
R. March 3, 1757   Page 263

Scott, William: Leg.- wife Elizabeth; son William;
land in Southampton County; son Robert; daughter Mary;
daughter Elizabeth, unborn child. Exs., wife, Thomas
Pretlow and Joseph Scott
D. 11 mo. 13, 1756   R. March 3, 1757
Wit. Mary Pretlow, William Maycock, James Tyrie
                                            Page 264

Vance, Hugh. Estate appraised by William Hodsden,
William Harrison, Joseph Jones
R. March 3, 1757   Page 265

Briggs, James: Leg.- daughter Katherine; son Robert;
friend Richard Baker to be guardian for son Robert; wife
Elizabeth; son William; daughter Priscilla Clayton; daugh-

ter Catherine. Ex., friend, Richard Baker
  D. November 30, 1756   R. June 2, 1757
  Wit. Benjamin Baker, Mary Clayton   Page 268

Lawrence, William: Leg.- daughter Penelope; son John;
wife Sarah; son John land in Southampton County; daughter
Molly; daughter Ann; daughter Sally; son Miles. Exs.,
wife and brother-in-law Arthur Applewhaite
  D. September 8, 1756   R. June 2, 1757
  Wit. John Darden, Jesse Watkins, Joshua Council
          Page 269

Babb, Mary: Leg.- son William; daughter Mary Driver;
to Thomas Pinner; daughter Patience Pinner; daughter
Sarah Gay; grandson John a legacy in the possession of
his father Joshua Gay; granddaughter Martha Gay; son
Robert. Ex., son Robert Babb
  D. September 23, 1754   R. July 7, 1757
  Wit. John Driver, Sarah Driver   Page 273

Pitt, John. Account estate, debtor to the estate of
Joseph Pitt decd. Examined by Willis Wilkinson,
Nicholas Parker   R. July 7, 1757
          Page 274

Person, Samuel. Account estate, examined by Richard
Baker and Dolphin Drew. Signed, Thomas Pretlow and
Jordan Thomas   R. July 7, 1757
          Page 276

Gutre, Daniel: Leg.- son Benony; son Reuben; wife
Jane to maintain my younger children
  D. February 2, 1757   R. July 7, 1757
  Wit. John Bowden, Jacob Thomas   Page 278

Marshall, Robert: Of Nansemond County. Leg.- son
Robert the land adjoining that of my brother John
Marshall; daughter Mary Cashwell; daughter Priscilla
Collifer; daughter Elizabeth; to Rachell Marshall; to
Jesse Godwin Marshall. Ex., daughter Rachell Marshall
  D. February 29, 1756   R. July 7, 1757
  Wit. Thomas Applewhaite, Jesse Marshall, Mary Frizzell
          Page 280

Briggs, James. Estate appraised by William Harrison,
Benjamin Harrison, Michael Smelly (?)   R. July 7, 1757
          Page 281

Pitt, Henry: Leg.- son Henry; rest of estate to be
divided among all of my children. Exs., wife Mary
and Nicholas Parker
  D. June 14, 1757   R. August 4, 1757
  Wit. James Channel, Joseph Whitley, Samuel Bagnall
                                        Page 282

Barlow, Thomas. Account estate, examined by
Richard Hardy and Edward Goodrich
  R. August 4, 1757   Page 285

Pope, William. Account estate, examined by Robert
Holland and William Segraves. Among items, funeral
expenses for William Pope, Garlent Pope and his son
William Pope   R. August 4, 1757   Page 286

Pitt, Henry. Estate appraised by Joseph Copeland,
Tristram Norsworthy and Thomas Parker. Signed, Nicholas
Parker and Mary Pitt
  R. October 6, 1757   Page 287

Hail, Elizabeth: Leg.- daughter Mary; son Thomas;
grandson Joseph Hail; daughter-in-law Hannah Hail;
daughter Sarah; son Joseph; son John; daughter
Elizabeth Turner. Ex., son John Hail
  D. October 16, 1756   R. October 6, 1757
  Wit. Benjamin Pynes; Tabitha Haile, Martha Bell
                                        Page 289

Everitt, Joseph: Leg.- daughter Elizabeth; wife; to
Joshua House; son Joseph. Ex., son Joseph Everitt
  D. June 27, 1756   R. October 6, 1757
  Wit. Joseph Meredith, Alexander Young, Joseph
        Darden, John Darden   Page 290

Hail, Edward: Leg.- son Benjamin; son Edward; son
Joshua; son Joel; son James; son Reuben; son Jesse;
daughter Rebecca; daughter Naomi. Extx., wife
Elizabeth
  D. September 19, 1757   R. October 6, 1757
  Wit. Benjamin Pynes, John Cook, Thomas Hail
                                        Page 291

Council, Susannah: Leg.- daughter Susannah; daughter
Christian Daughtry; daughter Mary Brantley; son Joshua;
daughter Martha Fowler; daughter Lucy Johnson; daughter
Ann Lawrence; son Charles; son Michael; granddaughter

Selah Council; grandson Willis Council; granddaughter
Sarah Lawrence; son Hardy. Exs., sons, Charles and
Joshua Council·
   D. April 19, 1756   R. October 6, 1757
   Wit. William Murphree, Robert Johnson   Page 294

Wright, John: Leg.- son John; daughter Ann Green;
daughter Sarah Butler; daughter Elizabeth West; daughter
Juliana Driver; granddaughter Juliana Green; to Sarah.
Alderson. Ex., son John Wright
   D. September 1, 1753   R. November 3, 1757
   Wit. Richard Reynolds, Martha Wright, William
         Brantley   Page 297

Robinson, Richard: Leg.- loving wife my whole estate,
at her death to be divided between Edward Miller and my
God-daughter Betty Wilson. Ex., son-in-law Thomas
Miller
   D. September 20, 1757   R. November 3, 1757
   Wit. George Wilson, Rebecca Miller   Page 299

Gibbs, Ralph: Leg.- sister Sarah Gibbs; wife Mary;
son John. Exs., wife and Giles West
   D. July 8, 1757   R. November 3, 1757
   Wit. Richard Reynolds, William Richard, Micajah
         Wills   Page 300

Everitt, Joseph. Estate appraised by Samuel Mathews,
Thomas Pinner, Samuel Everitt
   R. December 1, 1757   Page 301

Johnson, Robert: Leg.- daughter Sarah Britt; son
Robert; daughter Mary Williford; son James; daughter
Amelia. Exs., wife Ann and son Robert Johnson
   D. November 3, 1757   R. December 1, 1757
   Wit. Anthony Fulgham, Barnaby Little   Page 304

Wright, John. Estate appraised by James Benn, George
Benn, Giles West
   R. December 7, 1757   Page 305

Almand, James: Leg.- son Moses; son Lewis; son Aaron,
land in Nansemond County; granddaughter Mary Fleming;
grandson James Fossith; grandson Perrin Almand; grandson
Thomas Almand; granddaughter Peggy Almand; daughter
Sofia Rand; daughter Millison Fleming; wife

Exs., sons Moses, Lewis and Aaron Almand
   D. April 6, 1757   R. December 2, 1757
   Wit. Edward Goodrich, Benjamin Bidgood, Mary
         Humphry   Page 306

   Wrenn, John. Estate appraised by Edward Goodrich,
George Wilson, John Miller
   R. December 2, 1757   Page 308

   Jones, Abraham: Leg.- son Mathew; son John; son
Abraham; daughter Ann Pitman; daughter Martha Delk
Exs., sons Mathew and John Jones
   D. March 28, 1757   R. January 5, 1758
   Wit. Thomas Pretlow, Benjamin Gwaltney, James
         Gwaltney   Page 310

   Applewhaite, Ann: Of Newport Parish.¹ Leg.- Thomas
Wills, the son of ----- Wills, sister Mary Wills; to
Thomas Applewhaite, Jr.; brother Josiah Applewhaite
Ex., Miles Wills
   D. October 16, 1757   R. January 5, 1758
   Wit. James Fulgham, Sarah Tuell   Page 312

   Lawrence, John: Leg.- grandson Elisha Lawrence
Ballard land in Southampton County; to John Lawrence,
my brother's son land in Southampton County; granddaughter Honour Ballard; granddaughter Ann Ballard;
daughter Ann Ballard. Ex., son-in-law Elisha Ballard
   D. March 2, 1757   R. January 5, 1758
   Wit. Hardy Lawrence, Joseph Lawrence, William
         Moore   Page 313

   Wrenn, John. Account estate, examined by John
Mallory and William Glover. Signed, John Wrenn
   R. January 5, 1758   Page 315

   Norsworthy, Joseph: Leg.- granddaughter Carziah
Godwin; son-in-law Robert Kinder; wife Rachel; son
Joseph; daughter Mary Gross; daughter Elizabeth
Reynolds. Ex., son Joseph Norsworthy
   D. May 3, 1757   R. February 2, 1758
   Wit. Thomas Gale, Jethro Gale, Thomas Gale, Jr.
                                                    Page 316

   Dodgson, Christopher. Estate appraised by James
Easson, Robert Johnson, Miles Wiles. Ordered,
January 6, 1758
   R. February 2, 1758   Page 317

Bridger, Joseph, Jr. Additional appraisal by Richard
Reynolds, Samson West, Thomas Miller
R. February 2, 1758   Page 325

Scott, William. Estate appraised by James Hough,
Michael Eley, Daniel Herring. Estate appraised in
Southampton County by Miles Cary, Henry Blunt, William
Taylor
R. February 3, 1759   Page 326

Hail, Elizabeth. Estate appraised by John Morris,
Philip Moody, Thomas Turner
R. March 2, 1758   Page 364

Powell, William. Estate appraised by John Bowden,
Henry Johnson, William Gay. Ordered, December 1, 1757
R. March 2, 1758   Page 366

Miniard, Barnaby. Estate appraised by Samuel
Whitfield, John Whitfield, Nicholas Parker. Ordered,
August 6, 1757   R. March 2, 1758   Page 368

Johnson, Robert. Estate appraised by Moses Almand,
Arthur Turner, Barnaby Little. Signed, Robert Johnson,
Jr.   R. March 2, 1758   Page 370

Tomlin, Benjamin. Estate appraised by John Moore,
Adam Brown, Arthur Turner. Ordered, November 3, 1757
R. March 2, 1758   Page 374

House, George. Estate appraised by James Watson,
Arthur Applewhaite, Bartholomew Lightfoot
R. March 2, 1758   Page 375

Gibbs, Ralph. Estate appraised by Joshua Hunter, John
Wright, William Richards
R. November 3, 1758   Page 377

Parker, Wilkinson: Leg.- Thomas Parker. Ex., brother
Thomas Parker
D. March 19, 1758   R. April 6, 1758
Wit. Tristram Norsworthy, Henry King   Page 378

Wilson, George: Leg.- daughter Mary Wilson, bonds in
the hands of Jordan Thomas and Richard Baker; daughter
Betty; daughter Honour; daughter Ann; son Solomon; daugh-
ter Ridley; wife Judith; my mother to live where she now
does, paying no rent. Exs., wife and brother Samuel
Wilson
   D. February 20, 1758   R. April 6, 1758
   Wit. Richard Jordan, Thomas Miller, Thomas Goodson,
      Rebecca Miller   Page 379

Casey, Thomas: Of Newport Parish. Leg.- granddaugh-
ter Sarah Miller; William Miller; to Samuel Morgan; to
William Richards; to Martha, daughter of John Miller;
nephew Thomas Casey. Ex., friend Nicholas Miller
   D. March 23, 1758   R. April 6, 1758
   Wit. William Hodsden, Samuel Morgan   Page 282

West, Elizabeth. Estate appraised by Bartholomew
Lightfoot; William Allmand, Christopher Reynolds
   Ordered, March 21, 1758   R. April 6, 1758
                                    Page 383

West, Everitt. Account estate, examined by Bartholomew
Lightfoot, Christopher Reynolds, William Allmand. Among
items, to widow and three children
   R. April 6, 1758   Page 384

Butler, John. Estate appraised by Bartholomew
Lightfoot, Christopher Reynolds, William Allmand.
   Ordered, March 2, 1758   R. April 6, 1758
                                    Page 385

Smith, Jesse. Estate appraised by Robert Tynes,
Thomas Brock, Christopher Reynolds, James Watson
   Ordered, March 2, 1758   R. April 6, 1758
                                    Page 387

Pyland, Elizabeth. Estate appraised by John Carrell,
Richard Hardy, Peter Fiveash
   R. May 4, 1758   Page 388

Applewhaite, John: Leg.- son Benjamin; son John;
wife Mary; daughter Mary. Exs., wife, Mr. Richard
Baker, Mr. Charles Fulgham and brother Arthur
Applewhaite
   D. March 1, 1758   R. May 4, 1759
   Wit. Charles Driver, Joseph Cutchins, Anthony
      Holladay   Page 390

Casey, Thomas. Estate appraised by William Hodsden, Thomas Whitfield, John Bidgood
R. May 4, 1758   Page 391

Wilson, George. Estate appraised by William Harrison, William Carrell, James Dering
R. May 4, 1758   Page 395

Wright, John: Leg.- sister Sarah Butler; to Charles; John and Ann Butler; to Julina Bailey; to William, Ann, Juliana, George and Sarah Green; to Olive Driver; to Selia West; to Ann and Randall West; debts to be paid John Butler. Ex., Augustine King
D. June 9, 1758   R. August 3, 1758
Wit. John Conner, Hannah King   Page 400

W Whitfield, Samuel: Leg.- wife Elizabeth; son George; daughter Jemima; son Mathais land in Nansemond County adjoining that of Thomas Witfield; daughter Elizabeth; daughter Margaret Lad. Exs., wife and son George Whitfield
D. March 27, 1758   R. August 3, 1758
Wit. John Sawyer, Arthur Benn   Page 401

Allmand, James. Estate appraised by John Hodges, John Gray, Henry Harrison
R. August 3, 1758   Page 403

Holliwood, Christopher. Estate appraised by Samuel Whitfield, Richard Bagnall, Nicholas Parker. Signed, Joseph Copeland
Ordered, April 7, 1757   R. August 3, 1758
       Page 406

Penny, John. Estate appraised by James Channell, George Whitfield, Joseph Copeland. Signed, Robert Lawrence
Ordered, May 4, 1758   R. August 3, 1758
       Page 407

Norsworthy, Joseph. Estate appraised by Richard Reynolds, Samuel Holladay, Jonathan Godwin
R. August 3, 1758   Page 409

Smith, Mary. Estate appraised by Bartholomew Lightfoot, Robert Tynes, Charles Driver. Ordered, March 2, 1758
R. August 3, 1758   Page 411

Hail, Edward. Estate appraised by William Jordan,
Andrew Sykes, Anthony Crocker
R. August 3, 1758 Page 412

Applewhaite, John. Estate appraised by Richard
Reynolds, Giles Driver, Charles Driver. Signed, Mary
Applewhaite Page 414

Holladay, Jonas. Estate appraised by James Benn,
George Benn, John Morris. Ordered, May 12, 1758
R. August 3, 1758 Page 418

Hodsden, William: Leg.- son Henry, all my estate in
Great Britain, he paying the balance due Robert Irvin;
son William all my estate in Virginia. Exs., son
Henry Hodsden in Great Britain and son William Hodsden
in Virginia, with friend James Ridley
D. June 13, 1758 R. August 3, 1758
Wit. Andrew Mackie, Robert Johnston Page 419

Briggs, Charles: Leg.- son Inglish; son Charles;
son Elias; daughter Sarah; daughter Priscilla; son
James; wife Ann. Extx., wife Ann Briggs
D. April 24, 1758 R. August 3, 1758
Wit. Ann Smith, James Dering Page 420

Glover, William: Leg.- son William; son John land in
Nansemond County; son Richard; son Benjamin; wife Ann;
daughter Sally. Exs., wife and son William Glover
D. May 27, 1750 R. September 7, 1758
Wit. James Baker, R. Baker Page 422

Jones, Abraham. Estate appraised by Benjamin
Gwaltney, Peter Woodward, Jr., James Gwaltney
R. September 7, 1758 Page 423

Wiggs, Luke. Estate appraised by Robert Tynes,
John Woodley, Mathew Jones
R. September 7, 1758 Page 426

Briggs, Charles. Estate appraised by William
Harrison, Henry Harrison, John Barlow
R. September 7, 1758 Page 427

Lawrence, William. Estate appraised by Daniel Herring,
Michael Eley, Joshua Council
   R. September 7, 1758   Page 429

Miniard, Barnaby. Account estate, examined by James
Jordan Scott and William Haynes
   R. October 5, 1758   Page 432

Whitfield, William. Account estate, examined by Miles
Wills and Nicholas Parker
   R. November 2, 1758   Page 434

Daughtry, Elizabeth: Leg.- son William; son Richard,
legacy which formerly belonged to my brother Elisha
Williams; daughter Sarah Holland; son John; son Joshua;
son Moses; son Benjamin. Ex., son Richard Daughtry
   D. July 26, 1758   R. November 2, 1758
   Wit. Benjamin Whitfield, Robert Whitfield, Louisa
       Hedgepeth   Page 435

Wheadon, James. Estate appraised by Richard Hardy,
Peter Fiveash, Samuel Wilson
   R. November 2, 1758   Page 437

Brock, Benjamin: Of Johnston County (N.C.?) Leg.-
wife Elizabeth, who is to maintain my children
Extx., wife
   D.   R. November 2, 1758
   Wit. Robert Reynolds, Dorothy Brock, Richard Braswell
                               Page 440

Fones, Robert: Leg.- wife Elizabeth; son John
Ex., son John Fones
   D. March 1, 1753   R. November 2, 1758
   Wit. James Shelly, George Wainwright   Page 442

Shelley, Jane: Leg.- son Thomas; daughter Ann White;
granddaughter Sylvia Carrell; grandson Thomas Phillips;
grandson John Shelley; son James. Ex., son James Shelley
   D. March 17, 1758   R. November 2, 1758
   Wit. Benjamin Phillips, Benjamin Carrell, Ann White
                               Page 443

Daughtry, John, and Elizabeth Daughtry his wife. Es-
tate appraised by Joshua Council, James Council, Peter
Butler
   R. December 7, 1758   Page 444

Whitfield, Samuel. Estate appraised by Joseph
Copeland, John Norsworthy, Anthony Fulgham
  R. December 7, 1758   Page 446

Parnall, Thomas. Estate appraised by Adam Brown,
William Jordan, Anthony Crocker. Ordered, January 10,
1758
  R. December 7, 1758   Page 448

Jordan, John: Leg.- son John, money in the hands of
Richard Jordan, Jordan Thomas and James Jones; grandson
Edmund Jordan; daughter Mourning; daughter Elizabeth
Thorpe; daughter Margaret Sebrell; son Joseph; son
Billingsley; son Joseph. Exs., sons Joseph and
Billingsley Jordan. Overseers to will, James Jordan
and James Pitt
  D. October 28, 1757   R. December 7, 1758
  Wit. James Jordan, James Pitt   Page 449

Whitley, George. Estate appraised by Jonathan
Godwin, John Godwin, Nicholas Fulgham. Ordered,
November 18, 1758
  R. December 7, 1758   Page 451

Askew, Thomas. Account of sale, returned by John
Eley, Jr.   R. December 7, 1758   Page 453

Brock, Benjamin. Estate appraised by James Watson,
Bartholomew Lightfoot, Arthur Applewhaite
  R. December 7, 1758   Page 455

Wiggs, Luke. Account estate examined by Robert
Tynes, Bartholomew Lightfoot
  R. December 8, 1758   Page 456

Teasley, Richard: Leg.- brother John. Ex., bro-
ther John Teasley
  D. January 8, 1752   R. January 4, 1759
  Wit. John Sellaway, Sampson Underwood, John Powell
                                                  Page 457

Clayton, John: Of Newport Parish. Leg.- son George
and his wife; son William and his wife;daughter Elizabeth

Miller; granddaughter Elizabeth Miller; grandson John
Pinhorn; grandson Robert Pinhorn; grandson Benjamin
Miller; daughter Mary Vellines; daughter Susannah
Williamson; daughter Rebecca and her husband Thomas
Miller; son John Clayton and his wife. Exs., son
John Clayton and Twait Vellines
D.   1756   R.   January 4, 1759
Wit. Thomas Williamson, Charles Cosby   Page 458

Wright, John. Estate appraised by James Benn, Giles
West, William Richards, John Morris
R.   January 4, 1759   Page 460

Tomlin, John. Estate appraised by Adam Brown, John
Harris, Thwait Vellines. Ordered, November 2, 1758
R.   February 1, 1759   Page 462

Brock, Susannah: Leg.- son John; grandson Peter Best;
grandson Robert -----; to James Brock the son of
Benjamin Brock; to James, the son of Robert Brock; to
Jacob, the son of William Mandling (?); son Thomas
Brock. Ex., son Thomas Brock
D. October 18, 1757   R.   February 1, 1759
Wit. Benn Willett, Elizabeth Parrie (?), Sarah Hawks
                                                Page 463

Brantley, Benjamin. Estate appraised by Benjamin
Harrison, William Harrison, William Wrenn. Ordered,
January 5, 1759
R.   February 1, 1759   Page 465

House, James. Estate appraised by John Pitt, Samuel
Godwin, Joshua Godwin, William Weston. Ordered,
December 1, 1757
R.   February 1, 1759   Page 465

Smith, Joseph. Estate appraised by Nicholas Smith,
William Hawkins, Thomas Murry
Ordered, February 1, 1759   Page 468

Jordan, John. Estate appraised by John Marshall,
Robert Driver, John Newman. Signed, Joseph and
Billingsley Jordan
R.   March 1, 1759   Page 470

Barlow, Benjamin: Of Newport Parish. Leg.- estate to

be divided between my four brothers, viz.- John, James,
Thomas and William Barlow and sister Priscilla Barlow's
son Nathaniel Barlow. Ex., brother Thomas Barlow
  D. December 26, 1757   R. April 5, 1759
  Wit. James Dering, Samuel Bowden, Martha Dering
Page 474

Powell, William. Account estate, examined by John
Eley and John Darden. Signed, Elizabeth Powell
  R. April 5, 1759   Page 475

Barlow, Benjamin. Estate appraised by James Dering,
Francis Wrenn, Samuel Wilson
  R. May 3, 1759   Page 476

Fones, Robert. Estate appraised by James Dering,
James Shelley, Samuel Wilson
  R. May 3, 1759   Page 478

Shelley, Jane. Estate appraised by James Dering,
Henry Harrison, Samuel Wilson
  R. May 3, 1759   Page 480

Gibbs, Ralph. Account estate, examined by Richard
Reynolds and Augustine King
  R. May 3, 1759   Page 481

Davis, William: Of Newport Parish. Leg.- son William,
land bought of Theophilus Williams; son John, land
bought of Joseph Jones; son James; wife Deborah
  D. August 28, 1757   R. May 3, 1759
  Wit. Benjamin Pynes, Elizabeth Britt, Amey Britt,
      Susannah Smith   Page 482

Jones, Britain. Estate appraised by Richard Jones,
Benjamin Atkinson, Joseph Mangum.
Ordered, April 5, 1759   R. May 3, 1759
Page 484

Clark, Joseph: Of Newport Parish. Leg.- wife
Johnnna; son Henry, among all my children
  D. September 17, 1758   R. May 3, 1759
  Wit. Henry Mitchell, Caspar Mintz   Page 485

Frizzell, James. Estate appraised by Joseph Driver,
Anthony Fulgham, Thomas Channell.
Ordered, February 1, 1759   R. June 7, 1759
Page 486

Mitchell, Henry. Of Newport Parish. Leg.- wife
Rebecca, land purchased of Richard Bray. Extx., wife.
    D. July 4, 1758   R. June 7, 1759
    Wit. Joseph Clark, Jesse Atkinson, Thomas Crocker
Page 487

Smith, Mary. Account estate, examined by Augustine
King and Giles West.
    R. June 7, 1759   Page 489

Davis, William. Estate appraised by William Blunt,
William Crocker, John Morris.
    R. June 7, 1759   Page 489

West, Elizabeth. Account estate, examined by John
Wills and Bartholomew Lightfoot. Paid estate to three
children
    R. July 5, 1759   Page 491

Best, Peter. Estate appraised by George Norsworthy,
George Whitfield, Richard Bagnall, Samson West. Signed,
Cornelius Ratcliff. Ordered, June 7, 1759
    R. July 5, 1759   Page 492

Clark, Joseph. Estate appraised by Joseph Atkinson,
Moses Exum, John Thomas
    R. July 5, 1759   Page 494

Cutchins, Joshua. Estate appraised by William
Richards, Nicholas Wail, Samuel Weston. Signed,
Elizabeth Cutchins. Ordered, March 1, 1759
    R. July 5, 1759   Page 495

Williams, Joseph. Estate appraised by John Baldwin,
John Marshall, John Richards. Signed, Jethro Gale.
Ordered, June 3, 1756   R. July 6, 1759
Page 497

Jones, Elizabeth. Estate appraised by John Jordan,
John Newman, John Wright. Signed, John Wrench. Ordered,
May 3, 1759   R. July 5, 1759
Page 500

Benn, George: Leg.- daughter Nancy; wife Mary, my
children; unborn Child.   Extx., wife Mary Benn
   D. February 25, 1759   R. August 2, 1759
                                          Page 502

Casey, Thomas. Account estate, examined by Joseph
Bridger and Robert Tynes
   R. August 2, 1759   Page 503

Glover, William. Estate appraised by John Mallory,
William Carrell, Edward Goodrich
   R. August 2, 1759   Page 504

Brock, Susannah. Estate appraised at the house of
Thomas Brock by Robert Tynes, Bartholomew Lightfoot,
Charles Driver   R. September 6, 1759   Page 507

Goodrich, Edward: Leg.- son John land purchased of
Thomas Hill and the right to a deed of gift made my
wife in 1754 by her father; son Edward; unborn child;
daughter Elizabeth a plantation purchased of Col. John
Ruffin; sister Ann Gray; to John Miller; legacy to the
widow Davis (in the Bay), the widow Bell, the widow
Bell (relict of Charles Briggs), the widow Rosser and
the widow Pollard; wife Juliana; to Simpkins Dorman
Exs., William Davis and Richard Hardy. Trustees, John
Goodrich and Thomas Day
   D. July 17, 1759   R. September 6, 1759
   Wit. John Hodges, Moses Allmand, William Bidgood
                                          Page 508

Hunter, Seth: Of Newport Parish. Leg.- wife Mary;
daughter Frances; daughter Rodith Hunter, the child
which I had by Priscilla Braswell; son Seth; son
Emanuel
   D. May 2, 1759   R. September 6, 1759
   Wit. Richard Baker, Benjamin Pynes, John Day
                                          Page 511

Benn, George. Estate appraised by Giles West,
Anthony Fulgham, Augustine King
   R. September 6, 1759   Page 514

Davis, Edward: Leg.- son John; son Thomas; son
Edward; to all my children. Exs., Robert Tynes and
daughter Ann Davis
   D. March 14, 1759   R. October 4, 1759
   Wit. Benjamin Davis, Edward Davis, Easter O'Neal
                                          Page 515

Hunter, Seth. Estate appraised by Richard Jones,
Samuel Jones, Francis Wrenn
R. October 4, 1759   Page 517

Clark, John: Leg.- Mary Ingram; grandsons, Yarret
and John Lucks; son William; friend Elizabeth Carrell
to live with my daughter Mary Ingram. If my heirs
should die without issue, my estate to the widows and
orphans in this county
D. October 6, 1759   R. December --, 1759
                                                     Page 518

Barlow, Benjamin. Account estate, examined by Robert
Fry and James Dering. Signed, Thomas Barlow
R. December 6, 1759   Page 520

Teasley, Richard. Estate appraised by Jacob Jones,
William Raiford, Jr., William Segrave
R. December 7, 1759   Page 521

Wheadon, James. Account estate, examined by John
Mallory, Richard Hardy. Among items, to a legacy
received of the executors of Joyce Wheadon to Mary and
John Wheadon, the children of James Wheadon, decd.
R. December 7, 1759   Page 522

Glover, William. Account estate, examined by Dolphin
Drew and William Davis. Signed, Ann Glover. Among items,
paid Rosamond Wilson and Richard Jordan for schooling
children
R. January 3, 1760   Page 525

Smith, Arthur. Account estate, examined by John Wills
and Charles Fulgham. Signed, Elizabeth Smith
R. January 3, 1760   Page 526

Stuckey, Simon. Estate appraised by Joseph Norsworthy,
Jonathan Godwin. Ordered, November 1, 1759
R. January 4, 1760   Page 529

Gale, Thomas: Leg.- son Jethro; son Thomas; daughter
Ann; younger daughters, Tabitha and Alice; daughter Elizabeth
if she does not marry Joshua Jenkins; daughter Mary Spencer;

friend John Marshall, Jr. to have the care of Thomas, Tabitha and Alice Gale. Ex., friend John Marshall, Jr.
D. January 1, 1760   R. February 7, 1760
Wit. John Baldwin, Lewis Baldwin, Ann Marshall
                                              Page 530

Fulgham, Mary: Leg.- cousin John, the son of my brother John Fulgham; cousin Anthony Fulgham, Jr. Ex., cousin John Fulgham
D. April 6, 1759   R. February 7, 1760
Wit. Daniel Herring, Edmund Fulgham, Ann Harris
                                              Page 534

Pitt, Captain Henry. Account estate, examined by Giles Driver and Joseph Coupland
R. February 7, 1760   Page 535

Mitchel, Henry. Estate appraised by Thomas Crocker, William Crocker, William Blunt
R. February 7, 1760   Page 537

Jones, Abraham. Account estate, examined by Arthur Williamson, Philip Moody and Adam Brown
R. March 6, 1760   Page 538

Sanders, Solomon. Estate appraised by George Whitley, Richard Reynolds, Jonathan Godwin
D. April 3, 1755   R. October 2, 1758
                                              Page 198
Account of his estate examined by Charles Fulgham and Richard Reynolds
R. November 7, 1755   Page 204

Read, William. Account estate examined by H. Edmunds and John Person
R. November 6, 1755   Page 199

Holleman, Susanna. Estate appraised by Edward Portis, Britain Jones, Peter Woodward
R. November 6, 1755   Page 200

Whitfield, John. Estate appraised by Tristram Norsworthy, Thomas Parker, Henry King
D. October 5, 1758   R. November 2, 1758
                                              Page 434

Errata

Page 3. Will of James Webb, Exs., William Wilkinson and
         wife, not William Webb and wife.

Page 9. Will of Mary Davis, witnesses, William Green,
         Sarah Murry, Thomas Davis.

Page 11. Will of George House, dated April 16, 1714,
         recorded April 24, 1721.

Page 14. Will of Pool Hall, witnesses, William Price
         and Thomas Uzzell.

Page 24. Daughter Sarah Weston omitted will of Robert
         King.

Page 31. John Linsey's will R. August 28, 1727.

Page 35. Will of Mathew Jones, Henry Sumerling not Thomas.

Page 39. Boykin, Edward: Leg.- son John; wife Ann,among
         all my children. Exs., wife and son John
              D. January 4, 1725/26   R. May 27, 1728
              Wit. James Atkinson,Mary Atkinson,John Dunkley
                                   Will Book 3, p. 98

Page 48. Daughter Elizabeth omitted in will of John Scott.

Page 64. John Johnson, not John Turner, witness Anthony
         Fulgham.

Page 79. Uncle Thomas, not William Joyner,will of Mathew
         Kinchen.

Page 84. Adm., Robert Moxson, John not Robert Pitt.

Page 85. James Baker not James Barlow, Thomas Ryall's Acct.

Page 87. James Carrell and Richard Hardy, Exs.,Jeremiah
         Ingraham's will.

Page 89. Daughter Martha Applewhaite, omitted will of
         Mary Green.

Page 130.Granddaughter Mary Murphry omitted in will of
         Elizabeth Neaville.

Page 132.Should be son Henry Applewhaite deceased in will
         of Ann Applewhaite.

Page 134.John Edward's will recorded, August 11, 1748.

Page 184.Edward called son of Thomas Miller in will of
         Richard Robinson.

Page 195.Nicholas Parker, James Benn, wits. George Benn.
Page 196.Mary Broadfield, Wm. Morgan, Lewis Conner,
         Elizabeth Carrell, wits. will of John Clark.

INDEX

Hargrave,
  Benjamin ------------- 172
  Jesse ---------------- 172
  Lemuel --------------- 172
  Samuel --------------- 172
Harris,
  Amos --------------- 100(2)
  Ann ----------------- 68, 98
            100(2), 123, 197
  Catherine ------------ 20
  Charles -------------- 98
  Cherry --------------- 98
  Daniel --------------- 68
  Edward -------- 14(2), 51
              55, 68(2)
              100(3), 105
  Elizabeth ----------- 7, 9
  Francis -------------- 43
  George -------------- 7(2)
  Hannah --------------- 52
  Hardy --------------- 100
  Henry -------- 14, 52, 56
            59, 67, 87, 89
            90, 134, 150
  Jacob --------- 68, 89, 90
  James ------------- 68, 98
  Joel --------------- 100(2)
  John --------- 5, 68, 91
          136, 157, 173, 192
  Joseph ------------ 7, 98
  Joshua --------------- 52
  Lewis --------------- 100
  Martha ------------- 7, 25
  Martin ---------------- 7
  Mary -------------- 52, 68
            100, 105, 179
  Mathew ------------- 14, 98
  Michael -- 31, 98(2), 123
  Nathan ------------- 68(2)
  Rebecca ------------- 101
  Robert ----- 7, 14, 98, 99
  Sarah ----------------- 7
  Simon ---------- 125, 136
  Thomas ----- 12, 14, 20, 48
            52(2), 56, 59
            68, 104, 149, 173
  West ----------------- 68
  William ------- 7, 101, 139
Harrison,
  Ann -------------- 127, 140
  Benjamin --------- 182, 192
  Henry --------- 78(3), 136
            141, 142, 143, 145
            156, 188, 189, 193
  John ------------- 26, 62(2)
            118, 140

Harrison (cont'd)
  Josiah --------------- 64
  Temperance ---------- 120
  William ------- 6, 36, 38
            43, 66, 77(2), 78
            89, 91, 98, 101
            112(2), 113, 120(2)
            124, 133, 135(2), 136
            138, 139(2), 140(2)
            143(2), 152, 154, 158
            160, 162, 163, 169(2)
            177, 181, 182, 189, 192
Hart,
  Widow --------------- 134
Haslep,
  Elizabeth ----------- 100
Havett,
  William -------------- 21
Hawkins (Hawkings),
  John -------------- 23, 40
  Joseph -------------- 156
  Mary ---------------- 139
  William ------- 11(2), 30
            38, 43(2), 70, 99
            139, 141, 167, 192
Hawks,
  Sarah --------------- 192
Hayes,
  Arthur --------------- 10
  Elizabeth ------------ 10
  Peter ---------------- 10
  Robert ------------- 10(2)
Heard,
  John -------------- 37, 41
Hedgepeth,
  Henry --------------- 144
  Louisa -------------- 190
  Priscilla ----------- 160
Herbert,
  Buller --------------- 37
Herring,
  Daniel ----------- 48, 105
            156, 157, 158, 163
            165, 167, 168, 174
            179, 186, 190, 197
Hickman,
  William ---------- 48, 132
Hicks,
  Robert --------------- 33
Hiden(Hyden),
  Elizabeth ---------- 37(2)
  Ephraim ---------- 37, 40
  Sarah ---------------- 37
Higginson,
  Humphrey ------------- 25

Pinner,
    John -------------------- 173
    Patience ---------------- 182
    Thomas -------------- 18, 61
                          182, 184
Pitman,
    Ambrose ----------------- 54
    Ann ------------ 4, 54, 185
    Arthur ------------------ 54
    Edward ----------------- 125
    Elizabeth ----------- 4, 54
    Faith ------------------- 54
    John -------------------- 54
    Joseph ------------------ 54
    Lettis ------------------- 4
    Lucy -------------------- 54
    Martha ----------------- 125
    Olive ------------------- 54
    Pratta ------------------- 54
    Robert -------------- 54, 91
    Samson ------------------ 54
    Samuel --------------- 4; 54
    Thomas ------- 4, 54(3), 55
    W. ---------------------- 77
Pitt,
    Edmond ----------------- 137
    Elizabeth -------- 127, 137
    Esther ------------------ 72
    Henry ------------- 1, 2(2)
                        7; 11; 18, 24
                        34, 41; 45, 61
                        69, 109, 135(3)
                        137(2), 146; 164
                        168, 183(3), 197
    James --------- 150, 191(2)
    John ----- 2(2), 72, 73(2)
                        74; 103; 124
                        125(2), 127; 128
                        135, 137(2); 141
                        170, 182, 192, 198
    Joseph ---- 2; 134, 137(2)
                        141, 171(2), 182
    Joseph Major ---------- 135
    Lidia ------------------ 137
    Martha ------ 72, 125; 134
    Mary ------------- 2; 3, 137
                        173, 183(3)
    Prudence ---------------- 72
    Rachel ------------------ 72
    Robert -------- 23, 84, 198
    Sarah ------------------ 134
    Thomas --------- 45, 69, 125
                        131, 135, 138
    William ---------------- 135
Pledger,
    Ann -------------------- 158

Pledger (cont'd),
    Martha ----------------- 158
    Mary ------------------- 158
    Mourning --------------- 158
    Thomas ----------------- 133
                          156, 158(3)
Pollard,
    Widow ------------------ 195
    Arthur ----------------- 163
    Mary ------------------- 137
Ponsonby,
    Ann -------------------- 132
    William ----- 89; 101; 103
                        113(2), 132, 157, 161
Pope,
    Ann -------------------- 173
    Charity ----------------- 67
    Edward ------------------ 42
    Garlent ---------------- 183
    Hardy ------------------ 139
    Henry ------------- 39, 42(2)
                        45, 67(2), 139
    Jacob ------------------- 42
    Jane -------------------- 67
    John -------- 10; 13; 42(3)
                        51, 81, 82(2)
                        83, 86, 87, 139
                        149(2), 160; 162(3)
    Joseph --------- 42, 139(3)
                        160, 162
    Mary ------------------- 175
    Mourning ---------------- 42
    Nathan ----------------- 173
    Patience --------------- 118
    Priscilla ----------- 162(2)
    Richard -------- 13; 42, 52
                        67(2), 148; 173(2)
    Samuel ------- 42, 139; 160
    Sarah ---------- 20, 39, 42
                        67(2), 139
    Thomas ------------ 42; 157
    William ----------- 8; 42
                        44, 49, 66, 69, 71
                        86, 90; 100
                        105, 115, 118; 149
                        162, 175, 183(3)
Porter,
    Charles ------------ 47, 75
Portis --------------------- 197
Portlock,
    Mr. -------------------- 151
    Charles ---------------- 110
                        113, 115, 129, 142
                        160(2), 165, 178(2)
    Nathaniel ------- 160, 178

Ricks,
Richard -------------- 116
Robert -------------- 20
53(4), 66,82
115(2), 116, 121
William -------------- 53
Riddick,
George ----------- 5, 14
16, 30, 44
Ridley,
Ann ---------------- 132
Elizabeth ----------- 1(2)
James -------------- 20
93, 95, 101, 102
103, 105, 108,118
124, 130, 151, 189
Jane ---------------111
Lydia --------------- 1
Mary --------------- 1
Nathaniel ----------- 1(2)
2, 14, 20, 70
73, 93, 94, 100
101(2), 123, 139
Priscilla -------- 103, 132
Thomas -------------- 1
Riggin (Riggan),
Ann --------------- 15, 22
41, 43, 76
Daniel ---- 4, 15, 41, 118
Patience -------------- 41
Sarah --------------- 22
Riggs,
John ---------------- 61
Rives,
Mary --------------- 33
Roberson,
Elizabeth --------- 86, 97
James ------- 86, 100, 141
Jonathan -------- 86, 141
Roberts,
John ---------- 33, 53, 94
145, 148, 151
Thomas ---------- 15, 148
Robinson,
Richard --------- 184, 198
Rochell (Rotchell),
John -------- 50, 75, 127
Rochester,
Ann ---------------- 139
Catherine ----------- 139
Charity ------------- 139
Joshua -------------- 139
William -------- 139, 155
Rodes,
Elizabeth ------- 132, 174

Rodway,
Mary --------------- 159
Susannah ---------- 159(2)
John ---------- 40, 50, 51
61, 78, 100, 104
107(2), 109, 113, 115
120, 126, 152, 159
Rodwell,
John -------------- 4
Rogers,
Bridgett ------------ 34
Michael ------------- 22
Rose,
Henry -------------- 125
Rosser,
Widow -------------- 195
Thomas ---------- 17, 51
99, 119, 136
Row,
John --------- 66, 71, 89
Rue (Rew),
John Anthony ------- 34, 43
133, 135, 152
Ruffin,
John -- 117, 126, 173, 195
Robert -------------- 28
Rutter,
Mary ------------- 44, 56
William --- 40, 44, 50, 56
Ryall,
Charles ------------- 36
Thomas ---- 16, 85(3), 198

Salmon,
James ---------- 55(3), 57
John --------------- 55
Mary --------------- 55
Phillis -------------- 55
Sarah --------------- 55
Thomas -------------- 55
William ------------- 55
Salter,
Wil. ------- 120, 129, 136
Sammon,
James -------------- 103
Sampson,
Barcroft ------------ 36
Elizabeth ----------- 36
James ------------ 6, 36
39, 67, 147
Margaret ------------ 36
Sanders (See Saunders)

www.ingramcontent.com/pod-product-compliance
Lightning Source LLC
Chambersburg PA
CBHW021859020426
42334CB00013B/402